SUPPORTING NEW DIGITAL NATIVES

Children's Mental Health and Wellbeing in a Hi-Tech Age

Edited by
Michelle Jayman, Maddie Ohl and Leah Jewett

Foreword by
Pooky Knightsmith

T0366789

First published in Great Britain in 2021 by

Policy Press, an imprint of Bristol University Press
University of Bristol
1-9 Old Park Hill
Bristol
BS2 8BB
UK
t: +44 (0)117 954 5940
e: bup-info@bristol.ac.uk

Details of international sales and distribution partners are available at
policy.bristoluniversitypress.co.uk

© Bristol University Press 2021

British Library Cataloguing in Publication Data
A catalogue record for this book is available from the British Library.

ISBN 978-1-4473-5645-5 paperback
ISBN 978-1-4473-5646-2 ePdf
ISBN 978-1-4473-5647-9 ePub

The right of Michelle Jayman, Maddie Ohl and Leah Jewett to be identified as
editors of this work has been asserted by them in accordance with the Copyright,
Designs and Patents Act 1988.

Cover design: Robin Hawes
Front cover image: Violeta Stoimenova/iStock

Bristol University Press and Policy Press use environmentally
responsible print partners

Printed in Great Britain by CMP, Poole

For all the new digital natives who were the
inspiration for this book and for Jay and Danny
who gave me the motivation to complete it – MJ

For Andrew, Jan, Lily and Ahri for their
love and encouragement – MO

With love to Dare and Cope – my teenage
kids who live up to their names – LJ

In memory of Professor Marcia Worrell, greatly
missed by her colleagues and friends

Contents

List of figures and tables

Figures

Tables

Glossary

Adventure education – the promotion of learning through adventure-centred experiences; this includes a wide variety of activities due to the different ways people experience adventure.

Affordances – all actions that are made physically possible by the properties of an object or an environment. Users should be able to perceive affordances without having to consider how to use the items.

Agency – the capacity for human beings to make choices and act on those choices; an individual's ability to determine and make meaning from their environment through purposive consciousness and reflective and creative action.

Attention restoration theory (ART) – this asserts that exposure to nature can help improve one's focus and ability to concentrate; even looking at scenes of nature can be beneficial in this respect.

Audacity – a type of computer software for audio functions.

Avatar – in computing, a graphical representation of a user or the user's character or persona.

Behaviour change drivers – procedures or techniques which influence behaviour change and can be identified as underlying processes to explain the effectiveness of a specific intervention.

Biomedical model (of health) – dominant in modern western societies and one that underpins policies and practice. Ill health (including mental ill health) is seen as being caused by individual biological factors which require treatment for recovery.

Blended learning – a method of teaching that combines online educational materials and opportunities for interaction online with traditional place-based, face-to-face classroom activities.

Buddy system – used in schools; where a child gets paired with another child, usually one who is older and of higher abilities. The aim is to help promote friendship and support academic work and behavioural and social needs. A buddy system can foster a greater sense of belonging and a more inclusive school community.

Child-centred method – one that places the child at the notional centre of the learning or research process, and in which they are active participants.

Children's Services – a public service with statutory duties to support and protect vulnerable children in England. This includes providing children and their families with extra help. Where children are thought to be at risk of harm Children's Services will take steps which aim to make sure they are kept safe.

Co-constructed learning – collaborative or partnership working between the teacher and the learner; to enable students to develop the skills and confidence they need to become highly effective independent learners, taking ownership of their own learning, including content and mode of delivery.

Cognitive behavioural therapy (CBT) – a talking therapy that can help one manage problems by changing how one thinks and behaves. Most commonly used to treat anxiety and depression but can be useful for other mental and physical health problems.

Collaborative meaning making – from a socio-cultural perspective this is a social and dialogical process; group members participate in collaborative activities and they are engaged in different types of discourse. Through these discourses members share information, interpret ideas, explore the problem and negotiate meaning, and finally reach a shared understanding.

Community of inquiry – a group gathered to examine a topic of common interest through investigation; usually comprises a mixed membership (eg teachers, researchers, students, pupils) that undertakes the research collaboratively and produces knowledge.

Competence enhancement models – these focus on building an individual's competencies or strengths, thus enabling them to be resourceful and resilient when they encounter adverse circumstances.

Comprehensive sex education (CSE) – a rights-based approach that seeks to equip young people with the knowledge, skills, attitudes and values they need to determine and enjoy their sexuality.

Constructivist theories – these propose that people construct their own understanding and knowledge of the world through experiencing things and reflecting on those experiences.

Convenience sample – one derived from a type of non-probability sampling method where the sample is taken from a group of people easy to contact or to reach.

Co-production – a methodological approach that involves professionals and stakeholders working in partnership to share knowledge and develop a service or type of provision.

Critical thinking – the process of skilfully analysing, interpreting, evaluating and forming a judgement about something; being active in one's own learning and questioning ideas, arguments and findings.

Cyberbullying – bullying that takes place over digital devices like mobile phones, computers and tablets. Cyberbullying occurs online where people can view, participate in or share content. This includes sending, posting or sharing negative, harmful, false or malicious content about someone else, sharing someone's personal or private information and causing embarrassment or humiliation.

Digital divide – the gap between those who have access to the latest digital technologies and are therefore able to benefit, and those who do not have access and do not share the same benefits.

Digital exclusion – unequal access and capacity to use digital technologies that are essential to fully participate in society. Digital exclusion can result from lack of both physical and financial resources, low motivation (due to poor understanding or appreciation of the benefits), and lack of skills and confidence.

Digital literacy – the ability and skill to find, evaluate, utilise, share and create content using information technologies and the internet.

Digital native – a person born after 1980 who grew up in the rapidly emerging digital age rather than having acquired familiarity with digital systems as an adult. This unique developmental experience purportedly changed the way this generation think and process information.

Digital play – play involving children's interactions with digital technologies and active use of technologies and digital media content. The range of digital play activities available to young children growing up in the digital age can also involve their online participation, with many toys being internet enabled.

Digital technologies – electronic tools, systems, devices and resources that generate, store or process data. Digital equipment such as a computer or smartphone, tablet or console can be used to access digital tools such as learning platforms and social media platforms, and digital resources such as lessons and games.

Digital wellbeing – having an awareness of how being online can make one feel and looking after oneself and others when online. This includes recognising the impact being online can have on one's emotions, mental wellbeing and physical health, and knowing what to do if something goes wrong.

Displacement theories – these propose that new forms of activities have replaced pre-existing ones. For example, digital technologies are seen as responsible for the decline in previous, more common activities such as children's outdoor play and traditional toys and games.

Early Intervention Foundation (EIF) – an organisation in the UK that champions and supports the use of effective early intervention to improve the lives of children and young people at risk of experiencing poor outcomes.

Ecological systems theory of development – this proposes that we encounter different environments throughout our lifespan that may influence our behaviour to varying degrees. This theory helps practitioners to consider the balance of influences such as the home, school or community environment (as well as wider society) which are likely to play a part in the development of any child.

Electronic media – media that use electronic methods to access the content. This is in contrast to static media, which today are most often created electronically but do not require electronics to be accessed by the end user in the printed form.

Emotional competence – the ability to recognise, interpret and respond constructively to emotions in oneself and others; emotional competence encompasses self-awareness, self-management, social awareness and applying social skills.

Empirical evidence – knowledge obtained through an experiment or observation and documentation of certain behaviours and patterns.

Focus group – a group of selected people who participate in a facilitated discussion to gather their perceptions and/or experiences about a particular topic.

Free play – an unstructured, voluntary, child-initiated activity that allows children to develop imaginative abilities while exploring and experiencing the world around them.

Gender role – a social role encompassing a range of behaviours and attitudes that are generally considered acceptable, appropriate or desirable for a person based on that person's biological or perceived sex.

Guided play – learning experiences that combine the child-directed nature of free play with a focus on learning outcomes and adult facilitation.

Habitus – socially instilled habits, skills, attitudes and behaviours, usually shared by people with similar backgrounds; this affects how individuals perceive the social world around them and react to it.

Human flourishing – a sense of fulfilment that arises from achieving one's full potential as a human being.

Intervention fidelity – the degree to which an intervention or programme is delivered as intended. Only by understanding and measuring whether an intervention has been implemented with fidelity can researchers and practitioners gain a better understanding of how and why an intervention works, and the extent to which outcomes can be improved.

Key stage 4 – in the education systems in England and Wales this refers to the curriculum for pupils aged 14 to 16 in secondary (high) school.

Labelling – the process of categorising; self-identity and the behaviour of individuals may be determined or influenced by the terms used to describe or classify them. Public perceptions can also be influenced by labelling, which can lead to stereotyping and stigma for individuals or groups.

Latency stage (Freud) – in classical psychoanalytic theory, the stage of psychosexual development in which overt sexual interest is sublimated and the child's attention is focused on skills and peer activities with members of their own sex.

Learner-centred processes – these are designed to engage learners as active agents, recognising that learners bring their own knowledge, past experiences, education and ideas which will influence how they take on board new information and learn.

LGBTQ+ – an acronym for lesbian, gay, bisexual, transgender and queer or questioning to describe a person's sexual orientation or gender identity, with the plus sign encompassing other identities such as intersex and asexual.

Mantle of the Expert (MoE) – an education approach that uses imaginary contexts to generate purposeful and engaging activities for learning. MoE is not designed to teach the whole curriculum all of the time but is rather an approach to be used selectively by the teacher along with a range of other methods.

Member checking – a technique for exploring the credibility of research results. Data or results are returned to participants to check for accuracy and resonance with their experiences.

Mental health – not simply the absence of mental ill health (which includes a wide range of mental disorders that affect mood, thinking and behaviour) but also a positive state of mind and body; feeling safe and able to cope, with a sense of connection with people, communities and the wider environment.

Mental health disorder/illness/ill health – used to refer to a wide range of mental health conditions that affect one's mood, thinking and behaviour. Examples of mental health disorders/illness include depression, anxiety disorders, schizophrenia, eating disorders and addictive behaviours.

Mental wellbeing – this represents the positive side of mental health and can be achieved by people with a diagnosis of a mental health disorder; it is personal and therefore unique and needs to be developed and nurtured; others, both individually and collectively, can support or hinder this process.

Mixed-methods approach – a type of research which combines elements of quantitative (involving numerical data collection and analysis) and qualitative (involving non-numerical data collection and analysis) research approaches.

More knowledgeable other (MKO) – someone who has a better understanding or a higher ability level than the learner with respect to a particular task, process or concept.

Multi-component intervention programmes – ones which incorporate two or more components. For example, an intervention to support changes in a child's behaviour might work with both the child and their parents/carers.

Nature deficit disorder – the human costs of alienation from nature; negative consequences include diminished use of the senses, attention difficulties and higher rates of physical and emotional illness.

New digital natives (NDNs) – those individuals born in the 21st century who have been introduced to digital technologies from their first experiences in the world and are highly active and immersed in the digital realm.

One-to-one therapy – therapy sessions, most usually counselling, with just two participants, for example a counsellor or healthcare practitioner and their client.

Para-social relationships – one-sided connections imagined with fictional characters/celebrities, common in childhood and adolescence and which can play a role in identity formation and autonomy development.

Parental engagement – the active involvement of parents/carers in supporting their children's academic or other learning.

Participatory action research (PAR) – a philosophy and methodology of research which seeks transformative change through the simultaneous process of taking action and doing research. PAR involves researchers and participants working together to understand a problematic situation and change it for the better.

Pedagogy/Pedagogical – the method and practice of teaching.

Peer rejection – a global term that encompasses the many behaviours used by children to exclude and hurt one another, including overt forms of control and exclusion and more subtle tactics such as gossiping and spreading rumours. It can take place both online and offline.

Positive psychology – a branch of psychology concerned with the scientific study of human flourishing and an applied approach to optimal functioning.

Primary school – the first level of mandatory education in the UK encompassing ages five to 11. It is the equivalent to elementary and grade school in the United States.

Problematic internet and social media use – the overuse of, and overdependence on, the internet and social media platforms.

Psychoeducation – instruction to provide better understanding of mental health issues for those who have them and those who work or live with those who have these issues (for example teachers and parents).

Psychometric measures – tests that measure psychological values such as aptitude, ability, personality, memory, happiness and intelligence, and are designed for and given in mental health, education and employment settings.

Pupil premium – a grant given by the government to schools in England to decrease the attainment gap for the most disadvantaged children.

Pupil referral units (PRU) – establishments in the UK that provide alternative education for children who are sick, excluded or otherwise outside of the mainstream schooling provision.

Pupil voice – pupils' participation, contribution and influence in a school context, enabling children and young people to have the opportunity to play an active role in decisions that affect them.

Quasi-Experimental Design (QED) – a type of scientific experiment that aims to examine a cause and effect relationship but, unlike a true experiment (see RCT), a quasi-experiment does not rely on random assignment.

Randomised Control Trial (RCT) – a type of scientific experiment that aims to examine a cause and effect relationship and to reduce certain sources of bias. Participants are randomly assigned to one of two groups: one (the experimental group) receiving the intervention that is being tested, and the other (the comparison group or control) receiving an alternative (conventional) treatment.

Relationships and sex education (RSE) – RSE is statutory in all secondary schools in England and relationships education is statutory in all primary schools in England. All schools are required to teach health education.

Resilience – a concept in psychological terms which refers to the ability to recover quickly from difficulties including traumatic events and to take things in one's stride.

Role model – a person or character whose behaviour, example or success is, or can be, emulated by others. A positive role model serves as an example, inspiring children, and therefore plays an essential part in a child's positive development.

SATs – national tests that children take twice during primary school education in England: at the end of key stage 1, when children are aged seven, and at the end of key stage 2, when they are aged 11.

Scaffolding – a variety of instructional techniques used to move students progressively toward stronger understanding and ultimately greater independence in the learning process.

School-based interventions – programmes or strategies designed to produce behaviour change or improve outcomes (for example a health promotion campaign) which take place in a school setting.

Secondary school – the second level of mandatory education in England and Wales covering ages 11 to 19.

Self-care – the practice of taking action to improve one's health and wellbeing.

Self-excluded – a term used in the UK to describe a child who is demonstrating school refusal and has chosen not to attend compulsory education.

Sense of belonging – psychological feeling of belonging or connectedness to a social, spatial, cultural, professional, educational or other type of group or a community. Belonging is a strong and inevitable human feeling and is a subjective experience that can be influenced by a number of factors both within the individual and from their surrounding environment.

Social and emotional development – the process by which children start to understand who they are, what they are feeling and what to expect when interacting with others, thus enabling them to form and sustain positive relationships, and experience, manage and express emotions.

Social anxiety – a condition sometimes referred to as social phobia; a type of anxiety disorder that causes an individual to experience extreme fear in social settings.

Social capital – the effective functioning of social groups through interpersonal relationships; a shared sense of identity, a shared understanding, shared norms, shared values, trust, cooperation and reciprocity.

Social constructivist (approach) – based on a theory of knowledge according to which human development is socially situated and learning is a collaborative process. Knowledge is constructed through interactions with others and with one's culture and society.

Social intelligence – the ability to successfully build relationships and navigate social environments; an awareness of informal rules, or norms, that govern social interaction.

Social justice framework – a way of seeing and acting aimed at resisting unfairness and inequality while enhancing freedom and possibility for all. Attention is given to how people, policies, practices, curricula and institutions may be used to liberate rather than oppress those who are least powerful.

Social learning theory – this describes the importance of observing, modelling and imitating the behaviours, attitudes and emotional reactions of others, and considers how both environmental and cognitive factors interact to influence human learning and behaviour.

Social media – internet-based interactive platforms such as Twitter, Facebook and Instagram that allow information and ideas to be shared.

Sociogram – a sociometric diagram representing the pattern of relationships among individuals in a group.

Sociometrics – a quantitative methodology for measuring social relationships.

Special educational needs and disabilities (SEND) – a child or young person has special educational needs and/or disabilities if they have a learning difficulty and/or a disability that means they need special health and education support.

Specialist education – the practice of educating students in a way that addresses their individual differences and special needs. Ideally, this process involves the individually planned and systematically monitored arrangement of teaching procedures, adapted equipment and materials, and accessible settings.

Spiral curriculum – one that regularly returns to the same topics, building on and deepening knowledge over time.

Strengths-based approach – a person-led, holistic philosophy which focuses on an individual's personal strengths as well as the wider social and community network to promote wellbeing (rather than attending to individual deficits).

Strengths and Difficulties Questionnaire (SDQ) – a brief emotional and behavioural screening questionnaire for children and young people aged 3 to 16 used widely in the National Health Service (NHS) in the UK and in education settings worldwide.

Student voice – the values, opinions, beliefs, perspectives and cultural backgrounds of individual students and groups of students in an education setting, and instructional approaches and techniques that are based on student choices, interests, passions and ambitions.

Team around the child (TAC) – a multi-disciplinary team of practitioners established on a case-by-case basis to support a child, young person or family.

Techno-utopia – an ideal society where the impact of technologies is extremely positive.

Thematic analysis – a qualitative research method that analyses data through identifying themes to create meaning and understanding.

Theory of change – an evaluation methodology that seeks to use theory, research and experience to theorise pathways to change.

Theory of loose parts – objects found in nature which promote development through encouraging creative and self-directed play.

Therapeutic alliance – the relationship between a practitioner and their client, how they connect, behave and engage with each other.

Therapeutic counselling – a change-oriented process that occurs in the context of a contractual, empowering and empathetic professional relationship which aims to improve a recipient's mental wellbeing and strengthen their relationship with themselves and others.

3D building environment – a virtual reality which has a figurative appearance and allows interaction with other (networked) individuals as well as the manipulation of objects.

Trefoil symbol – a golden three-leafed symbol on a deep blue background that globally represents Girl Guides.

Unconditional positive regard – the basic acceptance and support of a person regardless of what the person says or does without evaluating or judging them.

Virtual and digital (delivery) **modes** – methods of remote service provision without any traditional face-to-face interaction between provider and participant. This may include delivery via digital interfaces such as video conferencing and online training courses, as well as contact by phone, email or chatroom.

Voice of the child – children's unique perspective on their lives; this concerns the real involvement of children and young people in matters that affect them. It means more than seeking their views; it includes involving them in decision-making to create meaningful change and better outcomes as well as facilitating a sense of empowerment and inclusion.

Voice over Internet Protocol (VoIP) – a technology that allows people to make voice calls using a broadband internet connection instead of a traditional (or analogue) phone line.

Wellbeing – a multifaceted term which encompasses one's physical, mental and social wellbeing; positive wellbeing refers to a physically and emotionally healthy, contented and prosperous state.

Whole-school approach – cohesive, collective and collaborative action in and by a school community (including senior leaders, teachers and all school staff as well as parents/ carers) that has been strategically constructed to improve student learning, behaviour and wellbeing, and the conditions that support these.

Woodcraft Folk – a UK-based grassroots educational movement in which children and young people learn about the world and understand how to value the planet and each other.

Zone of proximal development – the difference between what a learner can do without help and what they can achieve with guidance and encouragement from a skilled partner or **MKO**.

Notes on contributors

Bronach Hughes is Pyramid Project Coordinator at the University of West London, leads on Pyramid Clubs – a school-based mental health intervention that supports children aged 7 to 14 – and has been involved with the project since 2001. As well as overseeing the delivery of clubs in London she supports licensed delivery organisations across the UK with materials and research. Bronach volunteers with Girlguiding UK as a Brownie and a Guide Leader and trains other adults within Girlguiding, particularly around safeguarding children. As a school governor for 20 years and the chair of a local schools' cooperative trust in Surrey, she also works closely with school staff and therefore understands the school environment well. In 2020 Bronach embarked on a Professional Doctorate in Education with the aim of exploring in more detail the role of schools in supporting children's mental health, particularly through group-work interventions.

Michelle Jayman is a Chartered Psychologist and a Lecturer in Psychology at the University of Roehampton. She has a background in education and extensive work experience in schools and higher education. She is a founder member and convenor of the British Education Research Association (BERA) Mental Health, Wellbeing and Education Special Interest Group and a champion for the British Psychological Society (BPS) Education Section. Her main research interests include children's and young people's mental health and wellbeing, and programmes and interventions to support and improve learner outcomes. Michelle's latest research focuses on blended learning models in education and the relationship between technology and wellbeing. She has two sons and is passionate about promoting and supporting mental wellbeing for all.

Leah Jewett is a writer, co-author of the game Sex Ed on the Cards and founding director of Outspoken Sex Ed – a social enterprise that encourages parents to talk openly with their children about sex and relationships issues. Having grown up in 1960s San Francisco, Leah became a freelance sub-editor on a range of youth-magazine titles in London. She took voluntary redundancy from the *Guardian* after 19 years as deputy chief sub-editor on the *Observer Magazine* where in 2008 she edited the *Observer Book Of...* series. Retraining as a relationships and sex education (RSE) facilitator, she became the Working Group Lead on RSE for the Women's Equality Party. She sits on the International Advisory Board of Media Matters for Women and on the Education Panel of Our Streets Now. Leah's main interests are the impact of pornography on young people and the interrelationship of pleasure and consent. She has a teenage daughter and son.

Jenny Lewis is a retired teacher and educational consultant. She worked in primary schools in London, Oxford and Norwich as a full-time teacher and member of school management teams, mainly involved in curriculum development. For the last ten years of her teaching career she used the Mantle of the Expert (MoE) pedagogy with students and helped to train teachers. Jenny also worked as a freelance educational consultant and trainer, going into schools to help teachers develop MoE and Imaginative Inquiry approaches with their classes. Additionally, she took part in workshops at conferences and worked with senior leadership teams to develop the practice in their schools. Jenny is particularly interested in how MoE can bring children who struggle with formal structures and academic skills right into the centre of their learning, empowering them and focusing on their wellbeing and personal development.

Toni Medcalf is an integrative psychotherapist and the director, founder and CEO of the Schools Counselling Partnership (SCP). In 2009 she set up the Ealing Schools Counselling

Partnership across five schools. After demand grew through word of mouth in other London boroughs, she established the SCP. Toni had previously spent years in the music industry; through her artist management company and record label, she represented bands, singer/songwriters, producers and writers, signing them to international labels. Since qualifying as an integrative psychotherapist she has worked for Adults Surviving Child Abuse, the Open Door Project and the BRIT School for Performing Arts. A mindfulness teacher in the Paws b programme for 7- to 11-year-olds and a trustee of DreamArts, Toni is also a mentor and group leader for BASE Babywatching and sits on its advisory board.

Harriet Menter is Education Manager at Scotswood Garden, where she has worked since 2007. Scotswood Garden is a unique community garden in Newcastle upon Tyne that provides a wide range of activities for people of all ages and backgrounds. Harriet is a Forest School leader and trainer, and an Accredited Practitioner of the Institute of Outdoor Learning. She has been running the Forest School Breeze Project since 2017 with funding from the St James's Place Foundation, Froebel Trust, British & Foreign School Society and the Wellesley Trust Fund and Ward Hadaway Fund at the Community Foundation of Tyne and Wear. She is interested in how we can use a Forest School approach to help children and young people who struggle in the classroom environment. Harriet is happiest when tending a fire.

Maddie Ohl is Professor of Child Mental Health and Wellbeing at the University of West London (UWL). In addition, she is currently Director of Studies in the Graduate Centre at UWL, where she actively does research and supervises doctoral research students. Her research interests centre on the mental health and wellbeing of children and young people, with a particular focus on mental health and wellbeing in learning environments ranging from primary school right through to university. She carried out early research into the primary school version of the Pyramid Club intervention for her own PhD and has been involved with Pyramid since 2002.

Kyrill Potapov is a PhD candidate in human–computer interaction at University College London. His research interests include personal data interpretation and the potential role of data technologies in scaffolding learning with adolescents. He has pursued a Vygotskian approach in supporting and analysing young people's collaborative meaning-making. His thesis is entitled 'Orchestrating the interpretation of personal informatics data in secondary school classrooms'. Kyrill is an English teacher at a secondary school in London, where he has taught since 2010. His teaching role has involved being an enrichment coordinator and facilitating extracurricular collaborative projects such as overseeing self-published student story anthologies, producing films, running charity campaigns, designing board games and forming debate teams. In 2019 Kyrill also trained and coordinated student mentors as part of an academic and pastoral buddy system.

Lucy Tiplady is a research associate in the Centre for Learning and Teaching at Newcastle University. Since 2005 Lucy has worked on a diverse range of projects and evaluations within education and has developed specialisms in the areas of practitioner enquiry: visual, participatory and co-produced research methods; outdoor learning; and children's and young people's wellbeing. Working collaboratively with schools, young people and the wider education community has led to her interest in how research methods can be used as tools for enquiry to aid practitioner and student learning and in how alternative learning environments can increase wellbeing and address educational disadvantage.

Phil Tottman is the CEO and senior founder of Book of Beasties Ltd and co-creator of Book of Beasties: The Mental Wellness Card Game. Graduating from the University of West London with a BA Hons in broadcast journalism, Phil went on to write for several media companies including Bauer, NewBay and Incisive. Phil was inspired to create Book of Beasties from personal experience of mental health difficulties and homelessness in his youth. He developed Book of Beasties, along with Tom Dryland and Nadia De Kuyper, to support children's wellbeing and to help children understand about emotions and mental health. Phil has led Book of Beasties to win multiple awards, worked with researchers to build an evidence base, and partnered with Great Ormond Street Children's Hospital Charity and its Play team. Book of Beasties' resources now support hundreds of UK schools.

Foreword

Pooky Knightsmith

When I was first asked to write this foreword, the world was a very different place for all of us, and especially for our children. Even pre-pandemic, the need was there to help us understand and navigate tricky waters with the next generation – but now, more than ever, we need help to know what we should be doing, and how, in order to help our children to grow, stay safe and thrive.

Supporting New Digital Natives: Children's Mental Health and Wellbeing in a Hi-Tech Age pulls together insights into how children and young people can be active co-producers in shaping their learning experiences. Not only is it helpful for thinking about the role new digital natives play in their own educational journey and for supporting their mental health and wellbeing in today's rapidly changing virtual climate, but the varied and innovative interventions and initiatives it outlines will surely continue to inspire and have relevance down the line. It can speak to teachers, parents and carers, educators, social workers and others who work directly with the new digital native generation, and crucially it can help make a real difference to the lives of those children and young people.

This book is a guide to what matters most right now. As both a parent and a professional, I found it full of the ideas, support and reassurance I need both to grow with my children and colleagues and to look towards an uncertain future with more confidence. The jumping-off point of wellbeing in the digital age is a perfect one. It tackles, head on, the issues that feel most pressing in a world where as a mother of primary school aged children I've had to come to peace with the idea of days made up almost entirely of screen time. Whether my children are learning maths, doing PE, reading with their cousins or playing dolls with their friends, it's all done via a screen.

The first chapter is reassuring and practical, and sets the scene for the rest of the book. Each chapter that follows shares new ideas and approaches with clear explanation and real-world examples. There are golden threads that tie it all together, creating a book of many credible, kind voices which unite in their message of pragmatism and hope. As one reviewer commented, 'This is one of the few books on this topic and it does what it says on the tin – I believe it will last long into the future.'

Maybe, like me, you feel a little lost and unsure right now, but you hold hope in your heart and you want to help the children and young people you work with or care for to find a way forward. If that sounds like you, then please hold onto that hope and allow the many expert voices in this book to help guide the way.

It's going to be OK. We'll make it so.

Preface

2020 was an extraordinary year. The global health crisis declared by the World Health Organization (WHO) in March in the wake of the COVID-19 pandemic heralded exponential change to our everyday lives with profound and devastating consequences for individuals, families, communities and nations worldwide. Unquestionably, with millions of cases and hundreds of thousands of mortalities across the globe, immediate attention was firmly focused on tackling the physical burden of the disease and stemming its tidal spread. As we continue to learn to live in the aftermath and adjust to a reshaped normality, the deleterious impact of the pandemic on our mental health and wellbeing is becoming increasingly evident. Some of us have been more directly affected by the virus than others, and likewise our capacity to maintain good mental wellbeing is uniquely related to our individual circumstances. The frequent refrain with respect to the pandemic: 'We are not all in the same boat. We are all in the same storm'[1] rings poignantly true. There is indeed a clear divergence of experiences across different ages, geographies and individual circumstances. Children and young people (CYP) are at higher risk of developing mental health problems – for many their mental wellbeing has deteriorated substantially during the pandemic, and increased rates of anxiety and depression are likely to persist for some time to come.

However, it is crucial for us to understand how the effects of the pandemic interplay with the longer-term trend in CYP's declining wellbeing: the original impetus behind this book. The authors are primarily concerned with CYP growing up in the early decades of the 21st century and how to support this unique generation to maintain mentally healthy lives. While the case studies presented here originate in the UK,

Figure 0.1: 'Gimme a break' – thoughts and feelings about COVID-19 and the lockdown (Emily, age 10)

the voices and experiences they represent will resonate across geographical borders.

Pre-coronavirus, there was an escalating mental health crisis – estimates at the start of the decade placed the percentage of CYP worldwide experiencing mental health difficulties in the region of 10 to 20 per cent. Furthermore, compared to our European neighbours, the UK performed particularly poorly on children's subjective wellbeing, with the nation's 15-year-olds reporting to be the saddest and least satisfied with their lives.[2] These findings present a snapshot of life in 2017–18 and reflect children's mental wellbeing before the 2020 pandemic hit – the subsequent full and longer-term implications are, of course, still unravelling.

When the idea to write this book first took shape, the ubiquity of digital technologies and their influence on the lives of children growing up at this point in history emerged as a central thread, and both positive and nefarious links to mental health and wellbeing have been convincingly made by researchers and academics. As editors, we have brought together a range of carefully chosen interventions for a broad readership interested in CYP's mental wellbeing which, in line with the Royal Colleges of GPs (RCGP), Paediatrics and Child Health (RCPCH) and Psychiatrists (RCPsych), we believe is 'everyone's business'. These eight case studies were selected because of their original contributions, each focusing on different aspects of CYP's lives which are inextricably linked to mental wellbeing, such as friendships and relationships, play and learning experiences, and opportunities for connecting with nature and the community. More than this, each chapter is a platform for raising CYP's voice, rightly placing them, as experts in their own lives, at the heart of mental wellbeing interventions and services.

Before the pandemic, connectedness to the digital world was broadly considered the major defining feature of a generation born in the new millennium. Sadly, an alternative discourse is burgeoning around the new 'COVID generation', highlighting widely held perceptions of the profound impact the pandemic has had, and will continue having, on CYP's lives. Emerging evidence shows that 12- to 24-year-olds are one of the worst-affected groups, particularly in terms of the labour market and mental health outcomes. Certainly we know that pre-existing mental health difficulties have worsened and many CYP have experienced a decline in wellbeing without access to informal support systems usually provided by friends or trusted adults, including teachers, due to lockdown restrictions. Nonetheless, the ubiquity of digital technologies is still a distinguishing feature of CYP's lives, albeit in a new, shaken and shifting landscape. Moreover, the potential for such technologies to operate as a force for good, or for bad, also remains a constant.

Friends were seen as the most helpful form of support for CYP during lockdown and access to media networks greatly magnified opportunities to stay connected. On the other hand, a spike in social media consumption was associated with negative behaviours and greater risk of adverse effects, for example technology-based social comparison and feedback-seeking, and heightened concerns over body image. This apparent dualism, inherent in digital technologies, is a common theme that reverberates through the case studies in this book. Crucially, as we see in the final chapter, digital technologies have rapidly assumed an integral role as more traditional forms of mental wellbeing support for CYP have become harder, or impossible, to access. This unexpected predicament raises important questions concerning how blended models of support might look in the future and what this means for our lives beyond the pandemic.

The enduring battle against the COVID-19 crisis has brought the plight of CYP's mental wellbeing further into the spotlight, with new as well as existing challenges to overcome. It is imperative that government policies and strategies worldwide are robust and well targeted to protect the mental wellbeing of all CYP and prevent the onset of more serious problems taking hold. This will require an understanding of the complex and intersecting nature of the issues facing CYP, many of which predate the pandemic. The purpose of this book is to highlight some of those crucial factors and, moreover, to showcase some innovative and insightful projects which offer simple, practical approaches to help ameliorate CYP's mental wellbeing. Undoubtedly, a global health crisis is likely to have a lasting impact across multiple areas of CYP's lives. Nevertheless, a true commitment to making CYP's mental health 'everyone's business' will ensure that the remainder of the decade is extraordinary too. The contributors to this book strongly believe that now is the time for instigating real change to improve children's and young people's mental wellbeing, and with it, to bestow optimism and hope for an unpredictable future.

Michelle, Maddie and Leah
November 2020

Notes
[1] British writer Damian Barr introduced this analogy.
[2] The Children's Society (2020) *The Good Childhood Report 2020*, London: The Children's Society.

1

Digital lives: growing up in a hi-tech world and staying mentally healthy

Michelle Jayman

Introduction

Children in the early decades of the 21st century are growing up in a social world remarkably different from that of their parents or grandparents.[1] While every generation is transitory by nature, a uniquely striking feature for children living in contemporary society is the proliferation of digital technologies and the unprecedented pace and scale of change such technologies bring. The opportunities and benefits afforded those born into a digitally rich environment are immense and can have a positive impact on many important areas of children's lives including education and learning, play and creativity, and relationships and social connectivity. However, casting a shadow over this vision of techno-utopia is a cloud of associated risks and potential harms which appear in guises unique to a digital environment, for example cyberbullying, online sexual exploitation and access to distressing content. While not all children are exposed to digital technologies equally, the modern world is constantly changing in complex ways, and digital technologies are an integral part of this shifting landscape. An increasingly interconnected digital world requires children to learn the skills and be given the support to navigate the complexities of a hi-tech environment and to feel safe and happy to live, learn and play within it. This book is concerned with how children can live mentally healthy lives, meeting the challenges inherent in a society increasingly dominated by digital technologies, while also harnessing the abundance of great opportunities this has to offer.

The original 'digital natives' became young adults at the beginning of the 21st century. This book addresses a younger generation of 'new digital natives' – today's children – whose formative experiences are shaped by a social world saturated with digital technologies. International research suggests that the use of digital technologies has increased exponentially worldwide while the age of first access continues to drop (Gottschalk, 2019). In the United Kingdom, 50 per cent of ten-year-olds owned a smartphone in 2019 (Ofcom, 2019) and the average age of first mobile ownership was seven (Childwise, 2020). Patterns of usage are also shifting. In 2018, 'tweens' (aged 9 to 12) reported digitally active lives resembling those of teenagers recorded just three to four years earlier (Chaudron et al, 2018). Electronic devices connecting children to the digital realm have pervaded our everyday lives, spurring speculation on the effects of prolonged and immersive use. Sensationalist headlines such as 'Not-so-smartphones: Technology rewiring our brains and harming our intellect' (Daly, 2017) and 'Social media addiction should be seen as a disease, MPs say' (Waterson, 2019) have contributed to the proliferation of 'neuromyths' while linking technology use with poor developmental outcomes. Nonetheless, genuine concerns regarding the potentially nefarious effects of digital technologies on children's mental health and wellbeing have been repeatedly raised by parents/carers, educators, practitioners and policy-makers alike. Research in this area is still in its infancy and children's relationships with digital technologies are complex, their experiences multifaceted and disparate. What is certain is that digital technologies will be a distinguishing feature of childhood. Understanding the power, potential and risks of digital technologies in children's lives is important for parents/carers, professionals working with children and policy-makers; but most crucially, for children themselves.

Introducing the new digital natives

Prensky (2001) is credited with popularising the term 'digital native', which he used to describe individuals who are highly literate and integrated in technology. Prensky's central premise was that, due to this technological singularity, digital natives 'think and process information fundamentally differently from their predecessors' (Prensky, 2001: 1). However, critics have argued that this term has often been misapplied to categorise an entire generation (Ernest et al, 2014). In this book, the term 'new digital natives' (NDNs) describes children growing up in a hi-tech age, acknowledging that experiences are not identical for all children. There is significant diversity in the technological skills, knowledge and interests of children, as well as in their exposure to and use of digital technologies, which reveals a more nuanced picture and exposes a number of digital divisions.

To understand children's formative experiences in a digital society, Bourdieu's (1983) concept of habitus is useful. At its core, this refers to the embodiment of our culture as a means of seeing and acting in the world. Growing up in a digitally rich environment offers children unique opportunities for constructing a 'technological habitus'. NDNs are inclined to develop a robust technological habitus as their behaviours are framed by their experiences with technology from a young age. Modern toys and games often have technologies embedded within them which leads to different experiences and dispositions towards play and learning. For example, a touch screen device can be used for drawing and creative play rather than traditional materials such as paper, crayons and glue. The human brain changes in response to novel experiences, and childhood in particular is a time of high susceptibility to experience-dependent change (Bavelier et al, 2010). Adults, without the type of formative experiences with digital technologies that children incur, may need to reconstruct existing ways of perceiving and operating to adjust to a hi-tech environment, as their technological habitus will be weaker.

Another distinguishing feature of the digital realm is that in terms of technological savviness, children often occupy the role of 'more knowledgeable other' (Vygotsky, 1978), thus causing unprecedented disruption to the traditional flow of knowledge from older to younger generations. Children are typically the 'expert' when it comes to digital technologies, readily embracing and mastering new products and innovations, with some also designing and developing their own technology-based ideas. Listening to children's voices and personal experiences is critical in gaining a fuller understanding of how digital technologies influence children's lives and, moreover, how to harness those technologies to optimise healthy development, manage risk and minimise harm.

The concern of this book is children's mental health and wellbeing. The World Health Organization (WHO, 2018) recognises mental health as being more than the absence of mental health disorder and incorporates the concept of positive mental health or wellbeing – the term mental wellbeing encompasses this holistic view. A wealth of evidence suggests that children's mental wellbeing is in decline (Sadler et al, 2018; The Children's Society, 2019, 2020), with numerous stressors linked to the digital technologies that pervade many children's lives. This has introduced new challenges for parents/carers, educators, practitioners and policy-makers. Grave concerns regarding children's widespread captivation with digital technologies have been voiced, not least because of the many social, biological, cognitive and psychological changes that occur during sensitive periods, particularly during early childhood and adolescence, and their impact on healthy development. The chapters that follow present a selection of programmes and initiatives designed to support the mental wellbeing of a generation of children growing up in a rapidly changing, hi-tech world. Some unique features of our 21st-century digital society and their influence on children's formative experiences are first briefly explored.

The changing nature of play in a digital world

Playful experiences contribute hugely to children's development and provide important opportunities to learn, particularly in the early years. Healey and Mendelsohn (2019) point out that increased screen time among younger children has coincided with a slump in active play and diminished regard for traditional toys such as dolls, action figures, puzzles and building blocks. Alongside this, electronic or virtual versions of well-established, popular games such as Scrabble for older children have been developed for use on mobile devices. Arguably, these technology-driven changes directly interfere with the interaction between adult carers and children, as social engagement through facial expressions, gestures and vocalisations is unavoidably diluted. This position is challenged by Sakr (2020) who points out the multidimensional nature of digital play, which should not be seen as either being isolated from other types of play or as displacing play-based interactions. Conversely, she argues that children are constantly moving across spaces and environments, and between digital and non-digital actions through 'connected play'. A simple example of this would be a child listening to a song on a smartphone while simultaneously interacting with others by dancing or singing and encouraging others to join in, effectively connecting digital and non-digital modes in a synergised play experience. According to Sakr, digital play is often not seen as *real* play by practitioners in early years settings, which she argues is evident in the lack of active strategies for integrating technologies within children's social play.

Tensions among authors clearly exist regarding how the changing nature of play affects young children's social and emotional development. Despite these disagreements, social play is unanimously regarded as essential for healthy psychological development. This enables children to 'learn how to make decisions, solve problems, exert self-control and follow rules' (Gray, 2011: 443). Children learn to regulate their emotions and acquire vital social skills in order to make friends and manage relationships with peers. For Gray, the steady decline in children's self-directed and outdoor play is inextricably linked to a concurrent rise in psychopathology. Another significant factor shaping play patterns is digital technologies being perceived by parents and carers as an easy and effective means of keeping children occupied and 'safe' inside, away from adult-perceived harms such as 'stranger danger' encountered outside in the real world.

The proliferation of digital, indoor play has been associated with children's increasingly sedentary lifestyles and rising obesity levels (Carson et al, 2016). Research by Clements (2004) revealed a significant decline in outdoor play habits in a generation when the play patterns of children were compared with those of their parents. International research involving more than 200,000 11- to 15-year-olds showed that the relationship between digital technology consumption and physical activity differed according to age, gender and nationality (Melkevik et al, 2010). Furthermore, the type of digital activity (not simply the amount of time spent) was influential on the outcome. Technology designers have increasingly explored opportunities to embed mandatory active components, such as dancing or exercise, within digital games. These efforts aside, the physical environment is important, and natural outdoor spaces are far superior for engendering spontaneous free play (Gray, 2011). In line with the concept of connected play, Sakr (2020) points to the growth in gaming apps that require players to physically explore the outside world. While this shows potential for harnessing technology to increase physical exercise in children, especially as they get older, it is certainly no substitute for traditional sports or fitness regimes (Gottschalk, 2019).

Developing and maintaining social relationships

Social engagement enhances children's socio-emotional skills, providing one of the essential building blocks for developing friendships and healthy relationships. In recent years, digital technologies have facilitated a seismic shift in how we communicate, and for NDNs, social media dominates patterns of social interaction. An inquiry by the House of Commons Science and Technology Committee (HoCSTC) identified 'a range of instances where social media was a force for good in the lives of young people' (2019: 17). Evidence suggested that social relationships can be stimulated by digital technology, and online communication shows a positive relationship with friendship quality and social capital (Kardefelt-Winther, 2017). Furthermore, online communication has been credited with encouraging NDNs to be more open and honest in conversations. In a similar vein, Peter et al (2005) found that introverts were more motivated to engage online, thus increasing their likelihood of developing friendships. Meanwhile, research by the charity YoungMinds suggested that children who are isolated – for example due to disabilities – can find their voice by joining an online community (HoCSTC, 2019). Despite these benefits there are, however, legitimate concerns relating to how and with whom children interact online (Pew Research Center, 2012). Research by the National Society for the Protection of Cruelty to Children (NSPCC, 2018), for example, found that one in seven children aged 11 to 18 had been contacted online and asked to send sexual messages or images of themselves.

Classic and contemporary scholars (eg Erikson, 1968; Arnett, 2015) agree that early adolescence is an intense period of identity formation. Heightened body consciousness and concerns about how one is perceived by others are common during this stage of development. NDNs use social media platforms to share updates and photographs, and to stay constantly connected online. A survey involving 3,000 school pupils aged 6 to 19 in the UK revealed that following friends' updates was the main reason that over a quarter (27 per cent) used social media (HoC, 2019). Sherman et al (2016) insist that the simple act of having a photograph 'liked' acts as a quantifiable social endorsement and that perceptions of photographs are significantly affected by popularity (for example the number of previous 'likes'). While children may be vying for online popularity, browsing the carefully constructed online personas of others can surreptitiously invoke feelings of envy (Verduyn et al, 2017) and inadequacy (Kardefelt-Winther, 2017).

Evidence also indicates that anti-social behaviours including cyberbullying are easily facilitated in the online realm. A national survey by NHS Digital (2018) reported that one in five 11- to 19-year-olds in England had experienced cyberbullying in the previous year, with girls more likely to have been victims than boys. Research suggests a strong link between off- and online bullying. While cyberbullying often presents a vehicle for perpetrators of traditional bullying for abusing their victims further, it has distinct characteristics: digital communication enables 24/7 exposure, denying victims any respite or safe haven; incidents can be shared and forwarded multiple times;

and online anonymity encourages disinhibition, prompting perpetrators to share increasingly extreme and harmful content. NDNs primarily engage in social media and internet use in private spaces using a smartphone (Frith, 2017). This thwarts the efforts of responsible adults to prevent children from encountering deleterious and inappropriate content including pornography, hate speech and violence, and websites normalising harmful behaviours. Pornography is reportedly 'one click away' from most UK children (BBC News, 2019, np), while survey findings revealed that 31 per cent of children aged 12 to 15 had seen online content they found worrying and 9 per cent had seen something of a sexual nature that made them feel uncomfortable (Ofcom, 2019). However, data from *EU Kids Online* (Haddon et al, 2012) indicated that 40 per cent of parents/carers whose children had seen sexual images online were unaware of this, indicating worrying discrepancies between adults' and children's accounts of NDN's experiences with digital technologies.

Digital technologies and children's mental wellbeing

Societal concerns that children are spending too much time on digital devices at the cost of more valuable activities such as outdoor play, physical exercise and face-to-face social encounters have spawned popular displacement theories alongside a growing body of research examining children's digital lives. One survey (Childwise, 2020) involving 2,200 UK children aged 5 to 16 revealed that the average amount of daily mobile phone use for children aged seven plus was three hours and 20 minutes. More than half of respondents admitted to sleeping with their phone next to their bed. A proliferation of studies has emerged highlighting the prominence of digital technologies and claiming that screen time negatively impacts on children's sleep, physical activity and psychosocial functioning (Frith, 2017).

Many of those responsible for policy decisions have tended towards a precautionary response, with the American Academy of Pediatrics (2016), for example, recommending a one-hour limit of high-quality screen content, co-viewed with a carer, for children under five. However, emerging research suggests that many studies looking at mental wellbeing outcomes are correlational and show small effect sizes (Gottschalk, 2019). Moreover, digital engagement does not necessarily displace positive developmental experiences (Przybylski et al, 2019), and longitudinal data has shown that simply restricting the time children spend on digital technologies does not directly translate to a greater uptake of physical activities (Kardefelt-Winther, 2017).

The Royal College of Paediatrics and Child Health (RCPCH, 2019) insist that there is simply not enough robust evidence to assert that digital activity or 'screen time', in and of itself, is harmful to a child's health at any age (RCPCH, 2019). Yet there is sufficient support for a link between extreme use and physical, psychological and behavioural difficulties in adolescents (Rosen et al, 2014).[2] According to Przybylski and Weinstein (2017), these findings suggest a 'Goldilocks effect' whereby moderate engagement is beneficial but too much, or too little, is detrimental. Review evidence showed that being digitally active helped to boost existing social relationships and initiate new friendships (Kardefelt-Winther, 2017). A minority of children with restricted or zero engagement may therefore be missing out on valuable opportunities to connect with peers and enhance their social capital (often associated with higher levels of wellbeing). Likewise, extreme use can be problematic, and is linked to social withdrawal and isolation. One study (OECD, 2017) involving 35 countries found a negative association between extreme use of digital technologies and life satisfaction, with participants (aged 15) reporting feelings of loneliness. Survey findings from *EU Kids Online* (Haddon et al, 2012) revealed that older children with emotional difficulties and higher levels of sensation-seeking were more likely to engage in excessive internet use and thus experience negative outcomes.

A distinction appears to exist between those children who can engage healthily in the digital realm and others who are more vulnerable. Findings from Sadler et al (2018) indicated that children aged 11 to 19 with existing mental health problems may be more susceptible to detrimental outcomes from online engagement. This group, particularly those with clinical levels of emotional difficulties, were more prone to daily social media use and to spending longer periods of time online compared with their peers. Girls reported a greater likelihood of comparing themselves to others on social media, while both girls and boys admitted that the number of 'likes' they received affected their mood. The group overall were more than twice as likely as those without existing difficulties to have experienced cyberbullying in the past year (41.5 per cent compared with 18.1 per cent) and were also more likely to be perpetrators of cyberbullying themselves (14.6 per cent compared with 6.9 per cent).

Challenges and opportunities in the era of new digital natives

The ways in which children connect with and experience the world is constantly shifting due to the rapid pace of technological change and innovation. Within the home, children's digital skills start to emerge at a young age, usually by their observing and mirroring adult carers and older siblings. A child's potential to develop their technological habitus is influenced by several interrelated factors including socio-economic status, exposure, and the skills, knowledge, attitudes and perceptions of their parents/carers (Chaudron et al, 2018). Early personal experiences which help children develop competencies and a healthy approach to the digital world are diverse and may become more uneven as children get older and enter education. Micheli (2015) examined the mediation of digital activities by social environment and socio-economic background for a group of Italian adolescents. Findings revealed that those from higher household income groups spent more time online doing schoolwork and acquiring new skills (capital-enhancing activities) compared with those from poorer backgrounds, who focused predominantly on socialising and gaming. Inevitably, children's online experiences cannot be studied in isolation from their lives in general, and examining these differences can foster a better understanding of how digital technologies impact on children in unique ways.

While multiple studies have examined the time children spend on digital devices, the content and context of usage has received much less scrutiny. Also, perceptions of 'how long is too long' shift over time and vary between generations. Ferguson (2017) points out that children's screen consumption often exceeds levels recommended by national policy guidelines, which are set according to adult estimates of appropriateness. More nuanced approaches that consider the various digital activities that children engage in, and why, have been called for to make recommendations grounded in children's lived experiences (Bavelier et al, 2010). UK guidelines from the RCPCH (2019) recommend that more attention should be given to how digital technologies can support child wellbeing (such as improving online safety) rather than to setting arbitrary age-appropriate time limits. Authoritarian policies, such as the ban implemented in France on mobile phones in schools for children under 15 (Willsher, 2017), reflect ongoing preoccupations with risks, even though these are not rooted in robust research evidence, rather than efforts to exploit the potential benefits such technologies afford.

More multidisciplinary research is needed to better understand the complex relationship between digital technologies and child outcomes. Due to the ubiquity of digital technologies, it is imperative that children develop good habits and make informed decisions so that the risks associated with online activities are minimised. Although they are technologically savvy, children may be less digitally resilient in terms of their ability to recognise danger and maintain a healthy off- and online balance in their lives. Digital technologies need to be harnessed effectively to promote mental wellbeing while encouraging those experiencing difficulties or in distress to seek support, either off- or online.

Supporting children's mental wellbeing in a digital age

Narratives around digital technologies and children's healthy development continue to provoke vigorous debate and to divide opinion. Nonetheless, evidence does suggest that children's mental wellbeing is in decline. On the cusp of the 2020s, one in eight 5- to 19-year-olds in England was identified with a diagnosable mental health condition and emotional difficulties were increasingly common (Sadler et al, 2018). Mental ill health affects both quality of life and life chances, with children from the poorest 20 per cent of households four times more likely to have serious mental health difficulties by age 11 than children from the wealthiest 20 per cent (Gutman et al, 2015). Despite these figures, estimates revealed that less than a third (30.5 per cent) of children diagnosed with disorders had accessed NHS-funded treatment, while others faced lengthy waiting times. Support was denied to many of those in need on the grounds that their condition was not considered severe enough (HoC, 2019).

Worryingly, these findings present only part of the picture, as national figures for children below diagnostic thresholds are not recorded. Research by The Children's Society (2019) which measured the subjective wellbeing of 8- to 17-year-olds concluded that children's happiness was in decline. Psychological distress was associated with academic and sexual pressures, social media, bullying and negative body image. Many debilitating factors were linked to children's online lives, highlighting the complexity of the relationship NDNs have with technologies that are so ingrained in daily life: 'I feel like technology is taking over and people are becoming too reliant on it. It acts as a blindfold and is hard to remove' (female, aged 14) (The Children's Society, 2019).

Undoubtedly, intervening at an early stage and preventing mental health difficulties from arising in the first place is better for children, their families, communities and society as a whole. Evidence suggests that wellbeing declines as children get older, underlining the need to equip children early in life with skills to support their own wellbeing, develop resilience and flourish (Khan, 2016). Early intervention and proactive approaches also make good economic sense; they are more cost-effective as they reduce the need for more intensive and expensive treatment later on (Layard and Clark, 2014).

The UK government has adopted a settings-based strategy underpinned by the ethos that responsibility for children's mental wellbeing is everyone's concern. The pivotal role of schools has been well documented (eg Department of Health (DoH) and Department for Education (DfE), 2017). A new relationships and health curriculum places statutory responsibility on schools to promote mental wellbeing, reduce stigma and provide appropriate support for pupils experiencing difficulties (DfE, 2019). However, a major challenge for school leaders and others tasked with implementing prevention strategies and early intervention initiatives is the limited knowledge available about the most effective and appropriate approaches, something this book hopes to shine some light on.

How this book is structured and an overview of chapters

The interventions and initiatives presented in this book offer an insight into a range of approaches which have the common purpose of supporting mental wellbeing for children growing up in a digital age. The contributions are eclectic and include the voices of practitioners, researchers, programme developers and, crucially, children themselves.

The theoretical framework of the book aligns with social models of mental health (eg Beresford, 2002) which contrast with the traditional biomedical focus on individual deficits and treatment approaches. Social models understand health as being determined by a broad range of social, environmental and economic factors and posit that prevention and recovery are best achieved in a holistic way. Therefore efforts are best channelled proactively to build personal strengths and develop resilience, which act as protective factors against potential difficulties. Positive child outcomes are at the heart of this book; each chapter is connected by a common thread that ties together factors known to enhance wellbeing and their resonance in a hi-tech age. Priority is given to the voice of the child throughout the book. In order to provide effective, appropriate and acceptable mental wellbeing interventions, children must undoubtedly be at the centre. This book showcases examples of inspiring and innovative work to support children's mental wellbeing and aims to offer both optimism and inspiration to readers.

Programmes and initiatives to support mental wellbeing in schools

The first three chapters introduce school-based initiatives, opening with a discussion of Pyramid Club in Chapter 2, a ten-week after-school programme targeted at children with socio-emotional difficulties. Positive wellbeing is highly associated with healthy relationships, and digital technologies have dramatically altered the nature and dynamics of social interactions. Friendships can be forged and sustained through multiple connections across time zones and distance; however, on the flip side, heightened peer pressure (eg social media comparison and the 'likes' culture) can have a detrimental effect on relationships and wellbeing. For children who experience socio-emotional difficulties, Pyramid Club can offer a sanctuary and help children to develop the competencies and skills needed to build friendships and maintain healthy relationships both off- and online.

Chapter 3 presents Book of Beasties (BoB) – a mental-wellness card game created in 2018 and embedded within a five-week programme. BoB aims to increase children's emotional literacy, destigmatise mental health and promote wellbeing. Digital technologies have contributed to a demise in children's interest in traditional toys and games which provide inherent opportunities for social play and learning. BoB has integrated popular features often associated with electronic games (for example the concept of an avatar) into an innovative card game. Children are encouraged to talk about their feelings within the realm of social play in the fantasy world of the beasties and they learn to regulate their emotions through practical activities such as yoga, origami and mindfulness.

Chapter 4 looks at the School Counselling Partnership (SCP), a service which embraces the whole-school community and is available to pupils, parents/carers and staff alike. The SCP model is underpinned by Bronfenbrenner's ecological systems theory (1979), which highlights the importance of the multiple interconnecting systems that affect a child's healthy development, the most pertinent here being home and school. The demand for children's counselling services in the UK has increased alongside rising levels of psychological distress. At the same time, digital technologies have facilitated an expanding online service which appears to align more closely with the technological habitus of NDNs. This raises important questions about how children navigate their way to mental wellbeing support and how schools and communities can provide support in appropriate, acceptable and meaningful ways.

Programmes and initiatives to support mental wellbeing at home and in the community

Chapter 5 explores the Forest School approach through the Breeze Project case study and illustrates the crucial function of outdoor play and connecting with nature for healthy child development. The rise in technologies is one of several factors associated with children spending less time outside, and while a direct relationship has been disputed, the link between physical and mental health is well supported (Harris, 2018). Physical activity and nature experiences like camping and canoeing are also associated with children's involvement in youth groups: Chapter 6 considers the global Girlguiding (GG) movement. Although GG was founded over a century ago, policies have been implemented more recently to embrace technologies alongside the organisation's commitment to change as the lives of girls change. Belonging to a group or community is another widely recognised factor contributing to healthy development (Miller et al, 2017). GG uses its international reach to raise awareness and share mentally healthy practices to girls worldwide. The UK *Girls' Attitudes Survey* is published annually, and in 2019 findings revealed that one of the main causes of stress among 11- to 21-year-olds was pressure from social media, with 45 per cent reporting they felt the need to check their phone first thing in the morning and last thing at night (Girlguiding, 2019).

Outspoken Sex Ed (Chapter 7) aims to encourage parents to talk openly with their children at home about sex and relationships issues. Children's highly digital lives have brought mounting concerns around their access to pornography, pressure to share images of a sexual nature and the proliferation of misinformation. Research suggests that children themselves are worried about what they might inadvertently encounter online, and pornography was identified as the type of online content that distressed children the most (Livingstone et al, 2013). The Royal College of Psychiatrists (2020) urges parents/carers to maintain a dialogue with their children about the negative and positive aspects of digital technologies, underlining the importance of parental/carer engagement in helping children gain a healthy off- and online balance in their lives.

Mental wellbeing support co-created and developed by users

The final two case studies illustrate the active role children themselves play in shaping mental wellbeing provision so that it is meaningful to their lives. This includes when, where and how support is given. Chapter 8 presents the Lift-Off programme from the educational charity Red Balloon. This offers an online platform and blended learning to educate and support children who have self-excluded from school due to bullying, assault or trauma. Teachers and students co-created an online learning community and the project extended Red Balloon's reach, benefitting more children by offering an online option of support which is more attuned to the technological habitus of the children it aims to help.

Finally, LifeMosaic (Chapter 9) is a wellbeing app designed, developed and evaluated by secondary school pupils. Children occupy the digital world with intensity and in ways that adults find hard to comprehend, but evidence suggests that children are more conscious of its drawbacks than might be expected. This places them in a pivotal position to look for ways to successfully navigate the digital realm and harness its potential. The impact of digital technologies is a crucial consideration in relation to children's mental wellbeing, while technologies are increasingly being drawn upon to both help understand and support wellbeing. Alongside this is a growing recognition of the valuable contribution of children – as users and beneficiaries – to the design, development and evaluation of programmes and initiatives targeted at them.

This book is written for a broad audience and a glossary has been provided for convenience. The editors hope that readers will find the collection inspiring and informative and that what they discover from exploring the selection of case studies will resonate beyond this text. At the end of each chapter the authors have provided links for information on individual projects and points for further reflection.

Notes

[1] The term 'children' used throughout this chapter includes young people.

[2] Defined by the Organisation for Economic Co-operation and Development (OECD) as more than six hours outside school on a typical weekday: http://www.oecd.org/edu/pisa-2015-results-volume-iii-9789264273856-en.htm.

References

American Academy of Pediatrics (2016) 'Policy statement: Media and young minds', *Pediatrics*, 138(5): 1–8, Available from: https://pediatrics.aappublications.org/content/pediatrics/138/5/e20162591.full.pdf.

Arnett, J.J. (2015) 'Identity development from adolescence to emerging adulthood', in K.C. McLean and M. Syed (eds) *The Oxford Handbook of Identity Development*, Oxford: Oxford University Press, pp 53–64.

Bavelier, D., Green, C.S. and Dye, M.W. (2010) 'Children, wired: for better and for worse', *Neuron*, 67(5): 692–701.

BBC News (2019) 'Pornography "one click away" from young children', BBC News, [online] 26 September, Available from: https://www.bbc.co.uk/news/technology-49837920.

Beresford, P. (2002) 'Thinking about "mental health": towards a social model', *Journal of Mental Health*, 11(6): 581–4.

Bourdieu, P. (1983) 'The forms of capital', in J.G. Richardson (ed) *Handbook of Theory and Research for the Sociology of Education*, New York: Greenwood, pp 241–58.

Bronfenbrenner, U. (1979) *The Ecology of Human Development: Experiments by Nature and Design*, Cambridge: Harvard University Press.

Carson, V., Hunter, S., Kuzik, N., Gray, C.E., Poitras, V.J., Chaput, J.P., Saunders, T.J., Katzmarzyk, et al (2016) 'Systematic review of sedentary behaviour and health indicators in school-aged children and youth: an update', *Applied Physiology, Nutrition & Metabolism*, 41(6): S311–27.

Chaudron, S., Di Dioia, R. and Gemon, M. (2018) *Young Children (0-8) and Digital Technology: A Qualitative Study Across Europe*, Belgium: European Commission.

Childwise (2020) *The Monitor Report 2020: Children's Media Use, Purchasing, Attitudes and Activities*, Norwich: Childwise.

Clements, R. (2004) 'An investigation of the state of outdoor play', *Contemporary Issues in Early Childhood*, 5(1): 68–80.

Daly, S. (2017) 'Not-so-smartphones: technology rewiring our brains and harming our intellect', ABC Action News, [online] 12 October, Available from: https://www.abcactionnews.com/news/science-and-technology/not-so-smartphones-technology-rewiring-our-brains-and-harming-our-intellect.

DfE (Department for Education) (2019) *Relationships Education, Relationships and Sex Education (RSE) and Health Education*, London: Crown.

Department of Health and Department for Education (2017) *Transforming Children and Young People's Mental Health Provision: A Green Paper*, London: Crown.

Erikson, E.H. (1968) *Identity, Youth and Crisis*, New York: W.W. Norton & Company.

Ernest, J.M., Causey, C., Newton, A.B., Sharkins, K., Summerlin, J. and Albaiz, N. (2014) 'Extending the global dialogue about media, technology, screen time, and young children', *Childhood Education*, 90(3): 182–91.

Ferguson, C.J. (2017) 'Everything in moderation: moderate use of screens unassociated with child behavior problems', *Psychiatric Quarterly*, 88: 797–805.

Frith, E. (2017) *Social Media and Children's Mental Health: A Review of the Literature*, London: Education Policy Institute.

Girlguiding (2019) 'Girls' Attitudes Survey 2019', [online] Girlguiding UK, Available from: https://www.girlguiding.org.uk/globalassets/docs-and-resources/research-and-campaigns/girls-attitudes-survey-2019.pdf.

Gottschalk, F. (2019) *Impacts of Technology use on Children: Exploring Literature on the Brain, Cognition and Well-being*, OECD Education Working Paper No. 195, Paris: OECD Publishing.

Gray, P. (2011) 'The decline of play and the rise of psychopathology in children and adolescents', *American Journal of Play*, 3(4): 443–61.

Gutman, L., Joshi, H., Parsonage, M. and Schoon, I. (2015) *Children of the new Century: Mental Health Findings from the Millennium Cohort Study*, London: Centre for Mental Health.

Haddon, L., Livingstone, S. and EU Kids Online (2012) 'EU Kids Online: national perspectives', EU Kids Online, London School of Economics [report], Available from: http://eprints.lse.ac.uk/46878/1/__lse.ac.uk_storage_LIBRARY_Secondary_libfile_shared_repository_Content_EU%20Kids%20Online_EU%20Kids%20Online%20national%20perspectives_2014.pdf.

Harris, M.A. (2018) 'The relationship between physical inactivity and mental wellbeing: findings from a gamification-based community-wide physical activity intervention', *Health Psychology Open*, 5(1): 2055102917753853.

Healey, A. and Mendelsohn, A. (2019) 'Selecting appropriate toys for young children in the digital era', *Pediatrics*, 143(1): e20183348.

HoC (House of Commons) (2019) *Mental Health Services for Children and Young People*, London: House of Commons.

HoCSTC (House of Commons Science and Technology Committee) (2019) *Impact of Social Media and Screen-use on Young People's Health. Fourteenth Report of Session 2017–19*, London: House of Commons.

Kardefelt-Winther, D. (2017) *How Does the Time Children Spend Using Digital Technology Impact their Mental Well-Being, Social Relationships and Physical Activity? An Evidence-Focused Literature review*, Innocenti Discussion Paper 2017-02, Florence: UNICEF.

Khan, L. (2016) *Missed Opportunities: A Review of Recent Evidence into Children and Young People's Mental Health*, London: Centre for Mental Health.

Layard, R. and Clark, D.M. (2014) *Thrive: The Power of Evidence-Based Psychological Therapies*, London: Allen Lane, Penguin Group.

Livingstone, S., Kirwil, L., Ponte, C. and Staksrud, E. and EU Kids Online (2013) 'In their own words: what bothers children online?', EU Kids Online, London School of Economics [report], Available from: http://eprints.lse.ac.uk/48357/1/In%20their%20own%20words%20%28lsero%29.pdf.

Melkevik, O., Torsheim, T., Iannotti, R. and Wold, B. (2010) 'Is spending time in screen-based sedentary behaviors associated with less physical activity: a cross national investigation', *International Journal of Behavioral Nutrition and Physical Activity*, 7(1): 46.

Micheli, M. (2015) *Communication and Information Technologies Annual: Digital Distinctions & Inequalities*, Bingley, UK: Emerald Group Publishing Limited.

Miller, K., Wakefield, J.R.H. and Sani, F. (2017) 'On the reciprocal effects between multiple group identifications and mental health: a longitudinal study of Scottish adolescents', *British Journal of Clinical Psychology*, 56(4): 357–71.

NHS Digital (2018) 'Mental health of children and young people in England, 2017: behaviours, lifestyles and identities', Available from: https://www.rcpsych.ac.uk/docs/default-source/improving-care/nccmh/suicide-prevention/monthly-clinic/(6a)mhcyp-behaviours-lifestyles-identities-(2017).pdf?sfvrsn=53d2b8dc_2.

NSPCC (2018) *How Safe are our Children? The Most Comprehensive Overview of Child Protection in the UK*, London: NSPCC.

OECD (2017) *PISA 2015 Results (Volume III): Students' Well-Being*, Paris: OECD Publishing.

Ofcom (2019) *Children and Parents: Media use and Attitudes Report 2019*, London: Ofcom.

Peter, J., Valkenberg, P.M. and Schouten, A.P. (2005) 'Developing a model of adolescent friendship formation on the internet', *CyberPsychology & Behavior*, 8: 423–30.

Pew Research Center (2012) *Parents, Teens, and Online Privacy*, Washington, DC: Pew Research Center.

Prensky, M. (2001) 'Digital natives, digital immigrants', *On the Horizon*, 9(5): 1–6.

Przybylski, A.K., Orben, A. and Weinstein, N. (2019) 'How much is too much? Examining the relationship between digital screen engagement and psychosocial functioning in a confirmatory cohort study', *Child & Adolescent Psychiatry*, [online], Available from: https://doi.org/10.1038/s41562-018-0506-1.

Przybylski, A.K. and Weinstein, N. (2017) 'A large-scale test of the Goldilocks hypothesis: quantifying the relation between digital screen use and the mental well-being of adolescents', *Psychological Science*, 28: 204–15.

RCPCH (Royal College of Paediatrics and Child Health) (2019) *The Health Impacts of Screen Time: A Guide for Clinicians and Parents*, London: RCPCH.

Rosen, L.D., Lim, A.F., Felt, J., Carrier, L.M., Cheever, N.A., Lara-Ruiz, J.M., Mendoza, J.S. and Rokkum, J. (2014) 'Media and technology use predicts ill-being among children, preteens and teenagers independent of the negative health impacts of exercise and eating habits', *Computers in Human Behavior*, 35: 364–75.

Royal College of Psychiatrists (2020) *Technology Use and the Mental Health of Children and Young People*, London: RCP.

Sadler, K., Vizard, T., Ford., T., Marcheselli, F., Pearce, N., Mandalia, D., Davis, J., Brodie, E., Forbes, N., Goodman, A., Goodman, R., McManus, S. and Collinson, D. (2018) *Mental Health of Children and Young People in England, 2017*, London: NHS Digital.

Sakr, M. (2020) *Digital Play in Early Childhood: What's the Problem?*, London: SAGE.

Sherman, L.E., Payton, A.A., Hernandez, L.M., Greenfield, P.M. and Dapretto, M. (2016) 'The power of the like in adolescence: effects of peer influence on neural and behavioral responses to social media', *Psychological Science*, 27(7): 1027–35.

The Children's Society (2019) *The Good Childhood Report 2019*, London: The Children's Society.

The Children's Society (2020) *The Good Childhood Report 2020*, London: The Children's Society.

Verduyn, P., Ybarra, O., Resibois, M., Jonide, J. and Kross, E. (2017) 'Do social network sites enhance or undermine subjective well-being? A critical review', *Social Issues and Policy Review*, 11(1): 274–302.

Vygotsky, L.S. (1978) *Mind in Society: The Development of Higher Psychological Processes*, Cambridge, MA: Harvard University Press.

Waterson, J. (2019) 'Social media addiction should be seen as a disease, MPs say', *Guardian,* [online] 18 March, Available from: https://www.theguardian.com/media/2019/mar/18/social-media-addiction-should-be-seen-as-disease-mps-say.

WHO (World Health Organization) (2018) 'Mental health: strengthening our response', *WHO* [online] 30 March, Available from: https://www.who.int/news-room/fact-sheets/detail/mental-health-strengthening-our-response.

Willsher, K. (2017) 'France to ban mobile phones in schools from September', *Guardian*, [online] 11 December, Available from: https://www.theguardian.com/world/2017/dec/11/france-to-ban-mobile-phones-in-schools-from-september.

2

Pyramid Club: building skills for healthy friendships and relationships in a digital age

Maddie Ohl

The importance of developing emotional competence and friendship skills in school-aged children cannot be underestimated (Rubin, Bukowski and Parker, 2006).[1] Friendships experienced in childhood provide us with a blueprint for relationships in adult life (Monsour, 2008). Not only do they offer support in coping with stresses encountered at home or in school, they also protect against the adverse effects of negative peer relations such as bullying (Cardoos and Hinshaw, 2011). Importantly, good-quality friendships can improve children's attitudes towards and engagement with school (Perdue, Manzeske and Estell, 2009). In the highly digital world which many children inhabit, the internet and social networking sites have opened up new avenues to make and maintain friendships both off- and online (Gluer and Lohaus, 2016). This development can be seen as both a force for good – enabling children to discover novel ways of establishing new friendships and communicating with existing friends – and a force for bad, as abuse of such technologies can lead to new and pervasive forms of social exclusion and bullying (Frith, 2017).

In particular, for those children who internalise their difficulties and tend to be quiet, anxious and withdrawn, securing a supportive peer group can prove challenging – and these children are more likely to be at risk of abuse and bullying

(Ohl, 2009). They may struggle to initiate peer interaction and as a result are more vulnerable to peer rejection and social anxiety. Furthermore, recent research in the Netherlands suggests that children with social anxiety are more prone to perceive that they are less likeable by their peers and to anticipate rejection even when this may not be the case (Baartmans et al, 2020), setting in train a self-perpetuating cycle of increased anxiety and low self-esteem. Socially anxious children are also more vulnerable to their anxiety persisting during adolescence and adulthood (Keller et al, 1992), often resulting in poorer future outcomes both educationally and personally (Fluori, Buchanan and Bream, 2000). Therefore, it is essential that all children are given the support they need during their childhood and adolescence to gain the socio-emotional skills required to build and sustain healthy friendships in school and outside, and for a generation of new digital natives (NDNs), both off- and online.

The first two decades of the 21st century have witnessed an increase in the number of school-based interventions designed to promote friendship skills and foster peer acceptance among children. This chapter presents a case study of a school-based socio-emotional intervention, Pyramid Club, which targets children who lack social skills and struggle with friendships. The original model was founded in the 1970s by an educational social worker, Kay Fitzherbert. Through her work in primary schools, Fitzherbert observed children who presented as withdrawn and lacking in self-esteem and social skills, which put them at risk of social isolation (Fitzherbert, 1997). This group of 'invisible' children was often overlooked by staff, and to offer much-needed support, the first iteration of Pyramid Club was developed for pupils aged seven to nine. The model was later adapted to extend Pyramid Club's reach and provide similar provision for older primary school aged pupils and young people in the early years of secondary education, up to age 14.

Digital technologies, wellbeing and social relationships

As outlined in Chapter 1, the mental health and wellbeing of children born since the start of the millennium has been a particular and growing concern both in the United Kingdom and globally

(Mackenzie and Williams, 2018). The ubiquity of technology in the lives of 21st-century children has prompted much research attention and there is burgeoning evidence linking poor wellbeing to technology use. According to the Royal College of Psychiatrists (RCP), high prevalence rates of problematic internet and social media use are indicative of digital technologies placing a new and substantial mental health burden on society (RCP, 2020). Research by Twenge et al (2018) revealed that spending more than a few hours per week using electronic media correlated negatively with self-reported happiness, life satisfaction and self-esteem among adolescents. Conversely, non-screen time – time spent on activities which involved, for example, face-to-face social interactions, sports, exercise, print media, homework, religious services and working at a paid job – correlated positively with psychological wellbeing. Technology has undoubtedly created a seismic shift in the way many children interact with their peers, and studies suggest that the majority of teenagers consider social media helpful for developing and sustaining friendships as well as being an important source of peer support (House of Commons Science and Technology Committee, 2019). While there were tangible benefits from social media use, research also identified associated stresses, the negative effects of reduced offline social interaction and diminished wellbeing through misuse and overuse of the online domain (Frith, 2017). Abi-Jaoude et al (2020) insist that the very nature of online interactions – which are effectively 'at arm's length' – creates a completely different friendship dynamic, and the online forum has made negative commenting both easier and more frequent compared with in-person interactions with peers.

Figures indicate that almost a third of UK children were age six or younger the first time they used the internet (Frith, 2017); moreover, the number of 3- to 11-year-olds going online has been steadily rising (RCP, 2020). As children's first exposure to the digital realm is happening at an increasingly younger age, there is mounting urgency to ensure a varied and balanced diet of social interaction both off- and online in order to foster positive wellbeing and essential social skills. Indeed, research indicates that when this balance is properly struck, friendships cultivated online enrich and increase the perception of friendship quality in both off- and online relationships (Gluer and Lohaus, 2016). Baiocco et al (2011) found that among 11- to 16-year-olds, friendships were reported as being closer and of better quality when physical contact with friends was complemented by communication online. Interventions such as Pyramid Club that help encourage such balance should be made readily available, particularly in schools, where the majority of children spend a large portion of their waking time (Weare, 2010).

The importance of friendship skills in middle childhood and beyond

Middle childhood spans the ages of 6 to 11 years and incorporates much of the period spent by children in primary school. Freud (1961 [1923]) described this as the latency stage, wherein the child acquires new social values from adults outside their family and also from play with same-sex peers. For NDNs, this period incorporates early experiences of school including first encounters with multiple peers of a similar age, and with this the opportunity to develop social bonds and forge friendship groups.

Between the ages of nine and 16, the importance of the peer group is in its ascendancy, and during this time children need to learn the social and emotional skills that will help them navigate their future relationships with others successfully (Ohl, 2009). Fundamentally, peer friendships are related to children's functioning in a multitude of ways – they can impact both positively and negatively on self-worth, school engagement, family life, psychological adjustment, how they view their friendships and indeed how they view themselves within those friendships (Maunder and Monks, 2019). As children grow up, they become more discriminating, and adolescents value their friendships more highly when there is reciprocated intimacy, trust and loyalty (Maunder and Monks, 2019). Furthermore, good-quality friendships made during early adolescence gain in importance over time and have been linked with higher levels of self-esteem and school adjustment and performance (Keefe and Berndt, 1996).

Friendships matter, as humans have a universal psychosocial need to belong (Maslow, 1987). A central tenet of Pyramid

Club is to foster a sense of belonging and group identity among members. The intervention targets both middle childhood and early adolescence as appropriate points within children's developmental span to intervene and nurture the growth of essential social competencies including friendship skills. The age range that Pyramid Club encompasses marks the beginning and end of middle childhood and, for the majority of children, a period of increased exposure to technology both at home and in school. Face-to-face interventions such as Pyramid Club are important for embedding fundamental skills for life which enable children to build and maintain healthy and satisfying friendships and social relationships both off- and online.

What is the Pyramid Club intervention?

Pyramid Club is a 10-week manualised programme which is both selective and preventive (Muñoz et al, 1996) and typically delivered as an after-school club. Its small therapeutic groups target quiet, socially withdrawn and anxious children who often have problems with friendships. By engaging in therapeutic activities including arts and crafts, games, food preparation and sharing, and circle time, children develop social skills and coping strategies; they become more confident and are happier in school. The informant-rated version of the Strengths and Difficulties Questionnaire (SDQ) is used to screen children and select those most likely to benefit from the intervention (Goodman, 1997). Suitability for Pyramid Club is defined by a high score in two of the subscales that indicate emotional issues such as poor self-regulation and anxiety (Emotional Symptoms) and problems interacting socially with peers (Peer Difficulties), and a low score on the subscale which indicates prosocial characteristics such as sharing readily with others (Prosocial Behaviour). Eight to ten children are invited per group and participation is voluntary. Weekly sessions last 90 minutes and are delivered by trained club leaders. The Pyramid Club model is underpinned by a theory of change (Hughes, 2014, cited in Jayman, 2017) which draws on elements of positive psychology (Seligman, 2002) and focuses on developing children's strength and resilience. The format of the programme has remained fairly consistent since its conception (see Table 2.1).

Table 2.1: The Pyramid Club intervention

Week	Focus	Therapeutic activities*	A typical club
Weeks 1 and 2	Forming the group: ownership and belonging Developing group identity and cohesion, and building trust	Circle time Arts/crafts activity Games Food preparation/snack time	Club members agree on a name for their club and decide on a set of rules An art activity, for example designing a club poster
Weeks 1 to 10	Encouraging friendship/social skills development Building confidence and self-esteem Regulating emotions and strengthening resilience	Circle time Arts/crafts activity Games Food preparation/snack time	Social and task-based skills are practised including working cooperatively with adults and peers A games activity, for example team or paired construction of a newspaper tower
Week 10	Closing the group: reflection and moving on	Circle time Arts/crafts activity Games Food preparation/snack time	A celebration of Pyramid Club with a party; children/young people and Club leaders say thank you and goodbye A circle time activity, for example rounds of 'What I'll take away from Pyramid Club'

Note: *Therapeutic activities:
Circle time: facilitates talking, listening and turn-taking; encourages expression of feelings
Arts/crafts: allows self-expression and fosters a sense of achievement
Games: creates a fun way to practise social skills and cooperation with others
Food preparation/snack time: encourages sharing, nurturing and prompts informal conversations
All activities are designed and planned to be age appropriate for Club members.

Source: Jayman et al, 2018

Does Pyramid Club improve children's socio-emotional wellbeing?

The effectiveness of the Pyramid Club school-based intervention is the subject of a considerable body of research (eg Ohl et al, 2008; McKenna et al, 2013; Jayman et al, 2018). Through its child-centred, non-clinical approach, this simple model has been shown to consistently improve the wellbeing of the majority of children who attend clubs both in primary school (Ohl et al, 2008; Ohl et al, 2012) and secondary school (Jayman et al, 2018). Early research concentrated on examining improvements in children's socio-emotional wellbeing using quantitative research designs and well-validated psychometric measures (eg the SDQ; Goodman, 1997). While these evaluations provided robust empirical evidence of the intervention's effectiveness, they did not identify *how* the Pyramid Club model might initiate change. Later research (Jayman et al, 2018) utilising a mixed methods approach addressed this gap in the literature.

As key stakeholders in the intervention, Pyramid Club children (recipients) and club leaders (delivery agents) possess a unique depth of personal experience which facilitates a more fine-grained evaluation and allows underlying process issues to be investigated. Qualitative research (Jayman et al, 2018, 2019) sought to scrutinise the 'active ingredients' of the intervention and gain an understanding of how Pyramid Club fostered children's socio-emotional development. Research findings identified behaviour change drivers which represent the elements of Pyramid Club associated with behaviour change. These were divided into two categories: behaviour change procedures (BCPs) which relate to contextual features that provide conditions favourable for success such as the setting (eg a welcoming physical space) and delivery aspects (eg a high adult-to-child ratio), and behaviour change techniques (BCTs) which refer to the underlying mechanisms that influence children's behaviour change, for example through demonstration and practice (eg modelling of desirable behaviours) and the provision of consistent social support (eg unconditional positive regard). Techniques were categorised according to the Behaviour Change Technique Taxonomy v1 (Michie et al, 2013).

Children's service satisfaction studies have traditionally relied on reports from parents/carers or teachers rather than seeking the views of children themselves (Stallard, 2001). However, as children are key stakeholders and main beneficiaries, their active contribution is increasingly recognised as an imperative component for effectively assessing and developing interventions and services targeted at them. In line with this rationale, focus group studies were conducted with Pyramid Club children (Ohl et al, 2013; Jayman et al, 2018, 2019) using the format of circle time – a technique used for encouraging children to express their thoughts and feelings (Heary and Hennessy, 2002). Circle time was also a practice that children were accustomed to from attending Pyramid Clubs. Children's perceptions of their Pyramid Club experiences are presented in the following section in their own words, alongside feedback gleaned from club leaders (pseudonyms have been used).

Supporting healthy friendships and relationships

The Pyramid Club environment, which comprises both the physical space and the ambiance, is hugely important to the club's success, and the regular weekly sessions provide children with consistency and a routine. The manualised format enhances that consistency but also provides flexibility to mould sessions to individual group's needs and preferences. In this way, faithful implementation of the intervention is maintained, and the unique needs of each Pyramid Club group can be accommodated (Ohl, 2009). A core objective of Pyramid Club is to provide children with a 'safe space' which they can make their own every week, creating a sanctuary away from outside stressors where they feel comfortable and calm: 'I liked to be able to have that time when you could just relax … when you don't have to worry about homework and you can just have fun' (Elsa, age 12). Small things that make the space special add to attendees' sense of comfort and belonging: 'When we came in instead of having normal cups, we had our own [personally decorated] mug' (Lucy, age 11). Children are encouraged to share responsibility for creating their own club, fostering a sense of ownership and shared connection with fellow members.

Important group bonding activities are facilitated from the outset – for example children decide on a name for their Pyramid Club and, to brand its identity, create a poster which can be put up in the room every week: 'We basically took the first letter of everyone's name and called it [our club] that [the combination of letters]' (Ariana, age 12). Some children may be slower than others to engage in activities, but by the end of the ten weeks a cohesive social group has been formed. This was recognised by club leaders: 'Towards the end [of the programme] we did an activity where they all thought of a compliment for each other and they had me in tears because it was really lovely and heartfelt' (club leader 3). Research suggests that when socialising processes are consistent, a social bond of attachment and connectedness develops among the individual, the group and the activities of the socialising unit (Catalano et al, 2004). 'It was amazing to see the girls as one big group at the very end of the last session sharing a group hug. You could see they had all made a special bond with one another' (club leader 1).

Pyramid Club's therapeutic activities are designed to practise targeted behaviours such as turn-taking, sharing and other social skills: 'I liked the games because it was like teamwork and you got to know each other' (Cookie, age 11). Group games, arts and crafts and cooking provide opportunities for children to learn to both give and take from the experience: 'There was a lot of sharing and you'd hear: "Is there any of that left to put on my cake?" Or, "That looks really good!"' (club leader 2). Children learn to negotiate and compromise: 'You had to club together and sometimes people might not agree, and well, that helped us' (John-Paul, age 13). Traditional activities are effective in engaging children and encouraging social interaction: 'A lot of those children just do not do those sorts of activities. They go home, they put the PlayStation on and they don't interact. They actually had to talk to each other [at Pyramid Club] and they actually enjoyed it' (club leader 2). Likewise, circle time provides an opportunity to share thoughts and feelings, and for anxious speakers to find their voice: 'You don't have to feel shy cos everyone is the same' (Becky, age 11). Children can learn how to regulate their emotional responses by observing and responding to the reactions of others. The supportive, nurturing environment encourages children to share their own stories: 'I used to get bullied and stuff which basically put me inside a shell, but Pyramid helped to break that shell' (Scooby, age 12). They can relate to common experiences such as being bullied and show empathy with their peers: 'At Pyramid we were all caring about each other ... you can share and not be embarrassed' (Hermione, age 13) and 'Say if you're having a bad week, I don't know at school, you know that you've got these people there [at Pyramid Club]' (Ainsley, age 12).

The children who attended Pyramid Club overwhelmingly reported having enjoyed the experience and identified several benefits from taking part. These included acquiring new skills which helped them to make friends and form positive relationships: 'It [Pyramid] helped with my confidence for making new friends' (Jessica, age 12) and 'I think most people here were shy before [Pyramid] to put their hands up' (Kawai, age 11). Pyramid Club offers a stress-free environment for children to rehearse social and communication skills which they can then transfer to the wider school environment: 'We're more confident [after Pyramid Club] ... we don't just walk past [peers] now we stop and speak' (Jeff, age 12). New competencies were applied in different social contexts: 'One of the girls is now taking part in volunteering work at school and she was the one who didn't have any confidence at the start' (club leader 1). These behaviours suggested that the immediate effects of the intervention would endure: 'I think it's about how [Pyramid Club] affected them in the long term, not just in the 10 weeks ... it's opened doors for them really' (club leader 2).

Club leaders observed how children's burgeoning friendships flourished over the 10 weeks of the programme: 'The friendships they formed. I mean they didn't talk to each other at the start and by the end they were walking home together and going to each other's houses over the weekend' (club leader 2). Pyramid Club was seen as instrumental in helping establish valued friendships by both attendees and club leaders: '[Without Pyramid Club] I'd never have met my dear friend, [name]' (Michael, age 11) and 'One of them said to the other: "I don't know if we would have been friends if we hadn't come here, so I'm glad we came"' (club leader 1).

The role of club leaders is integral to Pyramid Club's success and the child–adult relationship contributes fundamentally to the positive experiences of children who attend. Leaders were role models, popular and respected by attendees. According to Albert Bandura's (1977) social learning theory, observed behaviours are more likely to be emulated if the role model is held in high status by the observer, and at Pyramid Club evidence suggests that they were: 'She [the club leader] was like an older sister' (Kawai). Children recognised and appreciated the efforts of club leaders: 'I enjoyed circle time … talking … they [club leaders] were positive and made it fun' (John-Paul). The importance of establishing a trusting relationship was acknowledged by club leaders, who saw their role as essentially supportive: 'We were always there, trying to keep it light-hearted and positive … we were consistently like that which I think they felt was reliable' (club leader 2). The value of this relationship was expressed by the primary school children: 'The Club leaders say we should share our problems and they helped us, and they knew how we feel … and we can share everything with them' (Lana, age eight). The fact that club leaders were not in situ as authority figures or disciplinarians was key to the type of relationships they formed with the secondary school children: 'You're not their teacher, I think that really helped, there was no major hierarchy' (club leader 1). Away from the power dynamics of the wider school, older children described their relationship with club leaders as relaxed and informal: 'It was like getting to know a new friend or something' (Ariana).

When children are the main beneficiaries, responding to their feedback is imperative in effecting meaningful change to interventions and services aimed at them (Heary and Hennessy, 2002). Children were invited to discuss the things they liked best about their Pyramid Club and which aspects might be improved. The majority of attendees were extremely positive about their experiences, and one of the most frequent recommendations from primary school children was to extend the programme: 'I would like to change, um, that we get more time in Pyramid' (Charlie, age seven). Ellie, age eight, agreed and identified why she felt this would be useful: 'I think more [time] because it would make us feel even more confident … as much as others.'

Secondary school children also wanted Pyramid to go on for longer and were reluctant to say goodbye to club leaders, highlighting the strong bonds that had developed: 'The cards they wrote were so lovely … they were really sad about going' (club leader 2). Suggested improvements to clubs from older children included more opportunities to go outside and a greater variety of indoor activities. Requests tended to be for a broader selection within the existing core activities (eg more recipes or different games) rather than introducing novel ones. Only one child suggested bringing in technology: 'I would like it if we were allowed our phones' (Sunday, age 13) to which a peer responded: 'But if we had our phones all we would be doing is playing on them' (Perseus, age 13). Some children volunteered to talk to other pupils at their school about Pyramid Club: 'I would say about the activities and talk about the teamwork and encourage them all to come' (Ramsey, age 12) and 'So you feel you've helped them [the next group of children]' (Elsa). Club leaders observed that being an 'ambassador' could further benefit the children who had completed Pyramid Club while also raising awareness of wellbeing issues and helping support the growth of future clubs: 'The best thing really is to get them [pupils] to hear [about Pyramid Club] from other students [previous attendees]' (club leader 2). In this way, Pyramid Club can help mobilise pupil voice and simultaneously reinforce the message to children that there is no stigma in seeking wellbeing support.

Conclusions and future direction for Pyramid Club

Pyramid Club supports the mental health and wellbeing of children by helping them develop socio-emotional competencies, including friendship skills, which are transferable to their everyday lives in and outside of school. The ability to form and maintain friendships is a crucial life skill essential to the healthy emotional development of children (Catalano et al, 2004; Cardoos and Hinshaw, 2011; Clarke et al, 2015). For our current generation of NDNs, a vast array of digital technologies including social networking sites plays a major part in the formation and maintenance of peer relations (Frith, 2017). As the digital world continues to expand exponentially, it is increasingly important for children to learn how to strike a healthy balance between off- and online activities, as well as to be able to recognise and develop healthy friendships and social relationships (Gluer and Lohaus, 2016). School-based interventions such as Pyramid Club have an important role to play in enabling children to develop essential skills in the 'real world', thus providing a solid foundation from which to navigate friendships and relationships in the online world.

Pyramid Club is listed in the Early Intervention Foundation's *Guidebook* of validated interventions for improving socio-emotional wellbeing,[2] and clubs run across multiple school sites in the UK. Research is underway to investigate how technology can augment the Pyramid Club model and facilitate delivery both nationally and internationally while maintaining intervention fidelity and the quality of provision. One route involves digitalising resources so that club leaders and school staff can easily access training and materials online. This would help extend existing reach and provide many more schools with the opportunity to embed Pyramid Club within their existing mental health and wellbeing provision. Looking forward, it is anticipated that a systemic framework of evidence-based interventions, enhanced by digital technologies, will provide our NDNs with the support they need to develop into a mentally healthy generation with every opportunity to fulfil their potential in life.

Points for reflection
- How can we best support children to develop healthy friendships both off- and online?
- What can we learn from Pyramid Club group work involving traditional (non-digital) activities to help us support children's wellbeing both in school and at home?
- How can we exploit technology to extend the reach of school-based interventions to benefit the maximum number of children (including school non-attenders)?

Further information

To find out more about Pyramid Club visit https://www.uwl.ac.uk/business-services/pyramid-clubs-schools.

Contact Professor Maddie Ohl: maddie.ohl@uwl.ac.uk or Dr Michelle Jayman: michelle.jayman@roehampton.ac.uk.

Further reading

Jayman, M., Ohl, M., Fox, P. and Hughes, B. (2017) 'Beyond evidence-based interventions: implementing an integrated approach to promoting pupil mental wellbeing in schools with Pyramid club', *Education and Health*, 35(4): 70–75.

Notes

[1] The term 'children' used throughout this chapter includes young people.

[2] https://guidebook.eif.org.uk/.

References

Items marked with an asterisk (*) in the reference list are Pyramid Club publications or research.

Abi-Jaoude, E., Treurnicht Naylor, K. and Pignatiello, A. (2020) 'Smartphones, social media use and youth mental health', *Canadian Medical Association Journal*, 192(6): E136–41.

Baartmans, J.M.D., van Steensel, F.J.A., Mobach, L., Lansu, T.A.M., Bijsterbosch, G., Verpaalen, I., Rapee, R.M., Magson, N., Bögels, S.M., Rinck, M. and Klein, A.M. (2020) 'Social anxiety and perceptions of likeability by peers in children', *British Journal of Developmental Psychology*, 38: 319.

Baiocco, R., Laghi, F., Schneider, B.H., Dalessio, M., Amichai-Hamburger, Y., Coplan, R.J., Koszycki, D. and Flament, M. (2011) 'Daily patterns of communication and contact between Italian early adolescents and their friends', *Cyberpsychology, Behavior, and Social Networking*, 14(7–8): 467–71, doi: 10.1089/cyber.2010.0208.

Bandura, A. (1977) *Social Learning Theory*, Englewood Cliffs: Prentice-Hall.

Cardoos, S.L. and Hinshaw, S.P. (2011) 'Friendship as protection from peer victimization for girls with and without ADHD', *Journal of Abnormal Child Psychology*, 39(3): 1035–45.

Catalano, R.F., Haggerty, K.P., Oesterle, S. et al (2004) 'The importance of bonding to school for healthy development: findings from the social development research group', *Journal of School Health*, 74(7): 252–61.

Clarke, A.M., Morreale, S., Field, C., Hussein, Y. and Barry, M.M. (2015) 'What works in enhancing social and emotional skills development during childhood and adolescence? A review of the evidence on the effectiveness of school-based and out-of-school programmes in the UK', report produced by the World Health Organization Collaborating Centre for Health Promotion Research, National University of Ireland Galway, Available at: https://assets.publishing.service.gov.uk/government/uploads/system/uploads/attachment_data/file/411492/What_works_in_enhancing_social_and_emotional_skills_development_during_childhood_and_adolescence.pdf.

Fitzherbert, K. (1997) 'Promoting inclusion: the work of the National Pyramid Trust', *Emotional and Behavioural Difficulties*, 2(3): 30–5.

Fluori, E., Buchanan, A. and Bream, V. (2000) 'In and out of emotional and behavioural problems', in A. Buchanan and B. Hudson (eds) *Promoting Children's Emotional Well-Being*, Oxford: Oxford University Press, pp 48–68.

Freud, S. (1961 [1923]) 'The ego and the id', in J. Strachey (ed) *The Standard Edition of the Complete Psychological Works of Sigmund Freud* (vol. 19), London: Hogarth.

Frith, E. (2017) *Social Media and Children's Mental Health: A Review of the Evidence*, Education Policy Institute, Available from: http://dera.ioe.ac.uk/id/eprint/29528.

Gluer, M. and Lohaus, A. (2016) 'Participation in social network sites: association with the quality of offline and online friendships in German preadolescents and adolescents', *Cyberpsychology: Journal of Psychosocial Research on Cyberspace*, 10(2): article 2.

Goodman, R. (1997) 'The Strengths and Difficulties Questionnaire: a research note', *Journal of Child Psychology and Psychiatry*, 38: 581–6.

Heary, C.M. and Hennessy, E. (2002) 'The use of focus group interviews in pediatric health care research', *Journal of Pediatric Psychology*, 27(1): 47–57.

House of Commons Science and Technology Committee (2019) 'Impact of social media and screen-use on young people's health', [online] Available from: https://publications.parliament.uk/pa/cm201719/cmselect/cmsctech/822/822.pdf.

*Jayman, M. (2017) 'Evaluating the impact of a school-based intervention on the socio-emotional wellbeing and school performance of pupils in early secondary education', Unpublished Doctoral Thesis, London: University of West London.

*Jayman, M., Ohl, M., Hughes, B. and Fox, P. (2018) 'Improving socio-emotional health for pupils in early secondary education with Pyramid: a school-based, early intervention model', *British Journal of Education Psychology*, 89(1): 111–30.

*Jayman, M., Ohl, M. and Fox, P. (2019) 'Improving wellbeing for pupils in early secondary education with Pyramid Club: a qualitative study investigating behaviour change drivers', *The Psychology of Education Review*, 43(2): 29–36.

Keefe, K. and Berndt, T.J. (1996) 'Relations of friendship quality to self-esteem in early adolescence', *The Journal of Early Adolescence*, 16(1): 110–29.

Keller, M.B., Lavori, P.W., Wunder, J., Beardslee, W.R., Schwartz, C.E. and Roth, J. (1992) 'Chronic course of anxiety disorders in children and adolescents', *Journal of the American Academy of Child and Adolescent Psychiatry*, 31: 595–9.

Mackenzie, K. and Williams, C. (2018) 'Universal school-based interventions to promote mental health and emotional well-being: What is being done in the UK and does it work? A systematic review', *British Medical Journal Open*, 8: e022560.

Maslow, A. (1987) *Motivation and Personality* (3rd edn), New York: Addison-Wesley Educational Publishers Inc.

Maunder, R. and Monks, C.P. (2019) 'Friendships in middle childhood: links to peer and school identification, and general self-worth', *British Journal of Developmental Psychology*, 37: 211–29.

*McKenna, A.E., Cassidy, A. and Giles, M. (2013) 'Prospective evaluation of the Pyramid Plus psychosocial intervention for shy withdrawn children: an assessment of efficacy in 7- to 8-year-old school children in Northern Ireland', *Child and Adolescent Mental Health*, 19(1): 9–15.

Michie, S., Richardson, M., Johnston, M., Abraham, C., Francis, J., Hardeman, W., Eccles, M. P., Cane, J. and Wood, C.E. (2013) 'The behavior change technique taxonomy (v1) of 93 hierarchically clustered techniques: building an international consensus for the reporting of behavior change interventions', *Annals of Behavioral Medicine*, 46(1): 81–95.

Monsour, M. (2008) *Women and Men as Friends: Relationships Across the Life Span in the 21st century*, London: Lawrence Erlbaum Assoc.

Muñoz, R.F., Mrazek, P.J. and Haggerty, R.J. (1996) 'Institute of medicine report on prevention of mental disorders: summary and commentary', *American Psychologist*, 51: 1116–22.

*Ohl, M. (2009) 'The efficacy of a school-based intervention on socioemotional health and wellbeing of children in middle childhood: an evaluation', Unpublished Doctoral Thesis, London: University of West London.

*Ohl, M., Mitchell, K., Cassidy, T. and Fox, P. (2008) 'The Pyramid Club primary school-based intervention: evaluating the impact on children's social-emotional health', *Child and Adolescent Mental Health*, 13(3): 115–21.

*Ohl, M., Fox, P. and Mitchell, K. (2012) 'Strengthening socio-emotional competencies in a school setting: data from the Pyramid project', *British Journal of Educational Psychology*, 83(3): 452–66.

*Ohl M., Fox, P. and Mitchell, K. (2013) 'The Pyramid Club primary school-based intervention: testing the circle time technique to elicit children's service satisfaction', *Journal of Educational and Developmental Psychology*, 3: 204214.

Perdue, N.H., Manzeske, D.P. and Estell, D.B. (2009) 'Early predictors of school engagement: exploring the role of peer relationships', *Psychology in the Schools*, 46(10): 1084–97.

RCP (Royal College of Psychiatrists) (2020) 'Technology use and the mental health of children and young people', Available from: https://www.rcpsych.ac.uk/improving-care/campaigning-for-better-mental-health-policy/college-reports/2020-college-reports/Technology-use-and-the-mental-health-of-children-and-young-people-cr225.

Rubin, K.H., Bukowski, W. and Parker, J.G. (2006) 'Peer interactions, relationships, and groups', in W. Damon, R.M. Lerner, and N. Eisenberg (eds) *Handbook of Child Psychology: Vol. 3, Social, Emotional, and Personality Development* (6th edn), New York: Wiley, pp 571–645.

Seligman, M.E. (2002) *Authentic Happiness: Using the New Positive Psychology to Realize Your Potential for Lasting Fulfilment*, New York: Atria.

Stallard, P. (2001) 'Reducing parental dissatisfaction with a child and adolescent psychology service: a process of quality improvement', *Journal of Mental Health*, 10: 63–73.

Twenge, J.M., Martin, G.N. and Campbell, W.K. (2018) 'Decreases in psychological well-being among American adolescents after 2012 and links to screen time during the rise of smartphone technology', *Emotion*, 18: 765–80.

Weare, K. (2010) 'Promoting Mental Health in Schools', in P. Aggleton, C. Dennison and I. Warwick (eds) *Promoting Health and Wellbeing Through Schools*, London: Routledge, pp 24–41.

3

Supporting children's healthy socio-emotional development through play: Book of Beasties – the mental wellness card game

Michelle Jayman and Phil Tottman

Play in its variety of forms is intrinsically *fun*, rousing positive emotions which affect children's wellbeing and mental health. In fact, play is considered such an essential component of children's healthy development that it is recognised by the United Nations Convention on the Rights of the Child (UNCRC) as a right of every child (UN, 1989). Play has been broadly defined as any activity that displays features of non-literality, positive affect, flexibility and intrinsic motivation (Krasnor and Pepler, 1980). Simply put, it is enjoyable, voluntary and done for its own sake. The enormous physical, cognitive, social and psychological benefits of play for children from infancy to adolescence are well documented. A body of evidence indicates that incorporating a playful learning approach in the classroom is a highly effective pedagogical strategy for improving academic outcomes and increasing motivation (Weisberg et al, 2013). Moreover, pedagogies based on guided play (essentially child directed but incorporating adult-scaffolded learning objectives) have been shown to have a positive impact on socio-emotional development and emotional regulation (Ogan and Berk, 2009). Book of Beasties (BoB) – an award-winning school-based intervention which aims to develop children's emotional literacy and support wellbeing – utilises a guided-learning approach through the medium of a traditional card game.[1] Before this chapter explores BoB further, the concept of play and emerging modes of play for new digital natives (NDNs) will be briefly considered.

A radical shift in the nature of play has been linked with the exponential growth of digital technologies. Children growing up in digitally wealthy societies are exposed to technologies from an increasingly young age. A Canadian study which tracked nearly 2,500 two-year-olds revealed that their average weekly screen time was 17 hours, with some toddlers amassing up to 28 hours in a seven-day period (Madigan et al, 2019). Research suggests that electronic and virtual toys have diminished the popularity of physical, traditional modes of play, including board and card games typically played with others. A European Union study (Chaudron et al, 2018) revealed that, by the age of eight, girls in particular were ready to abandon play involving physical toys for digital alternatives. Changes in conventional play habits have been associated with a decline in the child-directed free play afforded by traditional toys and games (Healey and Mendelsohn, 2019). Evidence also suggests that over the last 20 years, opportunities for free play during the school day have been systematically reduced with shorter break times (Baines and Blatchford, 2019). These patterns have been considered alongside a concurrent rise in children's psychological difficulties – emotional issues in particular have seen an upward trend (Sadler et al, 2018). Restoring free play, according to Gray, is essential for children 'to grow up to be psychologically healthy and emotionally competent adults' (Gray, 2011: 459).

Research on children's screen time and use of digital technologies is still in its infancy. More work is needed to further investigate both the detrimental and positive effects on wellbeing which the extant literature indicates. Play is, nonetheless, unanimously regarded as a great facilitator for children as they grow and progress through important developmental stages. Through play, children develop interests and competencies, learn to problem solve and regulate their emotions. Moreover, play provides opportunities to practise essential communication skills and to learn about how to function effectively as social beings. Longitudinal research has demonstrated a correlation between social proficiency in middle childhood and adult wellbeing (Bagwell et al, 1998). Digital play, however, is often accused of encouraging sedentary behaviours. Furthermore, its two-dimensional interface relies primarily on sight and sound for children to interact, depriving them of vital primary experiences involving touch, smell and taste that conventional play can provide (Louv, 2005). Crucially, it is the impact that digital toys and games have on the social aspects of play which fuels concerns regarding children's healthy socio-emotional development. Critics insist that compared to 'real-world' games, virtual alternatives offer impoverished social encounters, with limited unscripted interactions, and rules and scripts that cannot be easily modified (Lancy and Grove, 2011).

For renowned developmental psychologist Jean Piaget (cited in Lancy, 2017: 60), 'children's games constitute the most admirable social institutions'. Traditional games are inherently social and provide ample opportunities for dispute, cooperation and negotiating rules. Ethnographic studies of conventional children's games have shown that they are less about players learning the rules and sticking to them and more to do with learning to negotiate. Through this process, children develop social intelligence (Lancy and Grove, 2011). The extent to which digital toys and games afford opportunities for children to practise the same skills and, like their traditional counterparts, support socio-emotional development requires careful scrutiny. This necessitates an objective lens and the impetus to understand how new ways of play can continue to facilitate healthy development for NDNs. However, the concern of this chapter is to investigate an intervention that utilises a physical card game to support children's socio-emotional development in an era when traditional games are becoming less and less a feature of modern childhood. Critical to the success of any intervention is its acceptability and appeal to participants. Book of Beasties has combined the social elements of traditional games with an original and contemporary design that captures the interest and imagination of children who may be more attuned to digital modes of play.

The Book of Beasties intervention

BoB is a mental wellbeing programme underpinned by the belief that every child should have the confidence to talk openly about their emotions and mental health. Delivered predominantly to children in UK primary schools aged 6 to 11, BoB utilises the format of a traditional card game combined with linked therapeutic activities to achieve three key aims: to raise children's emotional literacy, destigmatise mental health and promote wellbeing. The intervention can be facilitated by school staff who receive introductory training, and is designed for groups of five to six children. A programme of one-hour sessions is run over five consecutive weeks. There is an accompanying manual comprising five lesson plans. Although there are basic rules for playing BoB, the design is intentionally flexible to accommodate the unique needs of each group. An overview is presented in Table 3.1.

The Book of Beasties story is set in an imaginary world inhabited by ten uniquely designed characters, the beasties (see Figure 3.1). Each one is described as having specific features – for example self-consciousness or lack of energy – associated with emotional difficulties such as anxiety and depression. The objective of the game is for players to help the beasties by following *action* cards (with instructions for play) and locating *item* cards which present simple wellbeing exercises and are specifically linked to the difficulties the beasties are experiencing. Exercises include yoga, origami, arts and crafts activities and mindfulness practice. During turn-taking, players collect *comforts* (cards which help the beasties and can be swapped to assist another player) and try to avoid *minotaurs* and *fevers* (cards which hinder the beasties, for example by players missing a turn). At the start of each session, children are introduced to two beasties to look out for during play and encouraged to describe how the beasties might be feeling. Regular pauses are encouraged to allow for discussions when they naturally arise and to dedicate sufficient time for the linked activities in line with the preferences of the group.

Table 3.1: An overview of BoB: two beastie character examples

Beastie	Description	Character-istics	Item card	Action card	Comfort card
Populo	'Everyone has a foggy brain sometimes, especially poor Populo, who loses her puff and can't bring herself to do anything'	Loss of concentration; low mood	Bellows: 'Our breath has the power to calm us'	Make paper boats to race and use straws to blow (to practise deep breathing)	French rabbit (a cuddly toy for physical comfort)
Deki	'Deki is so conscious about how she looks that she goes around borrowing people's clothes to cover up'	Feelings of worth-lessness; isolation	Gogglys: 'The gogglys show us the best in everyone, you just have to look a little further than skin deep'	Discuss notions of 'beauty' and draw what 'inner beauty' might look like	Home (a place of safety and respite)

Source: Jayman and Ventouris, 2020

Figure 3.1: Populo card

Figure 3.2: The Tree (action) card

Theoretical underpinnings

The Book of Beasties intervention does not claim to align with a specific theoretical framework and developments have been largely practice driven. Nonetheless, there are several discernible influences including positive psychology (Seligman and Csikszentmihalyi, 2000) and programmes grounded in competence enhancement models (Durlak et al, 2011). A framework proposed by Hassinger-Das et al (2017) which incorporates games as a subset of playful learning experiences is also useful for understanding how an intervention such as BoB can enhance emotional literacy and contribute to children's wellbeing.

Play is sometimes described as being on a continuum according to the range and degree of playful behaviours on display. Spontaneous, child-initiated free play which encourages children to develop their imagination, creativity and self-expression has been positively associated with socio-emotional development. Nevertheless, guided play – which incorporates some degree of adult scaffolding but is still essentially child centred – has been shown to be more effective with both younger and older children for a range of learning outcomes than either free play or didactic methods (Weisberg et al, 2013). Children learn best in interactive environments which *invite them in* as active collaborators and include content which is meaningful to them (Chi, 2009). BoB employs guided learning – a social constructivist, assisted-discovery approach – to replicate this, thus creating a playful experience for socio-emotional learning. The following sections present emerging evidence to support BoB's effectiveness and give insight into some of the underlying processes 'at play'. Pseudonyms have been used throughout the text to protect the confidentiality of participants.

Practitioners' perceptions and experiences of delivering Book of Beasties

Nicole is an assistant head teacher and Aisha is a year 6 teaching assistant in a state-funded primary school in West London. Their reflections on delivering BoB to a group of five year 6 children (aged 10 to 11) were interwoven into the narrative using illustrative quotations.

The BoB programme can be delivered to universal groups of children or to groups of selected pupils who may be at risk of developing emotional difficulties: 'We started with a summer transition group as it is an anxious time for those children going to secondary school and finishing their SATs [exams]; they feel a bit lost' (Nicole). The two practitioners agreed that the level of training they had received for BoB was appropriate and both found the manualised programme accessible and amenable to different groups of children: 'It's not something that you need a lot of work to get your head round ... It is a flexible resource to use and can be adapted to how you see fit' (Nicole). Programme evaluation research (Durlak and DuPre, 2008) has shown that delivery agents' training and understanding of an intervention are crucial to the quality of implementation and intervention fidelity, and thus inextricably linked to programme outcomes.

In line with the guided learning pedagogy previously described, staff delivering BoB initiated the learning process and set the learning goals for each session. For example, they identified which beasties to look out for during play. The specific difficulties the beasties were experiencing were linked to selected discussion topics (such as feeling stressed) and therapeutic activities (for example doing a simple yoga stance to induce calm) (see Figure 3.2). While adults were responsible for setting and supporting the learning goals, the children were continuously active in their own discovery. '[BoB] thinks about what the child would want first rather than setting out a strict programme to follow' (Nicole) and '[Children] learn best through playing' (Aisha). An alternative programme also used in the school was brought up in the discussion as a comparison: '[The other programme] just isn't appealing or engaging for children and is so heavily adult led, whereas this [BoB] is child led and the adult just facilitates it' (Aisha).

Studies on the different roles that adults can occupy within the realm of children's play have indicated that sensitivity to the child's needs in the moment is paramount: adults should be flexible in the manner they intervene and always willing to take the child's lead (White, 2012). While the research suggests that interactions within play scenarios provide great benefits to children whether their partners are adults or peers, socio-emotional growth is nurtured not only through children's interactions but also through their ability to negotiate and compromise. Furthermore, it is imperative that learning occurs in a safe, anxiety- and risk-free environment where children develop confidence in their ability to solve a problem: 'Children [in the BoB sessions] feel they are in a safe space to play a game and talk about how they are feeling – it is very open' (Nicole).

Arguably, overt pretending or engaging in fantastical aspects of play diminishes significantly in middle childhood (Drewes and Schaefer, 2016). However, evidence suggests that older children are increasingly inclined to engage in fantasy in the context of technology-based games which incorporate avatars (a graphical representation of the player or an alter ego) and facilitate para-social relationships (Bergen and Williams, 2008). The overwhelming majority of 10- to 16-year-olds (93 per cent) in the UK play video games, with younger children playing for an average of two to three hours a day (Children's Commissioner, 2019). 'While they [the children] are very digital, I think they enjoy playing something that encourages interaction and involves other people around the table' (Aisha). In the virtual environment, the successes and failures experienced by avatars have been shown to have an impact on players (Wolfendale, 2007) while avatars with whom players identify create a more powerful affect (Vasalou et al, 2007). The imaginary world of Book of Beasties introduces avatar-type personas and, as typically happens within a virtual universe, players are tasked with a mission (helping the beasties) through problem-solving and resolution. Studies involving both younger children and adolescents have shown how engaging in fantasy or role play was associated with greater empathy and altruistic, prosocial behaviours (White, 2012).

According to Fisher et al (2011), children are better equipped to understand narratives and deal with situations when they have experienced similar concepts through play. 'They [children] find it difficult to understand what is happening with their emotions. Book of Beasties allows them to discuss the characters, and sometimes they associate with them' (Nicole). Socio-dramatic play increases children's perspective-taking abilities while also allowing them to master scripts for events they may encounter in their daily lives (Hirsh-Pasek and Golinkoff, 2003). '[BoB] involves social skills and is a way to practise some of the [coping] strategies such as yoga. Book of Beasties lets us know that we can do something about it when we are feeling a certain way' (Nicole). Both practitioners expressed their perception of BoB as a valuable and beneficial resource. Review evidence from programme evaluations has consistently demonstrated that 'buy-in' from school staff and the perceived benefits of an intervention are crucial factors involved in its potential success (Lendrum et al, 2013).

Children's perceptions and experience of participating in the Book of Beasties intervention

A child-centred method was utilised in a focus group discussion conducted with year 4 children (aged eight to nine) who had recently completed the five-week BoB programme at a second state-funded primary school in West London (Jayman and Ventouris, 2020). Such an approach enables the researcher to authentically capture children's voices (that is, what is meaningful to them), and regards them as 'articulate social actors' in the research process (James, 2007: 261). An effective strategy suggested by Punch (2002: 329) is to 'react to the children and follow their guidelines'. Particular care was taken when interpreting the data to remain true to the children's perceptions and intentions. To that end, children's words were 'privileged' in the analysis and comprise the core of the narrative that follows (Dorner, 2015).

Children described their BoB experience as 'fun' and reported an increase in subjective wellbeing: 'It cheered me up a lot' (Pug). Some children confessed to not understanding all the rules, but their enjoyment was not hampered by this. The game's main objective, helping the beasties, was engrossing enough for them not to be unduly concerned about strictly following the rules: 'The beasties were like people and they had worries [and we] try to help them to come up with ways to solve their problems ... I liked the beasties and how you can help them. I liked helping them' (Olivia). The linked therapeutic activities were perceived as fun and beneficial: 'I kind of just find drawing really calming… it's also really fun' (Olivia). A popular game was racing paper boats by blowing through straws, and although competition was involved, enjoying the activity appeared more important than winning. Likewise, having collectively helped as many beasties as possible in the game – 'When you help a beastie, put it in a separate pile and at the end you can count that pile and see how many [the group] saved' (Olivia) – was how 'success' was broadly perceived by players, as opposed to there being a single 'winner'. This aligns with research (Hughes, 1991) suggesting that during social play, cooperation goals and maintaining harmony within the group take precedence over competitive individual goals. Through social games like BoB, children learn how to function well within a team.

Children talked about their favourite beasties, showing empathy and an understanding of the worries each character had, which for some mirrored personal concerns: 'I also sometimes have a foggy brain; I need to take a deep breath in and so does Populo' (Bea); 'He [Bronze Child] is sometimes stressed and when you're stressed it kind of affects your life and I think it's worth helping him' (Dave). The concept of inner beauty, the need to fit in and the importance of 'just being happy' (Bea) were reflected upon: 'You help her [Deki beastie] to know that she's really beautiful [inside]' (Bea) and 'It's kind of annoying that people try to change themselves to fit in … you should just stay who you are' (Olivia). Children exhibited personal emotional awareness. For example, Pug described one of the beasties as having 'the same problems' as him while Bea expressed how '[BoB] helps us to talk about our feelings'.

Pretend play is positively associated with children's ability to cope and regulate their emotions. Imagining different experiences can help children manage similar content in real life (Phillips, 2010). A study by Christiano and Russ (1996) investigated a group of seven- to nine-year-old children who experienced an invasive dental procedure. Children who expressed greater affect and engaged more in fantastical play reported a higher number and variety of coping strategies and less distress during the procedure than children scoring lower on these factors.

BoB is fantastical by design, and in order to play children must knowingly and intentionally participate in a mentally represented alternative reality: 'I like the one [beastie] who goes into people's homes to get their clothes [Deki wants to change her appearance]' (Bea). Pretending requires children to operate at two levels: the real (external world) and the pretend (internal world) (Lillard, 1993). Reality is suppressed through pretending, which helps children develop inhibitory control (Bodrova and Leong, 1996), and studies have shown that pretend play improves children's self-regulation, including processes that regulate levels of emotional arousal (Blair and Raver, 2012). Therefore, pretending may encourage the divergent thinking required for children to overcome impulses and successfully control behaviour while providing an outlet to deal with stressors in the moment.

Several of the therapeutic activities that children were introduced to in the BoB sessions were given as examples of strategies children used when they felt worried or stressed: 'Every time I get annoyed or when I couldn't sleep I took deep breaths and it really helped because it calmed me down' (Olivia). Yoga, origami, arts and crafts and mindfulness exercises, built into the design of the game, were widely perceived as beneficial: 'It helps you to relax to do a tree pose [yoga stance]' (Bea). BoB activities are sensory focused and involve active learning. This aligns with authors (Durlak et al, 2011) who posit that interventions need to include participatory elements that concentrate on specific socio-emotional skills (for example self-regulation). Mindfulness tasks can foster tolerance and improve emotional regulation as they allow those who practise them to accept their thoughts and feelings in the present moment. A review by Burke (2010) concluded that interventions which used mindfulness practices were accepted and well tolerated by children. Some authors, such as Russ (2004), suggest that the symbolic nature of art may have similar effects on coping, as children can represent and deal with thoughts and feelings through artistic expression. A body of research supports the benefits of mindfulness training (Napoli, 2005), yoga (Hagen and Nayar, 2014) and arts-based activities (Irwin, 2006) for reducing stress and increasing socio-emotional resilience and wellbeing, especially when they are delivered in a non-prescribed manner such as through play.

Strategies for supporting friends and peers who might be experiencing socio-emotional difficulties were also put forward by the children: 'I would go and play with them [a peer in need of support] and try and get their mind off it [their worry]' (Bea) and 'I would probably just talk to them [a friend who was feeling low] and it would make them happy' (Dave). The children's responses revealed a proactive, problem-solving approach to supporting their classmates in the real-world context of school – an approach employing similar tactics to those they had used during the game to help the beasties: 'If I had a friend like Akky [beastie] with low self-esteem I'd tell them they don't have to worry about how they look and about what other people think of them and just remember they should just be happy' (Olivia). Perseverance and a positive outlook have been shown to improve one's ability to handle stress and challenges across the life course (Donaldson et al, 2015).

The children's preference to be supported rather than directed while playing BoB was evident in their lack of regard for strictly following the rules and their natural inclination to invent their own rules and suggest changes. Children have an inherent drive for agency, a critical component of learning through play (Zosh et al, 2017). Choice and agency are powerful tools, and within play situations children have the greatest opportunity to exert them. In contrast to most adult–child relationships, where adults are usually in charge, peer interactions have a relatively even distribution of power. Children are required to mutually establish the rules of the game. Through this action they practise the skills of planning, negotiation and cooperation and learn how to work in socially appropriate ways. They also become aware that others have intentions and desires that may not match their own. To successfully take the perspective of another, and to understand what they are thinking and feeling, is important for communication, altruism and empathy: 'I feel it's nice to help somebody [the beasties], to encourage them to do something even though I don't get encouraged well' (Olivia). All of the children's responses were consistently prosocial and supportive, regardless of their own personal, real-world experiences of receiving support.

Conclusions and future directions

Play is a cornerstone for developing emotionally healthy, joyful children: 'Social play makes children happy and its absence makes them unhappy' (Gray, 2011: 457). Deprived of social play, children fail to acquire the essential social and emotional skills for healthy psychological development. In a hi-tech age, the opportunities for children to benefit from quality play experiences can sometimes seem under siege. The UNCRC, mentioned at the start of the chapter, also stipulates that every child has the right to reach their potential (UN, 1989). This is fundamentally threatened if a child experiences poor mental wellbeing. This chapter has shown how Book of Beasties, based on a traditional card game, embeds a playful learning approach and offers a pedagogical tool for improving children's emotional literacy and supporting their wellbeing. The BoB programme offers a promising resource for staff and other professionals with responsibilities for mental health support in schools (for example educational psychologists) and can be easily implemented to complement existing provision.

In conclusion, children inhabit multiple social contexts, and in today's world traditional toys and games often hold less appeal than their digital counterparts. Nonetheless, technology-based games can be a powerful tool to promote the type of social learning enshrined in traditional modes of play such as card games. For instance, children are obliged to cooperate with one another to achieve goals in multiplayer digital games (Prensky, 2004). Moreover, the increasing sophistication of digital interfaces using different modalities (for example visual, tactile and auditory) can motivate children to play for longer periods and to stay on task. Desired learning outcomes therefore have more opportunity to be realised and exploiting digital technologies in this regard warrants further attention (Owston et al, 2009). Of even greater interest is how traditional and digital games can be cooperatively harnessed to optimise playful learning experiences and support children's socio-emotional development. Those who consider the realms of traditional and digital play to be irreconcilably distinct require a shift in thinking and an openness to hybrid solutions which are perceived as both acceptable and beneficial by the children they are targeted at. Finally, children should be at the heart of socio-emotional interventions, and this includes having the opportunity to be active contributors to their evaluation and development. The Book of Beasties case study has illustrated how this can be achieved in practice.

Points for reflection

- In which ways can the core elements of traditional games and their digital counterparts be effectively combined to optimise children's playful learning experiences?
- What opportunities are there to transfer some of the socio-emotional learning strategies used in Book of Beasties into the wider school curriculum?
- What practical steps can be taken to empower children to become active agents in the design, development and evaluation of programmes which are aimed at them?

Further information

To find out more about Book of Beasties visit https://www.bookofbeasties.com/ or contact philt@bookofbeasties.com.

Resources available: Book of Beasties: The Mental Wellness Card Game and the digital The Beastie Guide and lesson plans; Book of Beasties parent and teacher home-learning kits; free mindfulness resource.

For more about the Book of Beasties research contact Dr Michelle Jayman: michelle.jayman@roehampton.ac.uk.

Further reading

Jayman, M. and Ventouris, A. (2020) 'Book of Beasties: championing mental health in schools', *New Vistas*, 6(1), doi: 10.36828/newvistas.106.

Jayman, M. and Ventouris, A. (2021) 'Championing mental health in schools with Book of Beasties: the mental wellness card game', in M. Jayman, J. Glazzard and A. Rose (eds) *Researching Education & Mental Health: From 'Where Are We Now?' to 'What Next?' (BERA Bites Issue 6)*, [online] British Educational Research Association, Available from: https://www.bera.ac.uk/publication/bera-bites-issue-6-researching-education-mental-health.

Note

1   Awards include the Design in Mental Health Award 2019 and the Good Toy Guide badge of approval 2020.

References

Bagwell, C.L., Newcomb, A.F. and Bukowski, W.M. (1998) 'Preadolescent friendship and peer rejection and predictors of adult adjustment', *Child Development*, 69: 140–53.

Baines, E. and Blatchford, P. (2019) *School Break and Lunch Times and Young People's Social Lives: A Follow-Up National Study*, London: UCL Institute of Education.

Bergen, D. and Williams, E. (2008) *Differing Childhood Play Experiences of Young Adults Compared to Earlier Young Adult Cohorts have Implications for Physical, Social, and Academic Development*, Chicago: Association for Psychological Science.

Blair, C. and Raver, C.C. (2012) 'Child development in the context of adversity: experiential canalization of brain and behavior', *American Psychologist*, 67(4): 309–18.

Bodrova, E. and Leong, D. (1996) *Tools of the Mind: The Vygotskian Approach to Early Childhood Education*, Englewood Cliffs, NJ: Merrill.

Burke, C. (2010) 'Mindfulness-based approaches with children and adolescents: a preliminary review of current research in an emergent field', *Journal of Child and Family Studies*, 19: 133–44.

Chaudron, S., Di Gioia, R. and Gemo, M. (2018) *Young Children (0-8) and Digital Technology: A Qualitative Study Across Europe*, EUR 29070: Publication Office of the EU.

Chi, M.T. (2009) 'Active constructive interactive: a conceptual framework for differentiating learning activities', *Topics in Cognitive Science*, 1(1): 73–105.

Children's Commissioner (2019) *Gaming the System*, London: Children's Commissioner for England.

Christiano, B.A. and Russ, S.W. (1996) 'Play as a predictor of coping and distress in children during an invasive dental procedure', *Journal of Child Clinical Psychology*, 25: 130–8.

Drewes, A.A. and Schaefer, C.E. (eds) (2016) *Play Therapy in Middle Childhood*, Washington, DC: American Psychological Association.

Donaldson, S.I., Dollwet, M. and Rao, M.A. (2015) 'Happiness, excellence, and optimal human functioning revisited: examining the peer-reviewed literature linked to positive psychology', *The Journal of Positive Psychology*, 10(3): 185–95.

Dorner, L.M. (2015) 'From relating to (re)presenting: challenges and lessons learned from an ethnographic study with young children', *Qualitative Inquiry*, 21: 354–65.

Durlak, J.A. and DuPre, E.P. (2008) 'Implementation matters: a review of research on the influence of implementation on program outcomes and the factors affecting implementation', *American Journal of Community Psychology*, 41(3–4): 327–50.

Durlak, J.A., Weissberg, R.P., Dymnicki, A.B., Taylor, R.D. and Schellinger, K.B. (2011) 'The impact of enhancing students' social and emotional learning: a meta-analysis of school-based universal interventions', *Child Development. Special Issue: Raising Healthy Children*, 82(1): 405–32.

Fisher, K., Hirsh-Pasek, K., Golinkoff, R.M., Singer, D. and Berk, L.E. (2011) 'Playing around in school: implications for learning and educational policy', in A. Pellegrini (ed), *The Oxford Handbook of Play*, New York: Oxford University Press, pp 341–63.

Gray, P. (2011) 'The decline of play and the rise of psychopathology in children and adolescents', *American Journal of Play*, 3(4): 443–63.

Hagen, I. and Nayar, U.S. (2014) 'Yoga for children and young people's mental health and well-being: research review and reflections on the mental health potentials of yoga', *Frontiers in Psychiatry*, 5(35): 1–6.

Hassinger-Das, B., Toub, T.S., Zosh, J.M., Michnick, J., Golinkoff, R. and Hirsh-Pasek, K. (2017) 'More than just fun: a place for games in playful learning', *Journal for the Study of Education and Development*, 40(2): 191–218.

Healey, A. and Mendelsohn, A. (2019) 'Selecting appropriate toys for young children in the digital era', *Pediatrics*, 143(1): 1–12.

Hirsh-Pasek, K. and Golinkoff, R.M. (2003) *Einstein Never Used Flash Cards: How our Children Really Learn and Why They Need to Play More and Memorize Less*, Emmaus, PA: Rodale.

Hughes, L. (1991) 'A conceptual framework for the study of children's gaming', *Play and Culture*, 4(3): 284–301.

Irwin, E.C. (2006) 'Peter: a study of cumulative trauma, from robot to regular guy', in L. Carey (ed) *Expressive and Creative Arts Methods for Trauma Survivors*, Philadelphia, PA: Jessica Kingsley Publishers, pp 93–113.

James, A. (2007) 'Giving voice to children's voices: practices and problems, pitfalls and potentials', *American Anthropologist*, 109(2): 261–72.

Jayman, M. and Ventouris, A. (2020) 'Dealing children a helping hand with Book of Beasties: the mental wellness card game', *Educational and Child Psychology*, 37(4): 69–80.

Krasnor, L.R. and Pepler, D.J. (1980) 'The study of children's play: some suggested future directions', in K.H. Rubin (ed) *New directions for Child Development: Children's Play*, San Francisco, CA: Jossey-Bass, pp 85–95.

Lancy, D.F. (2017) *Raising Children: Surprising Insights from Other Cultures*, Cambridge, UK: Cambridge University Press.

Lancy, D.F. and Grove, M.A. (2011) 'Marbles and Machiavelli: the role of game play in children's social development', *American Journal of Play*, 3(4): 489–99.

Lendrum, A., Humphrey, N. and Wigelsworth, M. (2013) 'Social and emotional aspects of learning (SEAL) for secondary schools: implementation difficulties and their implications for school-based mental health promotion', *Child and Adolescent Mental Health*, 18(3): 158–64.

Lillard, A.S. (1993) 'Pretend play skills and the child's theory of mind', *Child Development,* 64(2): 348–71.

Louv, R. (2005) *Last Child in the Woods: Saving our Children from Nature-deficit Disorder*, Chapel Hill, NC: Algonquin Books.

Madigan, S., Browne, D., Racine, N., Mori, C. and Tough, S. (2019) 'Association between screen time and children's performance on a developmental screening test', *JAMA Pediatrics*, 13(3): 244–50.

Napoli, M. (2005) 'Mindfulness training for elementary school students: the attention academy', *Journal of Applied School Psychology*, 21(1): 99–125.

Ogan, A. and Berk, L.E. (2009) *Effects of Two Approaches to Make-Believe Play Training on Development of Self-Regulation in Head Start children*, Denver: Society for Research on Child Development.

Owston, R., Wideman, H., Ronda, N.S. and Brown, C. (2009) 'Computer game development as a literacy activity', *Computers and Education*, 53(3): 977–89.

Phillips, R.D. (2010) 'How firm is our foundation? Current play therapy research', *International Journal of Play Therapy*, 19(1): 13–25.

Prensky, M. (2004) 'The emerging online life of the digital native: what they do differently because of technology, and how they do it' [online], nd, Available from: http://www.marcprensky.com/writing/Prensky-The_Emerging_Online_Life_of_the_Digital_Native-03.pdf.

Punch, S. (2002) 'Research with children: the same or different from research with adults?', *Childhood*, 9(3): 321–41.

Russ, S.W. (2004) *Play in Child Development and Psychotherapy: Toward Empirically Supported Practice*, Mahwah, NJ: Lawrence Erlbaum Associates Publishers.

Sadler, K., Vizard, T., Ford, T., Goodman, A., Goodman, R. and McManus, S. (2018) *Mental Health of Children and Young People in England, 2017: Trends and Characteristics*, Leeds, UK: NHS Digital.

Seligman, M.E.P. and Csikszentmihalyi, M. (2000) 'Positive psychology: an introduction', *American Psychologist*, 55(1): 5–14.

UN (United Nations) (1989) *Convention on the Rights of the Child*, Geneva: United Nations.

Vasalou, A., Joinson, A.N. and Pitt, J. (2007) *Constructing my Online Self: Avatars that Increase Self- Focused Attention*, San Jose, CA: Conference on Human Factors in Computing Systems.

Weisberg, D.S., Hirsh-Pasek, K. and Golinkoff, R.M. (2013) 'Guided play: where curricular goals meet a playful pedagogy', *Mind, Brain, and Education*, 7: 104–12.

White, R.E. (2012) *The Power of Play: A Research Summary on Play and Learning*, Minnesota: Minnesota Children's Museum.

Wolfendale, J. (2007) 'My avatar, myself: virtual harm and attachment', *Ethics and Information Technology*, 9: 111–19.

Zosh, J.M., Hopkins, E.J., Jensen, H., Liu, C., Neale, D., Hirsh-Pasek, K., Solis, S.L. and Whitebread, D. (2017) *Learning Through Play: A Review of the Evidence*, Denmark: The LEGO Foundation.

4

The School Counselling Partnership: providing support and promoting self-care for school communities

Maddie Ohl and Toni Medcalf

The provision of counselling support in primary and secondary schools in the United Kingdom has increased exponentially since the 2000s. A report by Place2Be and the National Association of Head Teachers (NAHT, 2020) identified that between 2016 and 2019 school-based counselling support had risen from 36 to 66 per cent. This increased capacity in schools was a strategic response to the widely reported rise in psychological distress in both children and young people (CYP) (NHS Digital, 2018; The Children's Society, 2020), and is grounded in the belief that schools are best placed to deliver mental health and wellbeing support (Mackenzie and Williams, 2018). One provider, the School Counselling Partnership (SCP), is a locally developed service that delivers to both primary and secondary schools across London and is the focus of this chapter.

School counselling for 21st-century learners

The expansion of counselling services in schools has seen a concurrent rise in the use of virtual and digital modes of delivery. A review by the Early Intervention Foundation (EIF) (Wilson and Waddell, 2020) suggests that some interventions for CYP are being successfully implemented using online interfaces, including mental health and wellbeing programmes. This style of delivery would appear highly desirable to a generation of new digital natives who are already comfortable and conversant with online activities in other areas of their lives. However, the EIF's review of 21 virtual and digital mental health and wellbeing interventions urges caution in assuming CYP's inevitable engagement and reduced attrition (Wilson and Waddell, 2020). The online interventions that reported the strongest impact on CYP were those that adopted a cognitive behavioural therapy (CBT) technique (Grist et al, 2019). Through CBT, CYP are guided to rehearse adaptive behaviours to deal with, for example, anxiety or depression and to replace negative cognitions with positive ones. Specifically, internet-based cognitive behavioural therapy (ICBT) for youth anxiety is more developed than online treatments for other mental health problems (Pennant et al, 2015), while evidence suggests that higher levels of engagement are associated with programmes guided by a therapist, either virtual or real (Sauter et al, 2009; Beidas et al, 2014). This aligns with the EIF's findings which highlight the value of the practitioner–participant relationship in ensuring that CYP who participate in online interventions persist with the programme (Wilson and Waddell, 2020).

Although CYP reported a greater level of buy-in to all types of programmes when they felt a strong relationship with the therapist (Wilson and Waddell, 2020), several authors have questioned whether an effective and successful therapeutic alliance can be developed solely through technology and whether the well-supported benefits of the therapeutic relationship might be lost or diminished in online encounters (Richards and Viganó, 2013). Furthermore, the value of non-verbal cues and the intimacy of face-to-face interaction between counsellor and client must not be overlooked. This point is clear from the feedback given by a primary school child using the School Counselling Partnership service: 'The Space is an amazing [physical] place to talk about problems and [therapist's name] is so kind and understanding. It is also very great just to have a chat with someone once in a while, it makes you feel if there is something I don't like, I can share with a trusted person.'

The School Counselling Partnership: embedding holistic support

The SCP describe their service as 'a holistic approach to supporting children, young people, their families and the whole school community'. Therapeutic counselling is principally delivered face-to-face via drop-ins and workshops, but some online provision has been offered since 2020. The service dates back to 2011, when SCP chief executive officer Toni Medcalf was approached by a primary school head teacher. Medcalf, having worked in similar schools in areas of social deprivation, recognised that many of the children were likely to come from challenging backgrounds such as those known to Children's Services – and that therapy would only be fully effective if parents/carers and teachers also engaged in the process. The success of such approaches using multi-component intervention programmes has been acknowledged in the research literature (Goldberg et al, 2019). Without engagement from significant adults in both of the child's principal settings – home and school – intervention becomes a 'sticking plaster': it can support the child while they are in the therapy, but once therapy is over the plaster comes off and they may no longer feel the benefit. Therefore, in terms of sustainable support for CYP's mental wellbeing, a successful interface between home and school is crucial. The growing reliance on digital communications between educators and parents/carers (for example ParentMail, which connects them electronically) has made nurturing personalised school–home relationships more challenging and opportunities for face-to-face contact between school staff and parents less frequent, especially at secondary school level. Nonetheless, the SCP works extensively to bring parents/carers, school staff and CYP together in a cohesive partnership to help ensure the best outcomes for CYP are achieved.

Support for the value of the school–home dialogue can be found in the work of American psychologist Urie Bronfenbrenner. In his ecological systems theory of development, Bronfenbrenner suggested that children develop as a result of complex interactions between the principal settings in which they grow up (Bronfenbrenner, 1979, 1995), which for most children are home and school. Therefore it is essential that a high-quality relationship exists between these two micro systems; fundamentally this should be based on a level of communication that supports a rich dialogue between parents/carers and those who educate their child (Bronfenbrenner and Evans, 2000). This type of school–home dialogue helps to foster an ethos which promotes mental wellbeing for children within the school and also encourages the principle of self-care among the staff and parents/carers who make up the wider school community. On this basis the SCP works with each school's senior management team to identify how they can best build relationships with the parents/carers of the children who have been identified as most in need of help and slowly, through trust, bring them on board; unless there is parental buy-in there is little to work with. Sometimes this engagement involves therapy such as counselling and other times just meeting parents/carers regularly to talk about how they can best support their child. Extensive evidence (for example Wilson and Waddell, 2020) suggests that when parents/carers are engaged, CYP are more likely to stay the course of treatment.

Working to support the whole school community – the School Counselling Partnership's ecological structure

The SCP model of delivery is extremely flexible. According to Griffiths (2003), for counselling services to be youth friendly they need to be accessible, friendly and relevant, while counsellors working with CYP should be proactive and flexible in their style (Geldard and Geldard, 2004). The basic SCP framework consists of one-to-one therapy and drop-ins which take place throughout the day. Additionally, family assemblies and workshops are offered. Around this core service there is scope to adapt organically to meet the needs of each school. This makes sense, because schools are like micro communities, and what suits one school might not be appropriate for another. Often there are specific standout issues that emerge within individual schools, and the SCP will respond accordingly. Effective communication is clearly important in order to develop trust and this has taken time to build. Termly steering group meetings provide an open forum in which the SCP and partnership schools can discuss what is working well, what is not working well and how issues that have arisen can be resolved. Each school has a designated manager (normally a qualified child and adolescent psychotherapist) and either a qualified therapist or a trainee therapist. Some schools have the service for one day a week, some five and some three, depending on their budget and needs.

In 2020, because of the pandemic, bereavement was a major issue – one which is likely to be ongoing for some time. The SCP developed training for staff and developmentally appropriate programmes for teaching assistants to deliver to groups of CYP. Early on in their development the SCP encountered some critical incidents in schools, and the agility and sensitivity of their response helped the communities to understand the value of a counselling service like the SCP, especially during difficult times. This has not only cemented their reputation and increased the trust of the schools they work in, but it has also served to 'spread the word' and encourage other schools to approach them. The key is to give schools time, listen to see what that school community needs and to respond accordingly, and if these needs are met then trust will be forthcoming.

Supporting children and young people in school, at home and online

The SCP work to support CYP in the two main settings that they inhabit: home and school. Their principal offer is to provide wraparound support dependent on how the pupil's needs are perceived by all stakeholders: school, parents/carers and, most importantly, the pupil themselves. This approach gives CYP agency over deciding when and how to seek help. Some CYP will have one-to-one therapy, which may continue for quite some time. In fact, if therapy is deemed necessary to extend from primary to secondary school then therapists will 'move' with the pupil for continuity of support.

The SCP drop-in facility offers a haven for CYP seeking refuge: 'It feels safe here. Thank you!' (primary school pupil). Offering this type of access avoids the potential for stigma that one-to-one sessions might incur. The enhanced sensitivity of CYP to the perception of stigma is well supported in the literature (eg Draucker, 2005). Friends and peers serve as primary reference groups and thus CYP are highly sensitive to any negative assessment received from them. This results in reluctance to engage in behaviours which may be perceived as different. Furthermore, stigma may also be an issue for children whose family's cultural background means the concept of seeking mental health support is rejected (Gopalkrishnan, 2018). A principal aim of the SCP is to remove the stigma associated with therapy and for provision to be readily accessible for all those in need. To do this it is important to open up the conversation about mental health and be sensitive to cultural differences, encouraging everyone to know that it is OK not to be OK; it is OK to ask for help, and it is good to talk. Using this approach, the SCP have started to change the language and conversation in the schools and communities they work with.

New digital natives can express themselves and talk about their feelings through a range of different channels, and a significant number have turned to online therapy to address their mental wellbeing. Certainly this method allows service users to avoid the risk of stigma, and by reducing or eliminating such barriers online psychotherapy can reach CYP who might never have sought traditional in-person therapy (Kramer et al, 2013). This begs the question as to whether the desire for face-to-face therapeutic interactions has declined as a result. However, the SCP recognise that what children often want is an opportunity to speak and to be heard in a real space where they feel safe and unjudged: 'I don't talk about feelings, but I do in here!' (primary school pupil) and 'Going to lunchtime Space [drop-in session] has really helped me because it let me speak to people to make me feel better and tell them my worries. After going there, I felt less worried because I shared my feelings' (primary school pupil, North West London). Evidence such as this highlights the significance of the one-to-one relationship between counsellor and participant (Wilson and Waddell, 2020), while in general therapeutic skills used for in-person contact do not automatically translate into online therapeutic competencies. This begs another question concerning whether online psychotherapy is truly comparable to in-person treatment and whether it could ever replace traditional one-to-one therapy; many authors have expressed grave doubts in this regard (eg Richards and Viganó, 2013).

Empowering teachers to support children and young people

Importantly, the SCP emphasise the relevance of appropriate and adequate training for teachers. Staff must first understand the benefits of therapy and how this helps to release emotional blocks to learning. Teachers need to really look beneath the behaviour and ask: 'What is this child trying to communicate to me and how can I support them with that in the classroom?' The SCP help teachers to support children through psychoeducation (Adelman and Taylor, 2015). For example, if a child has been traumatised it is very difficult for them to become engaged academically until they can emotionally self-regulate and are ready to learn. By providing staff training around issues such as attachment, listening skills and bereavement, the SCP can cascade their reach beyond individual counselling support.

Informing best practice through evidence-based approaches

'A sociogram is worth a thousand words' (Contandriopoulos et al, 2018) and describes a sociometric measure that provides a visual representation of the interpersonal relationships within a social network (for example a school community) (Coie and Dodge, 1983). The SCP use a sociogram tool (developed by Robin Banerjee, professor of developmental psychology at the University of Sussex) when they go into a new school to create a 'map' of every class in the school. This is used in conjunction with the informant-rated Strengths and Difficulties Questionnaire (SDQ) (Goodman, 1997) to identify children who are experiencing social, emotional and behavioural difficulties (SEBD) and may need intervention. They then work with the school to tailor support which could be one-to-one therapy, mindfulness practice, or Friendship Group or Bereavement Group depending on the child's circumstances. Sociograms can capture aspects of social dynamism – changes in relationships or the movement of connections across different social contexts – and these visualisations can be used to extend social-network thinking to multiple stakeholders (Tubaro et al, 2016). For example, the SCP share the sociogram data they collect with school staff, informing the dialogue around appropriate support for a pupil and recommended changes in the classroom or across the school. Complex social dynamics are made intelligible through the sociogram method and unanticipated aspects can come to the fore, stimulating reflection (McCarty et al, 2007). Adopting this practice helps the SCP tailor their support to the unique needs of each school community. Moreover, it can uncover vulnerable groups that have remained 'hidden'. For example, in one school sociogram data indicated that new arrivals were struggling to adjust; this group had been overlooked as the school's attention was on children they suspected were suffering from neglect. This insight from the sociometric exercise prompted the school to revise its induction policy and set up a 'buddy system' for new pupils.

According to Cooper (2011) schools do not always make implementation decisions based on the strength of the evidence. However, the SCP embed evidence-based practice throughout their work with staff and parents/carers – running regular assemblies on themes such as kindness, gratitude, self-care, transitions, bereavement and loss – and help to foster a schoolwide culture of best practice. An example of this is the SCP's integration of the Flip Your Lid programme, which promotes a whole-school approach to listening. Derived from the book *Whole Brain Child* by Siegel and Bryson (2012), Flip Your Lid is about understanding your brain and what happens when you are anxious, worried or stressed and how to self-regulate. Recognising that parents/carers, as well as teachers, need to understand how to help their child self-regulate, this training programme has been offered universally – to teachers, children and parents/carers – which has altered the discourse in schools. This is well illustrated by one pupil's advice to a staff member: 'Miss, Miss, you are about to flip your lid – just get your upstairs brain to give your downstairs brain a hug.' Clearly CYP have adopted the language and shown a level of understanding about what happens when we struggle to self-regulate – adults and children alike.

'Team around the child': building a community of care

Many of the children the SCP work with come from chaotic home settings. This can be due to parent/carer illness – physical or mental – or a substance misuse problem, and sometimes because the child is in foster or kinship care. In these instances, the SCP build a 'team around the child' (TAC) to support them in school and at home. A TAC is a multidisciplinary team of practitioners established on a case-by-case basis to support a child, young person or family. TACs enhance good professional practice through joined-up working, information sharing and early intervention, and are widely used in Children's Services. A TAC in a SCP school consists of five key people: a senior leadership team member, a teacher, a key adult (usually a member of support staff), a parent/carer and one other member of staff chosen by the pupil themselves, thus ensuring that CYP's views are considered in planning support. For example, Sam would be introduced to 'Team Sam' and given a photo of the team – another is displayed in the staff room; when any issues with Sam arise a team member is called to respond. The team also share in Sam's successes, however small, and will acknowledge these with Sam when they see Sam in school.

For each pupil with a TAC, regular time is built in with their key adult during which they can engage in therapeutic play; this helps to build bonds and secure the relationship. A school/home book is kept in which the parent/carer is encouraged to be honest about their experiences at home. For example, if Sam did not sleep, having been awake all night playing video games, then staff can be prepared for any consequential behaviour in school the next day. Similarly, if Sam has had a disappointment, like a weekend with an absent father cancelled at the last minute, this can be useful information to support Sam emotionally at school. The approach is non-judgemental, transparent and built on mutual trust so that the team that covers the two most important settings for Sam – home and school – can really work together to be supportive in both environments.

The team also meets regularly to support one another and to make sure that no individual member becomes overwhelmed. Evidence from SCP practice suggests that a pupil with a TAC will love their team but also begin to challenge it, as they may not trust that everyone will be there for them all the time. The team needs to stay strong and ride out any storms that the pupil may throw in their path.

Prior (2012: 238) insists that engaging in counselling is not a single action but rather 'the outcome of a complex process of intra- and interpersonal negotiation and evaluation, in which the young person is the principal actor'. Therefore, counsellors and other key stakeholders need to attend carefully to issues of agency and choice for CYP. Nonetheless, the SCP have seen demonstrable success with their TAC approach, with some teams providing dedicated support to pupils across the entire school year, resulting in marked improvements in children's school adjustment and ability to stay on task in the classroom.

Supporting the wellbeing of teachers, school staff and parents/carers

A key tenet of the SCP is the concept of self-care, which can be defined as 'engagement in behaviours that maintain and promote physical and emotional wellbeing and may include factors such as sleep, exercise, use of social support, emotional regulation strategies, and mindfulness practice' (Myers et al, 2012: 56–7). Self-care is particularly important in addressing stress and supporting good mental health (Myers et al, 2012). In professions which demand high levels of emotional labour, such as teaching and healthcare, it is recognised that many staff do not take enough time and/or appropriate steps to exercise self-care.

Due to growing levels of anxiety among staff across SCP schools, monthly Self-Care Hubs were created. These allowed staff to pause and reflect on their own wellbeing, offering a space where they could be nourished with healthy food, herbal tea and essential oils, enjoy moments of stillness with guided mindfulness exercises and have time to indulge in some creative activities. The only proviso was: 'They can't discuss work.' Sessions ended with some thinking about how staff could build in self-care for themselves before the next hub. Positive follow-up actions included going for a walk with a colleague at lunchtimes instead of eating hunched over a laptop, or sharing lunches, while others made wellbeing boards for their staff room to create a more nurturing communal space. In addition to this initiative, the SCP also run drop-in sessions for teachers – safe havens where they can be heard. If therapy is deemed appropriate, staff are offered six weeks, or if there is a higher level of need they can be referred for additional support.

Self-care is extremely important for parents/carers too. In fact, Myers and colleagues (2012) recognise, quite rightly, that people cannot care properly for others if they don't look after themselves. Therefore, the SCP run drop-ins for parents/carers as well as staff. Congruent with Bronfenbrenner's model, here the aim is to ensure that CYP are always at the centre of everything that the SCP do and that they are able to work with important people in CYP's lives to support them (Bronfenbrenner, 1995). Parents/carers can come to unpick something with one of the team – maybe they have seen a change in their child's behaviour and they want to discuss this, or perhaps there has been a bereavement and they want to know how to talk to their child about it. Otherwise, it could be something that the parent/carer themselves needs support with personally; the SCP offer therapeutic support to them too. The SCP have a phone line that is available to parents/carers and CYP which is advertised by participant schools in their newsletters. Disseminating service details and providing contacts for the school's designated manager and therapist help to reassure the whole school community that there is always someone who can answer the phone or reply to their email.

The School Counselling Partnership: real-world outcomes for children and young people and their families

The SCP monitor everyone who uses their services. They log important demographic data for pupils such as gender, special educational needs and disabilities (SEND), ethnicity and recipients of pupil premium, and then compare this information to the school census data to build a profile of who *isn't* accessing the service. Strategies are developed to engage with any identified hard-to-reach groups to offer a service tailored to their needs while using language that neutralises any perceived stigma associated with seeking mental help services or concerns about being stereotyped. In this way the SCP develop organically within schools and ensure that the whole school community – CYP, parents/carers and school staff – feel comfortable and accepting of their service. If the SCP find that there is reticence among groups of parents/carers, they hold an informal event such as a coffee morning so any needs or concerns can be discussed candidly. In one instance it was discovered that some parents/carers were deterred from using SCP services because they were afraid of involvement by social services. This was quickly resolved by facilitating an informal meeting with social services representatives who were able to allay concerns. Other worries were linked to negative cultural perceptions of mental health problems and the stigma that might affect a family if one of their children was revealed to be having 'mental health issues'. Being alerted to these barriers to engagement enabled the SCP to be additionally sensitive in relation to how support was offered to these pupils.

Part of the SCP philosophy is to instil a sense of 'wraparound care' within schools. One acting head teacher described this feeling: 'The day that you are in it's like a veil of calm descends across the whole school. We all feel it. It is quite powerful.' Other school leaders have acknowledged the contribution of the SCP and how they have improved the quality of the pastoral support schools can offer: 'Joining the Schools Counselling Partnership has transformed the way we support students at [name of school]' (head teacher, West London secondary school). For parents/carers, the SCP offer an opportunity to work as a team to support their child when they are struggling, and with this comes a chance to be supported themselves: 'I cannot thank you enough for all you have done for us. The support for my child has been so valuable. I wish all parents could have something like this' (primary school pupil's parent); 'My weekly chats really help me to take control of my own anxieties linked to my everyday life, family and work' (parent, North West London school); 'Thank you for spending time to talk with me ... I was feeling very low and you managed to help me see a new direction in which I felt I could help my son' (parent, West London school).

A wealth of anecdotal evidence clearly shows that CYP feel supported and cared for by the SCP: 'You are the only one who hasn't told me what to do. You just listened' (primary school pupil); 'You are my knight dressed as a human' (primary school pupil). Feedback from CYP attending SCP-facilitated programmes such as Flip Your Lid (Siegel and Bryson, 2012) has provided evidence of socio-emotional learning, with participants showing greater awareness of how their developing brains function and a new understanding and willingness to describe how they are feeling: 'It was like there was a maze inside my head and I couldn't get out. Then you came along and unlocked the door' (primary school pupil). Uptake of the range of SCP support services for CYP is high (one in eight pupils in the North West London schools and one in six pupils in the West London schools) and the demographic of attendees is fairly equally distributed across ethnicity and gender (although boys in North West London are more highly represented in the one-to-one service). What is evident from the CYP is that they value the service highly and recognise that it provides them with a space where they can just be themselves and, most importantly, be heard: 'I wish we had the Space every day, my worries don't feel big when I share them' and 'Every school should have the Space because then children will all be happier and not have worries' (primary school pupils, West London schools).

Future directions: the Schools Counselling Partnership and therapeutic services for CYP

Technological innovation has led to rapid change in many professions, including counselling, bringing both benefits and challenges. Embracing technology allows service users more choice in how they receive support and can also remove barriers for those who want to seek help but are worried about others finding out. Digital modes of delivery extend professional reach to benefit more individuals as traditional boundaries of physical location are removed. Technology therefore can offer greater anonymity, flexibility, easier access to professional help and reduced waiting times. A survey of 742 professionals (University of Roehampton, 2020) showed that the number of CYP receiving school counselling halved between March 2020 (when COVID-19 lockdown restrictions first came into force) and July of the same year. This was largely attributed to school closures, with a reduction in the average hours of face-to-face therapy provided per counsellor from approximately 15 to three hours. Conversely, but perhaps not surprisingly, the amount of video, phone and text-based counselling activity increased. However, in some instances CYP who were prevented from receiving traditional support were also unable to access online therapy due to a lack of essential digital tools and/or an available private space.

During this tumultuous period of lockdown, the Schools Counselling Partnership responded with sessions for both CYP and staff on coping strategies entitled Understanding and Managing Anxiety in a School Setting, with an emphasis on self-regulation, self-care, what happens to us when we are anxious and ideas of how to create a sense of 'felt safe' in schools. The services and training that had transferred online to accommodate school closures were well received and subsequently integrated into the SCP portfolio of services. A six-week online CBT course for staff was popular and the virtual delivery mode seen as effective by participants: 'I thought that the training was first class, as it was tailored to the challenges that we face in school currently' (teacher, North West London school).

The Schools Counselling Partnership provide a holistic therapeutic service to whole school communities. They work with CYP, their parents/carers and staff to engender a community where exercising self-care is paramount. The SCP ethos is that self-care should be a priority in every school; they are trying to educate around mental wellbeing, and a lot of that education is about 'What can you do for yourself, and how can SCP support you?' In line with this rationale, the SCP are encouraging and empowering their partner schools to take ownership for some of the initiatives they introduce. This means that if the funding stops the work will carry on.

School counsellors occupy a critical role for CYP and the wider school communities they serve, not least during a global health pandemic. Their role is to listen and to support CYP during challenging times. However, the methods they use to do this are changing, with digital technologies offering a rage of alternative modalities. While there are keen advocates for the counselling profession to adopt a technology-based approach, equally there are critics, such as the SCP, who urge a more cautious response, insisting that therapeutic encounters online are fundamentally distinct from face-to-face experiences without affording the same or comparable benefits. Furthermore, online counselling may simply not be suitable, accessible or desirable for some CYP. Nonetheless, while some schools may favour the intimacy of in-person provision, and others prefer the flexibility of online support, a likely outcome is that schools will develop a hybrid service encompassing both. This, no doubt, will present a new set of challenges for school-based counsellors, but as we have seen with the SCP case study, through working in partnership with school communities, obstacles will be overcome and CYP and their families can receive the mental wellbeing support they need to thrive.

Points for reflection

- How can school communities work together to promote the importance of supporting CYP's mental health?
- How can schools develop and integrate the ethos of self-care into their communities for the benefit of all their members, including staff, CYP and parents/carers?
- How can we develop the online therapeutic relationship so that the delivery of school counselling becomes more flexible?

Further information

To find out more about the Schools Counselling Partnership visit https://www.schoolscounsellingpartnership.co.uk/ or contact tmedcalf.307@lgflmail.org.

References

Adelman, H.S. and Taylor, L. (2015) *Mental Health in Schools*, New York: Simon & Schuster.

Beidas, R.S., Edmunds, J., Ditty, M., Watkins, J., Walsh, L., Marcus, S. and Kendal, P. (2014) 'Are inner context factors related to implementation outcomes in Cognitive-Behavioral Therapy for youth anxiety?', *Administration and Policy in Mental Health*, 41: 788–99.

Bronfenbrenner, U. (1979) *The Ecology of Human Development: Experiments by Nature and Design*, Cambridge: Harvard University Press.

Bronfenbrenner, U. (1995) 'The bioecological model from a life course perspective: reflections of a participant observer', in P. Moen, G.H. Elder, Jr. and K. Lüscher (eds) *Examining Lives in Context: Perspectives on the Ecology of Human Development*, Washington, DC: American Psychological Association, pp 599–618.

Bronfenbrenner, U. and Evans, G.W. (2000) 'Developmental science in the 21st century: emerging questions, theoretical models, research designs and empirical findings', *Social Development*, 9(1): 115–25.

Coie, J.D. and Dodge, K.A. (1983) 'Continuities and changes in children's social status: a five-year longitudinal study', *Merrill-Palmer Quarterly*, 29: 261–82.

Contandriopoulos, D., Larouche, C., Breton, M. and Brousselle, A. (2018) 'A sociogram is worth a thousand words: proposing a method for the visual analysis of narrative data', *Qualitative Research*, 18(1): 70–87.

Cooper, P. (2011) 'Educational and psychological interventions for promoting social-emotional competence in school students', in R.H. Shute, P.T. Slee, R. Murray-Harvey and K.L. Dix (eds) *Mental Health and Wellbeing: Educational Perspectives*, Adelaide, AU: Shannon Research Press, pp 29–40.

Draucker, C.B. (2005) 'Interaction patterns of adolescents with depression and the important adults in their lives', *Qualitative Health Research*, 15(7): 942–63.

Geldard, K. and Geldard, D. (2004) *Counselling Adolescents: Second Edition*, London: Sage.

Goldberg, J.M., Sklad, M., Elfrink, T.R., Schreurs, K.M. and Bohlmeijer, E.T. (2019) 'Effectiveness of interventions adopting a whole school approach to enhancing social and emotional development: a meta-analysis', *European Journal of Psychology of Education*, 34: 755–82.

Goodman, R. (1997) 'The Strengths and Difficulties Questionnaire: a research note', *Journal of Child Psychology and Psychiatry*, 38: 581–6.

Gopalkrishnan, N. (2018) 'Cultural diversity and mental health: considerations for policy and practice', *Front Public Health*, 6: 179.

Griffiths, M. (2003) 'Terms of engagement: reaching hard to reach adolescents', *Young Minds Magazine*, 62: 23–6.

Grist, R., Croker, A., Denne, M., Stallard, P. (2019) 'Technology delivered interventions for depression and anxiety in children and adolescents: a systematic review and meta-analysis', *Clinical Child and Family Psychology Review*, 22: 147–71.

Kramer, G.M., Mishkind, M.C., Luxton, D.D. and Shore, J.H. (2013) 'Managing risk and protecting privacy in telemental health: an overview of legal, regulatory, and risk-management issues', in K. Myers and C.L. Turvey (eds) *Telemental Health: Clinical, Technical, and Administrative Foundations for Evidence-Based Practice*, Amsterdam: Elsevier, pp 83–107.

McCarty, C., Molina, J.L., Aguilar, C. and Rota, L. (2007) 'A comparison of social network mapping and personal network visualization', *Field Methods*, 19(2): 145–62.

Mackenzie, K. and Williams, C. (2018) 'Universal school-based interventions to promote mental health and emotional well-being: what is being done in the UK and does it work? A systematic review', *BMJ Open 2018*, 8: e022560.

Myers, S.B., Sweeney, A.C., Popick, V., Wesley, K., Bordfeld, A. and Fingerhut, R. (2012) 'Self-care practices and perceived stress levels among psychology graduate students', *Training and Education in Professional Psychology*, 6(1): 55–66.

NAHT (2020) 'Huge rise in number of school-based counsellors over past three years', Available from: naht.org.uk/news-and-opinion/press-room/huge-rise-in-number-of-school-based-counsellors-over-past-three-years.

NHS Digital (2018) 'Mental health of children and young people in England', 2017, Available from: digital.nhs.uk/data-and-information/publications/statistical/mental-health-of-children-and-young-people-in-england/2017/2017.

Pennant, M.E., Loucas, C.E., Whittington, C., Creswell, C., Fonagy, P., Fuggle, P., Kelvin, R., Naqvi, S., Stockton, S. and Kendall, T. (2015) 'Computerised therapies for anxiety and depression in children and young people: a systematic review and meta-analysis', *Behaviour Research and Therapy*, 67: 1–18.

Prior, S. (2012) 'Young people's process of engagement in school counselling', *Counselling and Psychotherapy Research*, 12(3): 233–40.

Richards, D. and Viganó, N. (2013) 'Online counseling: a narrative and critical review of the literature,' *Journal of Clinical Psychology*, 69(9): 994–1011.

Sauter, F.M., Heyne, D. and Michiel Westenberg, P. (2009) 'Cognitive Behavior Therapy for anxious adolescents: developmental influences on treatment design and delivery', *Clinical Child and Family Psychology Review*, 12: 310–35.

Siegel, D.J. and Bryson, T.P. (2012) *The Whole-Brain Child: 12 Revolutionary Strategies to Nurture Your Child's Developing Mind, Survive Everyday Parenting Struggles, and Help Your Family Thrive*, New York: Bantam.

The Children's Society (2020) 'The Good Childhood Report', Available from: www.childrenssociety.org.uk/good-childhood-report-2020.

Tubaro, P., Ryan, L. and D'Angelo, A. (2016) 'The visual sociogram in qualitative and mixed-methods research', *Sociological Research Online*, 21(2): 180–97.

University of Roehampton (2020) 'School counselling in the UK halved by Covid-19 restrictions', [online] 13 August, Available from: https://www.roehampton.ac.uk/psychology/news/school-counselling-in-the-uk-halved-by-covid-19-restrictions/.

Wilson, H. and Waddell, S. (2020) *Covid-19 and Early Intervention: Understanding the Impact, Preparing for Recovery*, London: Early Intervention Foundation.

5

The Breeze Project: supporting children and young people through Forest School

Lucy Tiplady and Harriet Menter

For some time there has been concern about the effects of children's disconnection from nature. In his book, *Last Child in the Woods*, Richard Louv coined the term 'nature deficit disorder', suggesting that the increasing use of digital technology and parental fear have contributed to 'endemic obesity, attention deficit disorder, isolation and childhood depression' (Louv, 2005: np). The growth of Forest School in recent years has, in part, been driven by a desire to reconnect children with nature (Leather, 2018) and to provide an alternative to the digital world experienced by today's children and young people (CYP).

Forest School was developed in the UK in the 1990s by early years practitioners at Bridgwater College, Somerset, who had visited Danish preschools and taken inspiration from Scandinavian models of *friluftsliv* (roughly translated as 'open air living'). It further draws on a rich history of outdoor learning in the UK, from the Romantics (for example Wordsworth and Ruskin) to the Scout movement, Woodcraft Folk and adventure education, and from a range of progressive educationalists such as Pestalozzi, Steiner, Froebel, Dewey, Isaacs, Montessori and McMillan (Cree and McCree, 2012). Forest School has evolved through a network of practitioners and, via consultation, established six principles:

1. Forest School is a long-term process of regular sessions, rather than one-off or infrequent visits; the cycle of planning, observation, adaptation and review links each session.
2. Forest School takes place in a woodland or natural environment to support the development of a lifelong relationship between the learner and the natural world.
3. Forest School uses a range of learner-centred processes to create a community for being, development and learning.
4. Forest School aims to promote the holistic development of all involved, fostering resilient, confident, independent and creative learners.
5. Forest School offers learners the opportunity to take supported risks appropriate to the environment and to themselves.
6. Forest School is run by qualified Forest School practitioners, who continuously maintain and develop their professional practice. (FSA, 2020, np)

The Forest School Association (FSA) was formed in 2012 and Forest School is now a popular outdoor learning approach used in schools and community settings throughout the UK. More recently the approach has been developed internationally, for example in Australia, New Zealand, Canada, South Korea and China, and adapted to local contexts and cultures (Knight, 2018). Research has demonstrated that experiences in nature can improve academic learning, personal development and environmental stewardship (Ernst and Stanek, 2006; Becker et al, 2017; Chawla and Derr, 2012), with Kuo, Barnes and Jordan arguing that there is now converging evidence of a cause and effect relationship (2019). Research into Forest School is still developing but a growing evidence base has shown that it can have several positive benefits for CYP, parents/carers, practitioners and school staff (Roe and Aspinall, 2011; Ridgers et al, 2012; Harris, 2017; McCree et al, 2018; Coates and Pimlott-Wilson, 2019; Kemp and Pagden, 2019; Tiplady and Menter, 2020).

Play is a central feature of Forest School, underpinned by principle six and the commitment to learner-centred processes. As highlighted in Chapter 1, play, and in particular outdoor play, is thought to be important in CYP's development of social skills and emotional regulation, and there is concern that the digital distractions of modern life have created a steady decline in these opportunities (Gray, 2011). Based in a natural woodland environment, Forest School is ideally placed as an alternative to the hi-tech world often experienced by CYP in their homes and schools. The forest environment includes an abundance of 'loose parts', for example sticks, stones and dirt. Nicholson (1971) first introduced the theory of loose parts: objects found in nature promote development through encouraging creative and self-directive play. Forest School's focus on learner-centred processes further ensures that CYP direct their own play and learning, supported by a trained practitioner. This is qualitatively different from most pedagogy found in UK classrooms, which tends to focus on adult-directed activities and learning (Waite and Goodenough, 2018).

However, there has been criticism that the growth of Forest School has resulted in a dilution of its principles in some practice (McCree, 2019; Sackville-Ford, 2019) and that there has been a tendency to overplay the evidence of the benefits, particularly in relation to confidence and self-esteem (Leather, 2018). This undoubtedly necessitates some caution, but practitioners and schools continue to reiterate their positive experiences and a growing body of research is being published. Evidence from the Breeze Project, outlined in this chapter, suggests that the benefits of Forest School are closely linked to its six principles (FSA, 2020) and are determined by the particular needs of the individuals who participate (Tiplady and Menter, 2020).

The Breeze Project

Scotswood Garden is a community garden in an economically deprived part of Newcastle upon Tyne, England. The site includes wildflower meadows, ponds, vegetable beds, heritage orchards and a small woodland where Forest School sessions take place. Since 1980 the organisation has provided services for and with the local community which currently include community open days, training and support to local adults including those with mental health issues, an older persons' project, youth work provision and an education programme. Scotswood Garden works with over 1,500 CYP every year through an education programme which includes environmental education workshops for local schools and Forest School delivery and training. Scotswood Garden has trained over 60 local teaching staff in Forest School delivery. All staff in the education team are trained to Level 3 in Forest School Leadership, the recognised industry standard to lead a Forest School programme.

The Breeze Project was conceptualised by Harriet Menter, Education Manager at Scotswood Garden, in response to a growing number of requests from local schools and individuals concerned about CYP's mental health. It was not designed as a clinical intervention but as an approach to support wellbeing. In partnership with five schools over three years and with CYP aged 5 to 16 years with a range of additional educational and support needs, Menter, a Level 3 qualified Forest School leader and trainer, co-delivered weekly Forest School sessions. Participants were chosen primarily because of their additional emotional and social needs and because their teachers believed that they would benefit from the high adult-to-student ratios available through the project.

The sessions, in accordance with the Forest School principles, used 'a range of learner-centred processes to create a community for being, development and learning' (FSA, 2020, np). In practice this meant that the group agreed ground rules together and that the CYP were given the opportunity to direct themselves with support from facilitating adults. The adults would often present ideas for activities, particularly at the beginning of the year, and taught the safe use of tools and fire lighting, 'scaffolding' new skills and then gradually withdrawing support as the CYP progressed (Bruner, 1977). Over time, most of the students were able to self-direct and come up with their own ideas for activities and projects. The adults also modelled good social communication skills, praised positive interactions among the CYP and supported interactions where necessary, for example by asking a student how their peer might be feeling after an altercation and engaging in conversations about how this could be resolved. In this way, social interaction was central to the learning process and the adults facilitated progress through the 'zone of proximal development' (Vygotsky, 1978) – the difference between what a learner can achieve on their own and what they can achieve with the support of a skilled helper. The voice of the CYP was central to the whole approach and, as seen in the following sections, this was very significant in their growth and development.

Case study school

The Breeze Project worked with five schools but here the focus is on a secondary specialist school which caters for young people (YP) with special educational needs and disabilities (SEND). Eight students aged 12 to 16 were selected for the project, all of whom had a degree of special educational needs and had an education, health and care (EHC) plan – a legal document outlining their special educational needs, the support they needed and the outcomes they wanted to achieve. All students had social and emotional difficulties resulting from their disabilities and/or traumatic experiences or lack of interaction and experiences in early life; two were looked-after children (LAC) living in group homes, and two had recently experienced parental deaths. These young people and three members of school staff attended sessions at Scotswood Garden from September 2018 to July 2019.

Theory of change

To assess the impact of the project, the Forest School practitioner and school staff worked with a researcher who used a co-production approach to plan and carry out the research. Co-production involves professionals and stakeholders working together, with a reciprocal transfer of knowledge and expertise, to develop provision (Needham and Carr, 2009; Hatzidimitriadou et al, 2012). Through in-depth interviews, the researcher, practitioner and school staff negotiated a theory of change. Theory of change takes individual contexts into account, is evidenced to be particularly effective in evaluating multistrand projects and enables beneficiaries and stakeholders to track change as it happens rather than having to wait to achieve long-term goals, for which conclusive evidence can often take years or indeed decades to become available (Dyson and Todd, 2010). The co-produced 'steps of change' diagram seen in Figure 5.1 demonstrates that the focus on developing YP's social skills and emotional resilience is central in supporting their emotional wellbeing and lifelong learning.

Figure 5.1: Anticipated steps of change for young people (YP) in Forest School (FS) case study

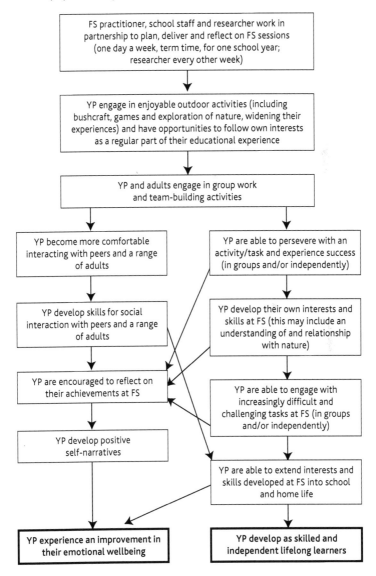

A data collection plan was produced, which aimed to utilise school and project data alongside researcher-collected data, to evidence (or contradict) the anticipated steps of change. This data included Forest School planning and evaluation documents; researcher observations; researcher interviews with the Forest School practitioner, school staff, YP and parents/carers; reflection activities with the YP (including photographs and visual methods) and Forest School diaries. The researcher was granted full ethical approval from her university institution and followed the British Educational Research Association ethical guidelines and the school's safeguarding policies at all times (BERA, 2018). All participants and stakeholders gave informed consent; for the YP, consent was obtained through initial parental/carer consent, followed by verbal consent during each session or individual encounter. This repeated confirmation of consent was important in ensuring that the research did not impinge upon the YP's experience of Forest School. The YP were further consulted on the ways in which they wished to engage with the research, whether that was through reflection activities, Forest School diaries or written articles, photographs and/or pictures or informal discussions or comments.

In analysing the data, the researcher used a combination of deductive methods to assess whether the data evidenced (or did not) the theorised steps of change and inductive methods using a more open thematic analysis to look for any unanticipated outcomes and general themes (Braun and Clarke, 2006). Figure 5.2 shows where there was judged to be substantial evidence to support the steps of change for all YP (light grey shading) and where there was either evidence for some, but not all, YP or where the evidence was judged to be suggestive rather than conclusive (dark grey shading). In no case did evidence refute the theorised steps of change.

Figure 5.2 shows that much progress was made in line with what was theorised through the steps of change, with many steps demonstrating substantial evidence for all YP (light grey shading). Where steps have the dark grey shading there was often evidence for some, but not all YP – for example some YP did engage with increasingly difficult and challenging tasks while at Forest School, developing tool skills or constructing

Figure 5.2: Evaluated steps of change for young people (YP) in Forest School (FS) case study

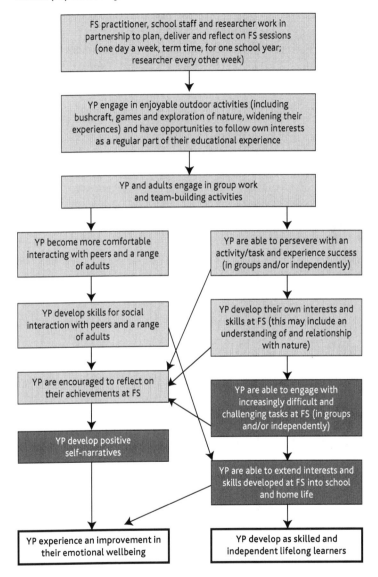

Key:

 Substantial evidence to support step of change for all YP

Some evidence to support step of change

complicated den structures. However, others concentrated on their social relationships with peers, learning how to integrate themselves into play situations or how to incorporate another member of the group who was struggling. In other cases there was often a desire to extend Forest School interests into their home lives, but practical barriers made this difficult. Many of the YP expressed enjoyment and pride in their Forest School activities and projects, which contributed towards a positive self-narrative, but they were also grappling with more negative experiences that inevitably affected the way in which they viewed themselves.

Thematic analysis of the integrated data from the YP, school staff and parents/carers provided insight into how the Breeze Project had achieved these steps of change (Braun and Clarke, 2006). Findings revealed that the Breeze Project had offered an alternative environment to both school and home life. This alternative environment was identified as both physically and pedagogically different. We now look at how this environment was experienced and how it impacted on the YP.

Physical environment

The Breeze Project provided a wooded, natural environment without access to the digital technology or devices that new digital natives (NDNs) are used to. Many of the YP had limited experiences of natural environments, with several commenting that they usually spent the majority of their time indoors, in their bedrooms and/or playing computer games. Some were initially anxious, but with support from staff they quickly adapted to the new setting, with many developing a connection to and interest in nature and/or bushcraft: 'I try to think what bugs go through every day ... I like the trees' (student, age 14); 'There's more to life than what you think, in a really good way' (student, age 14); 'He loves being outside all day, which is great because he has a lot of anxieties about being outside. It's very difficult to get him to go anywhere but not to Forest School. He really enjoys it' (parent/carer).

Spending time outdoors in nature was seen by parents, school staff and students to have many benefits. Some students talked about the opportunity to expand their sphere of experience and interests, for example in learning new skills and/or appreciating nature: 'It's exciting – you get to learn new things every week for projects that you want to do' (student, age 15); 'It gives him more of a choice of things to do, like being in nature and having other interests rather than computer games' (parent/carer). Meanwhile, others talked about the de-stressing effect of the natural environment, with Mark (see box) exemplifying how this played an important role in helping him to manage extremely difficult home circumstances.

Mark

Mark, age 15, is a calm, thoughtful young man who was dealing with a high level of stress. During the year he attended Forest School, he experienced a number of traumatic life events including his father's death, family turmoil and being removed from his mother's care. Mark enjoyed playing games – such as hide and seek, tag and eagle eyes – that used the whole forest area and involved running, chasing and hiding. He took an interest in den-making and woodworking activities; he also enjoyed using tools such as loppers, a sheath knife and a bow saw, often seeming more interested in the process than in the end product, although at times he was proud of his creations and would take them home. Tall and very strong for his age, he was always willing to help peers struggling with using the bow saw or moving heavy pieces of wood. Some days Mark arrived in a quiet mood and seemed more withdrawn. He would put up a hammock and lie quietly in it, seemingly just thinking. Because he faced a very structured school day, a chaotic home life and everyday adolescent pressures to interact with peers, staff members were aware of the importance of this quiet time and allowed Mark as much time as he needed. Mark told the researcher that he found Forest School 'peaceful' and that he appreciated the fact that 'no one bothers you'.

Time spent in nature is proven to lower cortisol levels (Roe et al, 2013) and attention restoration theory suggests that our brains require these kinds of rests through the 'comparatively effortless "soft" fascination of natural environments' (Goodenough and Waite, 2020: 12). In their book *Wellbeing from Woodland*, Goodenough and Waite summarise the four stages of restoration that Kaplan and Kaplan defined in their work on the psychological impact of time spent in nature as: '(1) "clearing the head", (2) recharging directed attention capacity, (3) random unbidden thoughts facilitated by soft fascination and (4) reflections on one's life, on one's priorities and possibilities, on one's actions and one's goals' (Goodenough and Waite, 2020: 12).

A rest allows the brain to recharge and offers a possibility to resolve issues. Mark, for example, would often rejoin the group for lunch and then get involved in some tool work in the afternoon; he told the researcher that he enjoyed Forest School as a 'place to be with friends'.

The woodland environment offered opportunities for play not found elsewhere in the students' lives. The chance to make dens, climb trees and run on an uneven surface supported their physical development by improving their balance, strength and dexterity. Another student, Tom (age 13), was often found picking up the largest, heaviest log he could find and throwing it as far as he could. Staff were unsure of the motivation behind these actions, and, having considered the safety of the group and the environment, continued to observe. Discussions with his key workers at school revealed that Tom experienced a certain amount of parental neglect and spent most of his time at home in his bedroom playing computer games or messaging friends. The school staff suggested that through throwing the logs he was getting sensory feedback, which he found satisfying. This was a young man with a rapidly growing body and little access to opportunities for exploring his high energy levels. In an interview with the researcher using photographs taken during Forest School sessions, Tom identified some logs and told the researcher: 'Lifting, you feel alive.' School staff commented that such experiences were particularly important for these students because they provided opportunities for physical development – for example increasing strength, stamina and 'hardiness' – otherwise lacking in their lives:

> The children in my school, in most cases, are brought to school in minibuses. They don't get the

opportunity to play out at break time if there is more than a light shower, they never play out with friends at home and if it's raining at the weekend, they stay in or go to the soft play or the Metrocentre [indoor shopping centre]. They aren't given the chance to become resilient. At Forest School the session goes ahead in all weather, unless it's not safe, and children are encouraged to wrap up warm, play games, build shelters and have a warm drink. I have seen children become more resilient to the weather in a short space of time. (school staff)

You get to run around – you don't have to stay in one place. (student, age 13)

Learner-centred pedagogy

Another central theme identified in the data was the learner-centred pedagogy of Forest School, in which the students were encouraged to follow their own interests rather than a predetermined scheme of work. The students made comments such as: 'You don't have teachers on your case; you can set your mind free. At school I just think about work' and 'You get to do what you like rather than being told by teachers.' However, for some students, the expectation that they would make their own choices was initially difficult: 'Choosing is different, you don't have pencils, sometimes you don't know.' The students were often not used to having to make their own decisions at school or home and many had low self-esteem, leading some to a reluctance to engage with activities and tasks.

Discussions between the Forest School adults and YP revealed that many of the students were typical NDNs, more comfortable in a digital world, and some began to use their digital experiences and knowledge as a bridge into Forest School. Some students began to incorporate their love of gaming into crafting activities, for example creating 'play buttons', wooden plaques with insignia or wooden characters from online games; at other times they would interact with each other in imaginative play, acting out scenes that drew inspiration from digital worlds. This imaginative play would then be extended, for example one young person acted out recent experiences of being physically restrained (Matthew, see box), and other more traditional games were played such as cops and robbers and chase. These opportunities for imaginative play were particularly important for these students, as many had had limited experiences as young children. Forest School provided a safe space in which they could be playful with one another and with staff. School staff commented that there was little opportunity for the students to play in this way at school and that many of the older students wouldn't feel comfortable outside of the Forest School environment for fear of not appearing 'cool'.

Once the students had settled into Forest School, many appeared to experience it as less stressful than school, enabling them to overcome anxieties and engage in learning through risk-taking. They developed tool skills and learned how to prepare, light and sustain a fire, tie knots and make dens and shelters. This freedom to choose, without having the option of digital distractions, allowed the students to fully immerse themselves in their play.

Play has long been recognised as a fundamental aspect of children's development. Froebel suggested that 'play is the highest expression of human development in childhood, for it alone is the free expression of what is in a child's soul' (Froebel, cited in Lilley, 1967: 84), while Andrews (2012) offers four perspectives on play (based on the work of Else and Sturrock, 2007):

- Physiological and biological perspective – in which the role of children's play is to develop their body and physical skills.
- Psychological perspective – in which play is a way of dealing with trauma and a tool to explore emotions and anxieties. Children may use play to express anger or grief or to act out conversations or arguments so that they can work through them in a more balanced state.
- Cognitive and developmental perspective – in which play is important for intellectual development, the development of thinking and understanding. Children use play to explore theoretical ideas in a practical way.

- Socio-cultural perspective – in which play performs the role of skills development and role practice for later life in a particular cultural context. Children may role play laying the table and making tea to practise skills they may later use in the home. (Andrews, 2012: 29)

During sessions the researcher and Forest School leader saw play that reflected all of these perspectives. A combination of the freedom to self-direct and the absence of choices that offer their own internal direction, such as a football game or computer game, allowed the students to use the time to meet their own developmental needs (although they were not necessarily aware that this was what they were doing). Just as a toddler will play at repeatedly dropping a cup from their highchair when their brain is starting to fathom gravity, a young person may throw heavy objects to develop awareness of their growing limbs (Tom, discussed previously) or act out traumatic experiences they need to make sense of (Matthew, see box).

Matthew

Matthew, age 16, was a LAC. He had recently experienced a number of traumatic events and struggled to negotiate adolescence and the uncertainty of his life without the support and safety of a family home; this had led to several incidents in school and in his care home which had resulted in him being physically restrained by staff. These incidents often ended in another upheaval for Matthew: a move to a new home or a different class without the time to debrief what had happened with the people involved. Matthew frequently returned to a game of physically restraining one of the teaching assistants, sometimes using rope and paracord, and sometimes using the same techniques that staff had used with him. He was never aggressive and seemed playful, enjoying using the names of the different 'safe-holding' techniques and calling for support as staff would have done. The teaching assistant himself had often been the one called on to support others in restraining Matthew and was able to talk to Matthew about what had happened.

At Forest School, playful experiences and time to 'hang out' together enabled the students to develop their social skills and to form friendships.

> During Forest School, I see children run and play who would not usually do so. I see children interact with others and make new friends, share experiences, support each other and depend on each other ... I still see children in school talking with the friends they made during Forest School, and we will often recount activities and memories of successes and failures. (school staff)

The Forest School ethos is designed to provide a supportive environment for students to develop good relationships with one another and with adults. The students who participated in the Breeze Project, some of whom struggled to have friendships in their school or home lives, identified the opportunity to spend time with peers and develop friendships as being important: 'You learn how to get along with people – good teamwork. Working on things you never normally do in school'; 'At Forest School you can hang out with friends'; 'At home I don't have anyone to hang out with, just family'. 'Hanging out' with friends is recognised as an important developmental stage of adolescence, when the main sphere of influence is moving from family to peers (Brown and Larson, 2009). A teacher from the school explained that the students, all of whom had additional needs, did not enjoy the same levels of independence as their peers in mainstream education, and the students' feedback emphasised how important this unstructured time at Forest School was to them.

Conclusions

Through its Forest School approach the Breeze Project offered an alternative educational environment that was physically and pedagogically different for participants. Time spent in nature and with fellow students and adults, away from digital distractions and the pressures of a school curriculum, allowed the YP to develop as individuals. For some this involved an appreciation of and connection with nature, for others it was about gaining bushcraft skills and for many it meant developing social skills and forming friendships. At times the YP's digital experiences and knowledge provided a bridge into Forest School activities, enabling them to incorporate their interests in a new environment. This demonstrated how central the digital world was to their lives but also how, given time in the right physical and pedagogical environment, the YP were able to adapt and redirect their creativity.

The Breeze Project provided the opportunity for these YP to be playful, which was facilitated by the woodland environment and learner-centred pedagogy. It enabled them to develop in ways which were important to them as individuals rather than being predetermined by adults. This learner-centred approach was central in enabling the YP to guide their own learning and development and establish a sense of freedom and control. The Breeze Project demonstrates how Forest School can provide an alternative environment for new digital natives by offering a range of opportunities that might otherwise be lacking in their lives and by placing children and young people at the centre of their development and wellbeing.

Points for reflection
- Forest School provides an alternative outdoor natural environment that is experienced as significantly different from school and home for many children and young people. How can schools learn from this approach to integrate practices into education more widely and benefit more students?
- Forest School offers opportunities for play that may be otherwise lacking in the lives of new digital natives. What other opportunities for play could be developed by schools to support children and young people's development and wellbeing?
- The learner-centred processes of Forest School enable young people to direct their own learning, supported by skilled practitioners, and to develop in ways important to them as individuals. How important is this in engaging children and young people in learning?

Further information

To find out more about the Breeze Project and its research methodology see Tiplady and Menter (2020) and Tiplady (2018).

References

Andrews, M. (2012) *Exploring Play for Early Childhood Studies*, Exeter: SAGE Publications.

Becker, C., Lauterbach, G., Spengler, S., Dettweiler, U. and Mess, F. (2017) 'Effects of regular classes in outdoor education settings: s systematic review on students' learning, social and health dimensions', *International Journal of Environmental Research and Public Health*, 14: 485, doi:10.3390/ijerph14050485.

BERA (British Educational Research Association) (2018) *Ethical Guidelines for Educational Research* (4th edn), London: BERA.

Braun, V. and Clarke, V. (2006) 'Using thematic analysis in psychology', *Qualitative Research in Psychology*, 3(2): 77–101.

Brown, B.B. and Larson, J. (2009) 'Peer relationships in adolescence', in R.M. Lerner and L. Steinberg (eds) *Handbook of Adolescent Psychology*, New York: Wiley, pp 74–103.

Bruner, J.S. (1977) *The Process of Education*, Cambridge, MA: Harvard University Press.

Chawla, L. and Derr, V. (2012) 'The development of conservation behaviors in childhood and youth', in S.D. Clayton (ed) *The Oxford Handbook of Environmental and Conservation Psychology*, Oxford: Oxford University Press, pp 527–55.

Coates, J.K. and Pimlott-Wilson, H. (2019) 'Learning while playing: children's Forest School experiences in the UK', *British Educational Research Journal*, 45(1): 21–40.

Cree, J. and McCree, M. (2012) 'A brief history of the roots of Forest School in the UK', *Horizons*, 60 (Winter): 32–4.

Dyson, A. and Todd, L. (2010) 'Dealing with complexity: theory of change evaluation and the full service extended schools initiative', *International Journal of Research and Method in Education*, 33(2): 119–34.

Else, P. and Sturrock, G. (2007) *Therapeutic Playwork Reader One 1995–2000*, Eastleigh, UK: Common Threads.

Ernst, J. and Stanek, D. (2006) 'The prairie science class: a model for re-visioning environmental education within the national wildlife refuge system', *Human Dimensions of Wildlife*, 11: 255–65.

FSA (Forest School Association) (2020) 'Principles of Forest School', [online] Available from: https://www.forestschoolassociation.org/what-is-forest-school/.

Goodenough, A. and Waite, S. (2020) *Wellbeing from Woodland: A Critical Exploration of Links Between Trees and Human Health*, London: Palgrave Macmillan.

Gray, P. (2011) 'The decline of play and the rise of psychopathology in children and adolescents', *American Journal of Play*, 3(4): 443–61.

Harris, F. (2017) 'The nature of learning at forest school: practitioners' perspectives', *Education 3–13*, 45(2): 272–91.

Hatzidimitriadou, E., Mantovani, N. and Keating, F. (2012) *Evaluation of Coproduction Processes in a Community-Based Mental Health Project in Wandsworth*, London: Kingston University/ St George's University of London.

Kemp, N. and Pagden, A. (2019) 'The place of forest school within English primary schools: senior leader perspectives', *Education 3-13*, 47(4): 501.

Knight, S. (2018) 'Translating Forest School: a response to Leather', *Journal of Outdoor and Environmental Education*, 21: 19–23.

Kuo, M., Barnes, M. and Jordan, C. (2019) 'Do experiences with nature promote learning? Converging evidence of a cause-and-effect relationship', *Frontiers in Psychology*, 10: 305.

Leather, M. (2018) 'A critique of Forest School: something lost in translation', *Journal of Outdoor and Environmental Education*, 21: 5–18.

Lilley, I. (1967) *Friedrich Froebel: A Selection from his Writings*, Cambridge, UK: Cambridge University Press.

Louv, R. (2005) *Last Child in the Woods*, New York: Workman Publishing.

McCree, M. (2019) 'When Forest School isn't Forest School', in M. Sackville-Ford and H. Davenport (eds) *Critical Issues in Forest Schools*, London: SAGE, pp 3–20.

McCree, M., Cutting, R. and Sherwin, D. (2018) 'The hare and the tortoise go to Forest School: taking the scenic route to academic attainment via emotional wellbeing outdoors', *Early Child Development and Care*, 188(7): 980–96.

Needham, C. and Carr, S. (2009) *Co-production: An Emerging Evidence Base for Adult Social Care Transformation*, London: Social Care Institute for Excellence.

Nicholson, S. (1971) 'How not to cheat children', *Landscape Architecture*, 62: 30–4.

Ridgers, N.D., Knowles, Z.R. and Sayers, J. (2012) 'Encouraging play in the natural environment: a child-focused case study of Forest School', *Children's Geographies*, 10(1): 49–65.

Roe, J. and Aspinall, P. (2011) 'The restorative outcomes of forest school and conventional school in young people with good and poor behaviour', *Urban Forestry & Urban Greening*, 10: 205–12.

Roe, J., Thompson, C., Aspinall, P., Brewer, J., Duff, E., Miller, D., Mitchell, R. and Clow, A. (2013) 'Green space and stress: evidence from cortisol measures in deprived urban communities', *International Journal of Environmental Research and Public Health*, 10: 4086–103.

Sackville-Ford, M. (2019) 'What does 'long-term' mean at Forest School?', in M. Sackville-Ford and H. Davenport (eds) *Critical Issues in Forest Schools*, London: SAGE, pp 33–44.

Tiplady, L. (2018) *Impacting on Young People's Emotional Wellbeing through Forest School: The Breeze Project, Pilot Year*, Research Centre for Learning and Teaching: Newcastle University.

Tiplady, L.S.E. and Menter, H. (2020) 'Forest School for wellbeing: an environment in which young people can "take what they need"', *Journal of Adventure Education and Outdoor Learning*, epub ahead of print, doi: 10.1080/14729679.2020.1730206.

Vygotsky, L.S. (1978) *Mind in Society: The Development of Higher Psychological Processes*, Cambridge, MA: Harvard University Press.

Waite, S. and Goodenough, A. (2018) 'What is different about Forest School? Creating a space for an alternative pedagogy in England', *Journal of Outdoor and Environmental Education*, 21: 25–44.

6

Promoting the mental health of girls and young women in the community: the role of Girlguiding

Bronach Hughes

This chapter will look at how the Girl Guides movement, and Girlguiding UK specifically, has embraced the opportunities and dealt with the challenges of the digital age and how it supports and promotes the mental health and wellbeing of girls and young women (GYW) through its network of volunteer leaders and its programme of relevant, fun but challenging activities.

The Girl Guides movement has responded to local need and culture but has at its core a common set of beliefs about the need to improve the lives of GYW through social action, self-development, leadership, female friendship and fun. The World Association of Girl Guides and Girl Scouts (WAGGGS) is a girls-only movement spanning 150 countries and including 10 million girls. WAGGGS' aim is to empower GYW to develop the skills and confidence to make positive changes in their own lives, in their community and in their country. As Dua, a 13-year-old from Pakistan describes:

> Being a part of Girlguiding is something else, especially living in a country with issues around women's rights. My favourite part of Guiding is how it empowers girls and shapes us into better versions of ourselves. It teaches us to love our sisters and stand up

for what is right. But most importantly, it teaches us to believe in ourselves. I have heard numerous stories of people transformed through Guiding, including being encouraged to speak out and never give up hope. (WAGGGS, 2020a)

WAGGGS uses digital technology to improve the lives of girls in a number of ways, including a partnership with GenU and UNICEF's U-Report (WAGGGS, 2020b), a free social media tool that allows local young reporters to use online polling to capture and report the views of under-represented groups in their community. The results of the polls can be analysed by gender, age and country in real time, allowing young people to connect with their political representatives and to influence the work of organisations like UNICEF. In Rwanda there is an initiative to review what girls would like to see from the Guiding programme and to establish more local Guide groups in secondary schools to support young people with disabilities, showing how technology can be used to improve the quality and relevance of face-to-face work.

The United Kingdom branch of WAGGGS, Girlguiding UK, sums up its four key aims as:

- We are for all girls.
- We give girls their own space.
- We give girls a voice.
- We change as the lives of girls change.

Clearly, this last item includes adapting to the needs of new digital natives (NDNs). This chapter will look at this community intervention that operates worldwide, is offered only to GYW and is shaped by the experiences of GYW. It will examine what difference it can make to their mental health and wellbeing and look at the opportunities it provides to ensure that the voices of GYW are heard.

The mental health of girls and young women

GYW's mental health seems to be particularly vulnerable, with girls at risk of emotional difficulties. Compared with other mental health disorders, these difficulties are on the rise and often increase as children get older. In 2017, 10 per cent of girls experienced anxiety, depression and other emotional disorders compared with 6.2 per cent of boys (NHS Digital, 2018). UK figures are in line with worldwide figures: the World Health Organization puts the level of all child mental health disorders at 10–20 per cent (WHO, 2020), with symptoms of half of lifetime mental health difficulties (excluding dementia) apparent by the age of 14.

In 2017 the Mental Health Foundation (MHF) issued a policy briefing in England which outlined the additional risks faced by GYW and called on the government to reinstate mental health support based on gender (MHF, 2017). Despite the fact that GYW are much more likely to suffer from a common mental disorder (self-harm, post-traumatic stress disorder, bipolar disorder, anxiety disorders and so on), government policy since around 2010 had ceased to promote specific strategies to support GYW, except in the case of perinatal support (see for example NHS, 2017). The divide between girls and boys has grown: while in 1993 girls in England were twice as likely to suffer from one of these disorders than boys (19.2 per cent versus 8.4 per cent), by 2014 they were three times more likely (26.0 per cent versus 9.1 per cent). Similar disparities are found in the other UK countries.

The MHF briefing examined potential reasons for this growing divide and concluded that issues like poverty (women were more likely to be negatively affected by government austerity policies), ethnicity (being from a Black, Asian or other minority ethnic group), not being heterosexual and an increase in domestic violence (cases were up 31 per cent from 2013–15) exacerbated GYW's problems. The other big issue was the presentation of GYW on social media, including the consumption of and ease of access to pornography by boys (and some girls) which offered up a very unrealistic view of GYW's bodies and of the nature of relationships, leading to issues of control, objectification, consent and sexual power.

A safe space for GYW

In the UK, Scouting was strictly for boys until 1976 but by 1991 girls were allowed to join; they now make up around 24 per cent of the membership (Scouts, 2019). Although the question of admitting boys to Girlguiding has been mooted over the years, it was felt that offering a girls-only space was important so that girls could talk openly about the issues affecting their lives and get support from other girls and women. The organisation's membership policy says that 'Girlguiding is a single-sex organisation in accordance with the provisions of the Equality Act 2010. Girlguiding believes that the needs of girls and young women are best met through an organisation catering specifically for girls and led by women' (Girlguiding, 2020). Girlguiding's inclusion policy allows for transgender girls and women to join; however, consultation with GYW about the programme update in 2018 confirmed that GYW themselves did not want boys to join.

In mixed-sex groupings girls often feel overpowered or compelled to act in different ways. While the reasons behind variation in behaviour are complex, the literature has identified differences in the ways that girls and boys behave and how that behaviour manifests in single-sex and mixed-sex groups. Booth and Nolan (2011) examined the way in which girls are less likely to compete in mixed-sex settings than boys but more likely to compete in single-sex settings. Edwards et al (2001) looked at the different styles of play that girls and boys engage in across many societies, and the increasing definition of interests and styles of play as being either for 'girls' or 'boys' as children move towards school age. Only in adolescence do these differences become less marked. In the most popular age range for Girlguiding members, five to 14, boys tend to gravitate towards noisier and more competitive play; to have more fixed ideas about what is suitable and to be punitive towards boys who wish to play with girls in peer groups. Girls, however, tend to want more choice, structure and flexibility of play options, which they find in single-sex Girlguiding units (Edwards et al, 2001). When it comes to digital games, and especially violent video games, the literature initially postulated an increase in aggression among young players. However, more recent research (Przybylski and Weinstein, 2019) finds little evidence to support that view, while still finding that around two thirds of boys but less than half of girls choose to play such games. Boys also spent longer playing than girls.

How Girlguiding's activities support girls' and young women's mental health and wellbeing

Outdoor and physical activities

Across the UK, groups meet weekly to provide a wide range of activities for GYW aged 5 to 18 (from age four in Northern Ireland). These meetings are run by local volunteers who are predominantly female. As described in Chapter 5, there are many benefits to being outdoors and close to nature, which happens both at weekly meetings and on residential events such as camps. Knots, whittling, gadgets, games, hikes, crafts and cooking are all essential parts of the Girlguiding heritage and may appear out of step with the digital age. It might be supposed that pitching tents and cooking over wood fires would be less appealing to NDNs, who are more inclined towards digital devices for entertainment, but despite the fact that technology is such a pervasive part of most children's lives it need not be mutually exclusive from a love of outdoor activities. Sustained high membership numbers in the UK and across the world certainly suggest that the organisation still appeals to NDNs. The technology is just a given, a natural part of NDNs' lives. While some adult volunteers might prefer girls to be using semaphore to send messages, most now recognise that girls can enjoy learning 'old' skills while simultaneously taking advantage of 'new' skills and resources. At times doing it the old-fashioned way and taking life at a slower pace comes as a welcome relief from screens and the constant pressures of technology; at other times the technology has enhanced activities and allowed more girls to participate, for example by accessing the free social media tool described at the beginning of the chapter.

Girlguiding UK organises camps at its training centres with an emphasis on the outdoors (such as Sparkle and Ice – a winter weekend camp) and physical adventure (such as Fearless Fun), prompting one Guide to write in a blog: 'The first day we did campcrafts [fire making, shelter building] which were epic! Great day! The next day we went on the traverse wall which I really enjoyed, and I made it all the way up hooray! Mostly fearless, totally fun!' (Eleanor, age 11). At the same time, it has set up partnerships with Google and Microsoft to engage with girls' love of technology and seamlessly inserted digital usage into its Wellies and Wristbands festival, as witnessed by Libby, age 14, who wrote in a blog: 'For anyone thinking of going next year, I would just say to try all of the opportunities [digital and non-digital] that are offered such as outdoor activities, media takeovers and band meet and greets!'

Creating a sense of belonging

For humans generally, but particularly for children, a sense of belonging is key to good mental health (Aked and Thompson, 2011). Research with Scottish adolescents (Miller et al, 2017) demonstrated how membership of multiple groups is linked to better health choices, and that the more groups that children identify strongly with, the better their wellbeing. This is particularly true if the groups share common values around behaviour and expectations, and works best the earlier that these connections can be established. As an organisation with a long history, Girlguiding features many symbols of belonging, from the promise that all members make and the badges and uniforms that they wear, to the songs they sing and its traditional ceremonies and celebrations. Certainly across the UK, any Brownie – aged seven to ten – would recognise another Brownie by her uniform, and on an international basis there are overlaps in the names used (Guides, Girl Scouts, Brownies) and the items of clothing worn (especially neckerchiefs and items incorporating the trefoil symbol). All Girl Guides and Girl Scouts celebrate their Founder's Day on 22 February each year as World Thinking Day – an opportunity to think about members across the world. Some members join at the age of four or five, move up through the sections, train to be adult leaders and then 'retire' to the associated Trefoil Guild, so the movement grows with them, supporting their wellbeing throughout the course of their lives.

Research with Italian adolescents (Albanesi et al, 2007) showed that those who took part in structured group activities (like Girl Guides) showed greater civic responsibility, developed more social capital and experienced better social wellbeing.

Creative, arts-based activities

The creative, arts-based activities that Girlguiding offer provide opportunities for self-expression and support mental wellbeing. There is a body of literature demonstrating how participating in structured group arts activities can have a positive impact on self-confidence, self-esteem, relationship building and a sense of belonging; all of which are associated with resilience and good mental health (for example Zarobe and Bungay, 2017).

Lifelong learning and challenge

Lastly, Girlguiding's adventurous activities protect girls against increased neuroticism or psychopathology as they offer a rehearsal for handling real-life risky situations through play (Sandseter and Kennair, 2011). Sandseter and Kennair identify six categories of risk, all of which appear in the Girlguiding programme – heights, speed, dangerous tools, dangerous elements (for example fire), rough and tumble and getting lost/being separated from adults – in a managed fashion that allows children to overcome their natural anxiety and to develop skills that will serve them well in the future.

A study carried out by the University of Edinburgh concluded that:

> Participation in Guides or Scouts was associated with better mental health and narrower mental health inequalities, at age 50. This suggests that youth programmes that support resilience and social mobility through developing the potential for continued progressive self-education, 'soft' non-cognitive skills, self-reliance, collaboration and activities in natural

environments may be protective of mental health in adulthood. (Dibben et al, 2017: 275)

How Girlguiding has embraced digital technology

Although the emphasis has always been on exploring and understanding the natural world and the wider community, the movement has kept pace with changes in technology. By 1995 both Brownies and Guides could complete a Computing badge; by 2003 there were references to keeping safe (mainly from 'bad people') online and the use of digital cameras was encouraged to complete badges. However, in the 2018 overhaul of the UK programme, technology really came into its own. Computing was no longer a separate badge but using technology underpinned how girls could complete badges, while the online safety advice addressed the trustworthiness of information on the internet, cyberbullying and data protection, as well as traditional personal safety advice. Girls are now encouraged to use technology to take part in activities and to use apps to support activities. Badges requiring the explicit use of digital technology (such as vlogging) were also introduced. In order to earn a badge completed outside of the weekly meetings, girls are asked to produce evidence. From Brownie age and up, technology is encouraged to record and present evidence, whether in the form of a film, playlist, blog, vlog, podcast, tweet or Pinterest board – the format is entirely the girl's choice, and she may prefer to provide something written, an art or craft, a performance or a presentation.

Despite leaders' own use of technology, and many finding that accessing the internet during meetings allows a wider range of activities to take place (for example using a stargazing app when out in a field at camp is fun, allows greater depth of learning and enables more girls to get involved), some leaders still feel uncomfortable about the girls using technology and have regular debates about, for example, whether girls should be allowed to take their mobile phones on residential events. There are concerns about data protection regulations and sharing photographs, cyberbullying, girls calling home and making homesickness worse, and phones detracting from opportunities to try new skills and enjoy the outdoors. Some leaders can be reluctant to get embroiled in issues arising from the use of smartphones or websites as they are not always confident about having the skills or the authority, despite the availability of training to support them.

There is a concern that the children's technological knowledge and expertise far exceeds the ability of the adults, leading to attempts to ban or minimise its use. This is not the organisation's policy – rather, Girlguiding UK has worked to highlight both the benefits and the risks of technology, and its safeguarding policies promote teaching girls how to use it safely rather than discouraging use. As the local units are run by volunteers of all ages from a wide range of backgrounds, the experiences of Girlguiding members vary quite widely. However, as more NDNs – young women who grew up with that technology – join the volunteer network, it is increasingly becoming the norm for the technology to be integrated into the wider work of Girlguiding.

Empowering girls and young women in the 21st century

Listening to GYW's voices has always been a key part of the Girlguiding ethos, so the programme introduced in 2018 was preceded by a major consultation with girls to find out what they wanted to see included. Overwhelmingly, it was more adventures, camping, skills for life, fun and having a voice. Some 26,000 members tried out the new activities in their unit meetings before they were finalised, 19,000 took part in online research and 1,000 participated in workshops. The Girlguiding Strategy (Girlguiding, 2020) was developed following consultation with girls, parents/carers, leaders and external stakeholders on what they thought the world would be like in 2020, what girls and young women would want from Girlguiding and therefore what Girlguiding should provide.

Using women to promote the rights and ambitions of GYW has been key to demonstrating the impact that being a Girl Guide can have on girls' lives. Many famous women who were members of the Girl Guides as children have come from the spheres of politics (Condoleezza Rice, Hillary Clinton and

Michelle Obama), sport (Venus Williams, Dame Kelly Holmes and Dame Tanni Grey-Thompson), the arts (Gwyneth Paltrow and Taylor Swift), literature (J.K. Rowling and Gloria Steinem) and the media (Martha Stewart). Less well-known names come from a range of inspirational backgrounds, such as Sally Ride (the first American woman in space), Sally Kettle (the professional adventurer who first rowed the Atlantic Ocean twice from east to west) and Colonel Lucy Giles (in charge of officer selection at the Royal Military College Sandhurst). Along with GYW's own local leaders, these women are important role models and show how women can have a significant impact on the world – a vital lesson to get across given some of the negative messages that GYW receive from the media and the high volume of recreational media consumption among NDNs facilitated through digital technologies.

Since 2008 Girlguiding has been surveying GYW in its annual *Girls' Attitudes Survey* (Girlguiding, 2018) to identify the issues that matter most to them, both as a prelude to raising public awareness and to prompt social action by Girlguiding members and others. Unsurprisingly, the role of technology has come to dominate these surveys. In 2013 the key issues were everyday sexism, body image and the unequal treatment of women in society: 75 per cent of 11- to 21-year-olds thought that sexism affected most areas of their life, with 87 per cent believing that women were judged for their looks more than their abilities. Girlguiding as an organisation and many individual members threw their weight behind the No More Page 3 campaign to persuade *The Sun*, a British family newspaper, to stop showing topless women on page three of each edition.

Mental health featured in the 2014 report, with three quarters of girls saying they knew girls their age who were self-harming or suffered from depression, and two thirds knowing someone with an eating disorder. Around 40 per cent were aware of the bullying of girls on grounds of race, sexuality or disability. This led to calls for better education in schools and elsewhere for girls around mental health, with one young member saying: 'There should be more education regarding mental health. I received none and when my friend became depressed and suicidal in Year 10 I did not know what to do' (Girlguiding, 2014: 7).

There were particular concerns around the media portrayal of women, with three quarters of older girls (aged 11 to 21) and half of younger girls (aged seven to ten) saying there were too many images of naked or nearly naked women in the media, including in music videos, and they called on government and media organisations to show a greater diversity of women – a campaign that continues. The link was made between such representation and violence against women ('The media should stop sexualising and objectifying women because this kind of culture makes men feel that sexual harassment is okay' (Girlguiding, 2014: 14)) and the victim blaming of women subjected to sexual violence was condemned. The impact of everyday sexism on girls made one in three feel embarrassed, degraded or less self-confident. Already, girls were feeling that it would impact their future career. What girls wanted to see was a change in the language used about women, girls not to be blamed for wearing the 'wrong' things and bringing sexual violence on themselves, and a move to teach girls from a very young age that the way they are presented in video games and pornography is not real. The girls felt that there was a double standard, with girls being criticised for the way they looked but then being called shallow if they took care about their appearance. While issues over the way women are presented in the media have always existed, these have escalated with the growth of technology – and the use of social media is having a very negative impact on girls in terms of body image and eating disorders (Perloff, 2014; Fardouly and Vartanian, 2015; Hogue and Mills, 2019; MHF, 2019). The 2019 MHF research report shows how dissatisfaction with their bodies has increased from one in ten women in 2013 to one in five feeling shame about their bodies in 2019, and just over a third feeling down or low because of their body. Among adolescents, 54 per cent said that images on social media caused them to feel less satisfied with their bodies. As a result of hearing comments like this, Girlguiding worked with the Dove Self-Esteem Fund to produce the *Looking at Me* resource for girls aged 10–14 (Girlguiding, 2007) and WAGGGS produced *Free Being Me* – empowering girls through improving body confidence and self-esteem – in conjunction with Dove (WAGGGS, 2019) for girls aged 7 to 14.

The 2014 *Girls' Attitudes Survey* reflected this pressure to conform to society's body image ideals, which mainly meant that girls should be thin. One girl commented that 'individuals need to see that the sort of image presented in the media isn't realistic and virtually impossible to achieve because the amount of modification done online is extreme – and that the way they look is okay and perfectly normal' (Girlguiding, 2014: 15). As early as 2008, Girlguiding was calling for an end to the media's airbrushing photographs of models, an issue it returned to in 2010 and 2017, citing the damaging and unrealistic expectations this placed on girls.

Two thirds of girls agreed that women often only appeared in the media because they were the girlfriend or wife of a famous man, and more than half felt there were not enough positive female role models. The sexual abuse of women on social media was a concern, with a quarter of girls worried that they could receive the same abuse online just for being a girl. That worry deterred them from wanting to be featured in the media themselves.

Direct support for girls' and young women's mental health

By 2015 girls' health concerns had moved away from smoking, alcohol and drugs to focus more clearly on self-harming and mental illness. Girls were concerned that the adults around them did not recognise the pressures on young people due to bullying (especially through social media) and exams. Almost 40 per cent had needed help with their own mental wellbeing but were very unsure of where to find it. The 2018 survey (Girlguiding, 2018) found that only 25 per cent of girls were very happy, down from 41 per cent in 2009, which had an impact on their confidence and relationships. It also showed that girls were socialising less and experiencing increased unkind behaviour online. On the plus side, they were getting more information about mental health through school and other sources and were feeling less awkward about talking about it, especially with peers, than they had in 2014. Social media, which had really taken off in 2013, was a new pressure, particularly with the rise of smartphones. In a comparison of causes of stress between 2011 and 2018, social media had gone from no girls experiencing it to 59 per cent. In terms of addressing mental health issues, peer support (which went from nothing in 2011 to 71 per cent in 2018) was felt to be a good source of help, as it brings people together who have had similar experiences to support one another.

Girlguiding issued a number of resources to help GYW to feel better about themselves. This included the *Think Resilient* resource which is delivered to Brownies, Guides and Rangers by Peer Educators (trained 14- to 25-year-olds), and *Me in Mind*, produced in conjunction with leading UK mental health charity YoungMinds, for leaders to use with girls aged ten and over (The Guide Association, 2009).

Specific badges relating to mental health and wellbeing were introduced with the 2018 programme. For the youngest girls, Rainbows (aged five to seven in England, Scotland and Wales, or four to seven in Northern Ireland), there is the Healthy Mind badge: to earn it, girls have to go on a sensory safari, taking note of things around them, practising mindful breathing and doing a digital detox by going for a day without using any digital devices – instead focusing on board games, arts or sports, or simply doing nothing but feeling calm. Brownies (aged seven to ten) can earn a Mindfulness badge which encourages mindful breathing while taking in nature, getting girls to recognise how their heartbeat reacts to exercise and rest, and listing ten things that they are grateful for. Guides (aged 10 to 14) can earn a Meditation badge: they need to do a body scan focusing on their body's relationship to its environment, practise clearing their mind and observe good bedtime routines, including putting their devices away an hour beforehand to allow them to reflect on their day and relax. The oldest girls, Rangers (aged 14 to 18), can earn a Self-Care badge, which requires them to analyse their use of time to see when they can free up some time for themselves, plan and spend an evening doing exactly what they would like to do, and connect with nature.

Activities in the meetings on the theme of positive mental health – Be Well – help GYW to understand the links between physical and mental health and to encourage the use of stress management and relaxation techniques. They allow leaders and girls to discuss issues such as stress, depression, anxiety, the importance of getting sufficient good-quality sleep, positive thoughts and feelings, and body image. This is all done in a low-key, fun way, but it opens up a conversation among supportive, non-judgemental adults and children that can help GYW to build resilience in a safe and informal environment.

How Girlguiding's volunteer leaders make a difference to girls' and young women's mental wellbeing

Training for UK leaders has been increasingly standardised since 2010, including an emphasis on safeguarding and providing the right sort of environment to allow GYW to grow in confidence. The concept of resilience is part of the training for unit leaders and links are made between levels of resilience and people's ability to cope when they are feeling vulnerable. A resilient person is described as having 'the knowledge, ability and the confidence to be actively involved in and responsible for their own safety and wellbeing and to cope with life's challenges' (Girlguiding, 2021). Resilience, it is explained, is a bit like an elastic band that allows people to twist when they face challenges but to bounce back from them and avoid becoming vulnerable. The elements of the Girlguiding programme that improve GYW's resilience include: volunteer leaders creating a warm and welcoming environment where GYW are listened to and feel safe to share concerns; empowering GYW through allowing them to choose the programme of activities and to lead activities themselves; giving GYW leadership roles within their Six (Brownie) or Patrol (Guide) group; creating opportunities for GYW to work with peers in a fun and relaxed environment; and offering an adventurous and challenging programme of activities that allows GYW to try new things and learn from their failures.

Although many Girlguiding volunteers have the same worries as other non-mental health professionals about supporting children's mental wellbeing, including concerns that they might 'get it wrong', they are, in fact, already doing the sorts of things that are considered best practice. The UK government department responsible for health promotes the framework developed by the New Economics Foundation which advocates five activities that are essential to wellbeing: 'Connect' by building social relationships and spending time with friends and family; 'Be active' by engaging in regular physical activity; 'Take notice' by being mentally 'present'; focusing on awareness and appreciation of the world around us; 'Keep learning' by maintaining curiosity about the world and trying new things; and 'Give to others' by getting involved in volunteering or helping other people (Aked and Thompson, 2011). All of these activities are fundamental to the delivery of the Girlguiding programme.

Conclusions

There is little doubt that poor mental health is a rising concern in many countries, and that girls and young women are particularly likely to suffer from emotional problems and eating disorders as they head towards adulthood. The rise of digital technology, and social media in particular, has had a negative impact on GYW in terms of sexist behaviour, bullying, body image confidence and self-confidence at a time when support for GYW's specific needs is no longer part of UK government policy. While schools are one setting where non-clinical interventions can be offered to GYW, it is also clear that community interventions such as Girl Guides can support GYW's mental wellbeing through a range of activities that research has shown are conducive to building good mental health (outdoor and physical activities, creative arts, group activities to promote a sense of belonging, and lifelong learning and challenge) in a girls-only safe space. Digital technology has been harnessed to supplement traditional activities – rather than being daunted by the complexities and constant changes of technology, Girlguiding has seen it as an integral part of life and sought to teach GYW how to be empowered, rather than overpowered, by it. By listening carefully to the real concerns of GYW through its annual consultations, Girlguiding has promoted the interests of GYW in the wider community and produced resources to support good mental health and normalise conversations. Furthermore, it has supported its volunteer leaders to feel confident in continuing to have those conversations.

Points for reflection
- While technology can bring benefits to children and young people, are there some benefits that can only be achieved, or which are felt more deeply, through face-to-face meetings with their peer group, whether in community or other settings?
- Volunteers, with a little bit of training and support, can have a significant positive impact on children's mental wellbeing.
- Not all children and young people have lost their appetite for non-digital activities just because they enjoy digital activities. Should we be encouraging all children to embrace both for the good of their wellbeing?

Further information

To find out more about Girlguiding visit: https://www. girlguiding.org.uk.

To find out more about the World Association of Girl Guides and Girl Scouts visit: https://www.wagggs.org/en/.

References

Aked, J. and Thompson, S. (2011) *Five Ways to Wellbeing. New Applications, New Ways of Thinking*, London: New Economics Foundation and NHS Confederation.

Albanesi, C., Cicognani, E. and Zani, B. (2007) 'Sense of community, civil engagement and social wellbeing in Italian adolescents', *Journal of Community & Applied Social Psychology*, 17: 387–406.

Booth, A. and Nolan, P. (2011) 'Choosing to compete: how different are boys and girls?', *Journal of Economic Behavior and Organization*, doi:10.1016/j.jebo.2011.07.018.

Dibben, C., Playford C. and Mitchell R.J. (2017) 'Be(ing) prepared: Guide and Scout participation, childhood social position and mental health at age 50 – a prospective birth cohort study', *Journal of Epidemiology & Community Health*, 71: 275–81, doi:10.1136/jech-2016-207898.

Edwards, C.P., Knoche, L. and Kumru, A. (2001) 'Play patterns and gender', *Encyclopedia of Women and Gender*, 2: 809–15.

Fardouly, J. and Vartanian, L.R. (2015) 'Negative comparisons about one's appearance mediate the relationship between Facebook usage and body image concerns', *Body Image*, 12: 82–8.

Girlguiding (2007) *Looking At Me: A Resource to Help 10–14 Year Old Girls Build A Positive Sense of Body Image and Self-Esteem*, London: Girlguiding UK.

Girlguiding (2014) 'Girls' Attitudes Survey 2014', [online] *Girlguiding UK*, Available from: https://www.girlguiding.org.uk/girls-making-change/girls-attitudes-survey/.

Girlguiding (2018) 'Girls' Attitudes Survey 2018', [online] *Girlguiding UK*, Available from: https://www.girlguiding.org.uk/girls-making-change/girls-attitudes-survey/.

Girlguiding (2020) 'Girlguiding Strategy', [online] *Girlguiding UK*, Available from: https://www.girlguiding.org.uk/globalassets/docs-and-resources/branding-and-resources/girlguidings-strategy-2020.pdf.

Girlguiding (2021) 'A safe space training resources', session presentation [online] *Girlguiding UK*, Available from: https://www.girlguiding.org.uk/making-guiding-happen/learning-and-development/information-for-trainers/training-resources/a-safe-space-training-resources/.

Hogue, J.V. and Mills, J.S. (2019) 'The effects of active social media engagement with peers on body image in young women', *Body Image*, 28: 1–5.

MHF (Mental Health Foundation) (2017) 'While your back was turned: how mental health policymakers stopped paying attention to the specific needs of women and girls', [online] December 2017, Available from: https://www.mentalhealth.org.uk/publications/mental-health-young-women-and-girls.

MHF (Mental Health Foundation) (2019) *Body Image: How we Think and Feel About our Bodies*, London: Mental Health Foundation.

Miller, K., Wakefield, J.R.H. and Sani, F. (2017) 'On the reciprocal effects between multiple group identifications and mental health: a longitudinal study of Scottish adolescents', *British Journal of Clinical Psychology*, 56(4): 357–71.

NHS (2017) *Five Year Forward View for Mental Health: One Year On*, Redditch, UK: NHS England.

NHS Digital (2018) *Mental Health of Children and Young People in England 2017*, London: NHS Digital.

Perloff, R.M. (2014) 'Social media effects on young women's body image concerns: theoretical perspectives and an agenda for research', *Sex Roles*, doi:10.1007/511199-014-0384-6.

Przybylski, A.K. and Weinstein, N. (2019) 'Violent video game engagement is not associated with adolescents' aggressive behaviour: evidence from a registered report', *Royal Society Open Science*, 6: 171474, doi:10.1098/rsos.171474.

Sandseter, E.B.H. and Kennair, O.L.E. (2011) 'Risky play', *Evolutionary Psychology*, 2011.9(2): 257–84.

Scouts (2019) *Annual Report and Accounts 2018–19*, UK: Scouts.

The Guide Association (2009) *Me in Mind*, UK: Girlguiding UK.

WAGGGS (World Association of Girl Guides and Girl Scouts) (2019) 'Free Being Me', [online] Available from: https://www.wagggs.org/en/resources/free-being-me-action-body-confidence-brochure/.

WAGGGS (World Association of Girl Guides and Girl Scouts) (2020a) 'Women here face many difficulties and problems but we remain strong', [blog], Available from: https://www.wagggs.org/en/blog/women-here-face-many-difficulties-and-problems-we-remain-strong/.

WAGGGS (World Association of Girl Guides and Girl Scouts) (2020b) 'Giving a voice to girls and young women in underrepresented communities', [press release] 22 July 2020, Available from: https://www.wagggs.org/en/news/wagggs-and-genu-partnership-upsfoundation/.

WHO (World Health Organization) (2020) 'Child and adolescent mental health', [online], *WHO*, Available from: https://www.who.int/mental_health/maternal-child/child_adolescent/en/.

Zarobe, L. and Bungay, H. (2017) 'The role of arts activities in developing resilience and mental wellbeing in children and young people: a rapid review of the literature', *Perspectives in Public Health*, 137(6): 337–47.

7

Supporting families to navigate the changing sex-education landscape: Outspoken Sex Ed

Leah Jewett

A generational divide exists between parents' understanding of what their children know about sex and relationships and what their children have experienced online and 'in real life'.[1] Ironically, although we live in a hypersexualised world, parents often do not realise that they are their children's sex educators and can be unaware of the consequences of relinquishing that role and responsibility to other influences. Children and young people (CYP) learn not only in the classroom, in the playground and from their surrounding culture, but also from what they find or are shown online (Livingstone et al, 2017). From an increasingly young age, children are exposed to sex and relationships topics through the media, social media, the internet, sexting and pornography. However, their moral compass will still be their parents' values and perspectives. In talking openly at home parents can improve their children's mental health, reinforce safeguarding and strengthen the parent–child connection. Parental engagement is the crucial missing link in sex education.

Outspoken Sex Ed – a social enterprise focused on giving parents the language, skills, knowledge and confidence to talk openly with their children about sex, bodies, consent and relationships – was founded on the conviction that CYP have a right to accurate information about sex and relationships that addresses their curiosity, desire and need to understand the bigger sex-education picture. In encouraging parents to look back at their own formative sex education and reflect on their current attitudes, it aims to help them take inspiration from their hopes for their children's positive sex and relationships experiences. 'The best support and protection parents can offer young people,' suggested author and comedian Sara Pascoe, 'is ensuring they have all the information they need to make decisions about their health, body, sexual exploration and emotions – which is what Outspoken is all about' (Outspoken Sex Ed, nd).

The need for informing CYP about sex and relationships topics is increasingly urgent. Continuing to make headlines are, for instance, the rise in unwanted touching at school (Women and Equalities Committee, 2016), in sexual harassment among children (National Education Union and UK Feminista, 2017) and in child-on-child sexual abuse – up by 71 per cent in 2017 (*Guardian*, 2017); the increase in boys' body image concerns (Williams, 2020) and pressures on boys to 'bulk up' (Katz and El Asam, 2020); the self-generated imagery that accounts for nearly a third of webpages featuring sexual images of children (Internet Watch Foundation, 2020); the fact that, with sexting, one in seven young people send sexual images while one in four receive them, often non-consensually (Madigan et al, 2018); and the prevalence of children seeing pornography from an early age (BBFC, 2019). Issues such as these have brought to worldwide attention the crucial importance of both sex education and parental engagement.

The most exciting developments in sex education involve a two-way street of communication – that is, between schools and parents, between young people (YP) and schools or organisations, and between parents and CYP. Such collaboration includes schools running polls during parent webinars and sharing lesson content and student survey results with parents; charities such as Fumble co-creating resources by YP for YP and Sexpression:UK using the 'near-peer' approach of university students teaching younger children; the consultancy Teaching Lifeskills having children present a sex-education lesson to their parents; and Outspoken Sex Ed encouraging parents to be proactive sex educators at home.

The right of children and young people to comprehensive sex education

Children, as set out in the United Nations Convention on the Rights of the Child (UNCRC) (UNESCO, 2018a), have a right to education and to reliable information. Comprehensive sex education makes the most impact when it is 'complemented with the involvement of parents' (UNESCO, 2018b), who are the 'primary source of information, support and care in shaping a healthy approach to sexuality and relationships' and who 'play a primary role in shaping key aspects of their children's sexual identity and their sexual and social relationships' (UNESCO, 2018a: 84). This view was corroborated by the UK government's *Sex and Relationship Education Guidance*, which called parents 'the key people' in teaching their children about sex, relationships and growing up, specifying: 'Parents need support in their role as sex educators' (Department for Education and Employment, 2000: 26). Its updated statutory guidance notably demoted parents to 'prime educators' (DfE, 2019b: 4).

Sex education begins at home – it is delivered, even inadvertently, through parents' attitudes, behaviour and language. Because parents are their children's most influential educators – 'a child's initial and powerful messenger about sex, sexuality and relationships' (Reed, 2017: 12) – parental engagement in sex education reinforces at home what is taught in school. YP want to be able to discuss sex and relationships topics with their parents and receive not only sexual information but also 'more insight ... about emotional intimacy: how to begin a relationship, establish mature love, how to avoid being hurt (or perhaps how to accept the potential for growth in pain), how to manage conflict, and how to deal with breakups' (Orenstein, 2020: 224). Although parents feel that they should talk openly with their children (NCB, 2011), these conversations do not always come naturally. Open communication is, however, a form of early intervention and ongoing prevention – a protective factor against the pressures and negative influences that CYP have to confront in a digital world, for example harmful online content and potentially risky social media activities (Livingstone et al, 2017). Meanwhile the Internet

Matters Cybersurvey of 15,000 UK children – which noted that from 2015 harmful content became a more prevalent and 'dominant' experience for CYP than cyberbullying – concluded that parents need the confidence to engage with 'and sustain the conversation with their teenager about online life' (Katz and El Asam, 2020). However, some parents fear that talking about the risks of digital technologies might 'trigger children's curiosity and prompt them to engage in risky activities' (European Commission, 2018).

The need for parental engagement in their children's sex education

Relationships and sex education (RSE) – which is taught in secondary schools in England – is the only subject that requires parental engagement in its development. How parents articulate their needs as their children's sex educators was the basis for an unpublished thesis by Outspoken Sex Ed co-founder and RSE teacher Yoan Reed (Reed, 2017). Her research revealed that parents have an explicit need to acquire the language, skills, tools and confidence to talk openly at home. Parents also expressed a need for sex and relationships resources, guidance and a framework; improved school-home communication; and parent education. Their implicit needs included understanding comprehensive RSE, gender approaches and family roles; challenging heteronormative and religious interpretations of sex education; and being able to access programmes to educate them about children's sexual development and lived experiences.

As Outspoken Sex Ed has discovered through its work – including a survey of 84 people on parents and sex education (Manning, 2020) – parents say they need help with learning about:

- what is age appropriate ('I would like nice simple messages about typical questions/issues/behaviour for different developmental stages' – survey respondent)
- how to start conversations ('Sentence starters for talking to children' – survey respondent)

- what to say ('Having phrases and questions for approaching topics would be a really useful starting point' – survey respondent)
- how to become confident ('It's made me realise how I fall into all the traps of avoiding dealing with awkward questions' – audience member; 'I want to be able to confidently educate, advise and discuss sex and relationships, without the squirming awkwardness that my generation grew up with' – survey respondent)
- their children's perspectives and digital experiences ('To be able to influence where she gets her info from [i.e. avoid peer group nonsense!]' – survey respondent)

Surveyed parents felt least confident in answering their children's questions about pornography and sexting, and most confident in addressing the topic of bodies and body image (see Figure 7.1).

Children's questions focused on the topics of babies, pregnancy and birth; body parts, and sex (see Figure 7.2).

Of the survey respondents, 87 per cent were women, with 91 per cent saying that they were the parent most likely to talk

Figure 7.1: Parent confidence levels in answering their children's questions

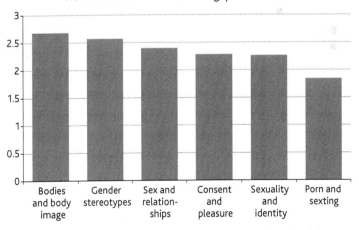

How confident we feel answering questions on...

0 = no confidence; 1 = little confidence; 2 = some confidence; 3 = good confidence

Source: Outspoken Sex Ed survey

Figure 7.2: Questions children asked their parents

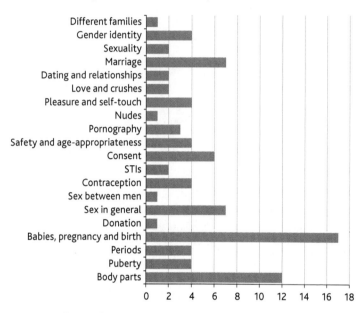

Topics: What are our kids' questions about?

Source: Outspoken Sex Ed survey

to their children about sex and relationships – a gender divide that correlates with findings from other studies. Interestingly, despite a growing awareness among some men of the need to engage with their children, primarily their sons, on the subject of pornography, they still leave their wives to be the 'providers' and 'gatekeepers' of their children's sex education (Reed, 2017).

Parents, along with schools, are YP's top two preferred sources of information about sex and relationships (Sex Education Forum, 2019). In a SEF poll, 48 per cent of YP rated the quality of RSE they received from their parents as 'good/very good' and 19 per cent as 'bad/very bad' (NCB, 2019). Many parents tend to be reactive rather than proactive – they might wait for their children to ask them a question, reach a certain age or be at a particular developmental stage. Barriers to talking openly can include parents' religious or cultural beliefs; a perceived need to have all the answers; embarrassment, shame, fear or past negative experiences; the assumption that sex and relationships topics are private or too personal; worries about driving their children away; a lack of openness modelled for them by their own parents; and/or concerns about other people being offended, judgemental or ostracising their children for being informed.

Commonly parents have fears around their children's emerging sexuality or of 'destroying their children's innocence', as reflected in this Outspoken Sex Ed survey respondent comment: 'How do I discuss porn and other unloving sex without ruining their innocent view of the world?' If parents believe that sexual knowledge is inappropriate for children and if they see sexuality as 'an aspect of adult subjectivity', innocence becomes 'a key discourse used to restrict and regulate children's access to knowledge … However, sexuality, in its broad sense of intimacies, relationships, desires and emotions, is very much part of children's lives and the development of their identities' (Robinson et al, 2017).

Learning about sex and relationships is a powerful protective and preventative measure, and maintaining CYP's ignorance leaves them vulnerable to abuse and liable to seek information from unreliable sources such as pornography or their peers. Take the erroneous assumption that sex education encourages YP to have sex: teenagers in Holland, which leads the way in best-practice sex education, generally have delayed first-time sexual experiences, often under their parents' roof and with parental awareness. Dutch parents tend to normalise discussions with their children around bodies, relationships, sexual health and pleasure. In fact, the quality of the Dutch parent–child connection 'can determine whether a child's first steps into adulthood, including sexuality will … be guided by openness, communication and mutual consideration with their parents' (Rough, 2018: 217).

Charting challenging territory: open communication at home

The age-old idea of parents having 'the talk' with their children has long been discounted – more effective than a 'one-and-done' lecture are casual, everyday mini-conversations that are normalised early on and form a foundation of trust.

Making use of humour, facts, relevant news stories, teachable moments, cultural prompts and other people's experiences as ways in, parents can try having frequent short conversations. Over time they will revisit topics, adding in age- and stage-appropriate information. This approach echoes the spiral curriculum advocated by SEF (Emmerson, 2018) in which themes are reinforced through being 'repeated multiple times with increasing complexity, building on previous learning' (PSHE Association, 2018). Even if parents feel awkward in being straightforward, and especially if they are honest about how difficult they find it, their willingness to reach out about 'off-limits' topics will telegraph the message that they are there for their children – an openness that their children will take on board at some level.

The importance of talking openly at home is acknowledged by both Dr Naomi Sutton, a National Health Service (NHS) sexual health consultant and star on the television programme *The Sex Clinic*, who declared about Outspoken Sex Ed: 'This is wonderful work and very much needed', and mental health and body-image campaigner Natasha Devon MBE, who commented: 'With pornography and social media, young people are exposed to a tsunami of false and damaging ideas and information. It's therefore our duty to provide young people with a healthy counter-narrative. The work of Outspoken – which provides resources for parents and teachers to have open, honest conversations about sex and relationships – is therefore more crucial than ever' (Outspoken Sex Ed, nd).

Outspoken Sex Ed focuses on six interrelated topic areas: sex and relationships, bodies and body image, pornography and sexting, consent and pleasure, sexuality and identity, and gender stereotypes.

Its live events include panel discussions ('So massively important to break the taboos. You totally have to have more of these events, bring more awareness' and 'It changed my attitude to how you think about your children and sex, and I didn't realise that I was probably quite [unnecessarily] scared about it all' – audience members), workshops ('As a parent I felt enabled and empowered to have age-and-stage appropriate conversations with my children after the Outspoken Sex Ed workshop. This suddenly felt like a challenge I could take on with gusto rather than shying away from' – Dr Pooky Knightsmith, child and adolescent mental health expert) and parent discussion groups which inspire experiential learning among peers ('My motivation was curiosity. Wanting to hear other parents' experiences. Trying to understand what was normal for us is not the same normal now. It can be very hard for an adult to communicate with a teenager – and there are very rare opportunities to talk to other parents' – participant).

'Encouraging peer support is important,' declared the charity School-Home Support (2015), citing the benefit of developing 'a space for parents to work together'. In comparing notes with peers and test-driving open communication, parents brave what can be problematic territory and come away emboldened to initiate conversation with their children ('It triggered a good discussion at home when I debriefed my son' – discussion group participant).

A go-to resource for parents, the Outspoken Sex Ed website offers tips organised by topic and by age, a range of expert opinion on how to confront tricky situations (entitled Mayday Moments) and a round-up curated from the latest news stories and including talking points for parents to use with their children. Its topical newsletter keeps parents and educators up to date on current thinking, debate, research, campaigns and articles around sex-education issues, signposting them to relevant television shows, podcast episodes, films, books and events ('I truly enjoy your newsletters. I have found so many resources for helping me and my daughter on various topics. I find myself always sharing articles. Thank you so much for helping parents such as myself who are always feeling like they are five steps behind!' – subscriber).

Outspoken Sex Ed also pioneered a lively, ice-breaking, LGBTQ+ inclusive card game published by Routledge – Sex Ed on the Cards – so that students aged 14+ can play their way through sometimes challenging sex and relationships topics (see Figure 7.3). The aim of the game, which encourages critical thinking and digital literacy, is for players to improve their knowledge, explore their values and prepare for real-life experiences. 'The prompts will help [new] "digital natives" to

Figure 7.3: A Question card from the game Sex Ed on the Cards

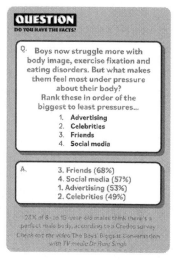

make sense of the images they have seen online,' commented Professor Pam Alldred of Nottingham Trent University, adding that the game 'flags the bravery of admitting to not knowing something'. Emily Harpham-Wells, age 18, had this to say: 'I learned a lot from playing this, especially with the Debate cards which provide an excellent way to start talking openly about topics that would be hard to bring up in a regular conversation.' The game's social action perspective (for example highlighting homophobia or questioning virginity as a social construct) aligns with new digital natives' interest in, for example, equality, diversity and social justice. Sex Ed on the Cards also meets the significant need for upskilling professionals – such as teachers, school staff, youth workers and social workers – around confidently tackling sex and relationships topics. According to Dr Emily Setty, an expert in YP and digital culture at the University of Surrey: 'This collaborative approach to relationships and sex education – in which both adults and young people have the opportunity to share their ideas and views – will help adults ensure that RSE resonates with young people and has the potential to meaningfully impact their lives.'

The benefits of parents talking openly at home about sex-education topics

Improving children's mental health

'Talk to your kids about mental health, just as you would about sexuality, or race, or gender, or physical health,' advised a *Guardian* piece (Parkinson, 2015) which stated that 55 per cent of parents had not discussed mental health with their children. Meanwhile one of the 11 points in the charity YoungMinds' manifesto on CYP's mental health noted the importance of resources 'to improve the emotional literacy of parents and help them identify and respond to mental health concerns' (YoungMinds, 2017).

Because mental health exists in a hard-to-calibrate matrix including emotional, physical and sexual health, parental engagement is crucial in talking openly about such topics as sex, sexuality, body image, the changing body, the developing brain, emotional issues and identity. Parents can discuss puberty before puberty hits, and if they talk positively about their own body it will encourage their children to mirror that body confidence.

It is by mirroring parents' behaviour that children develop digital skills, according to a Joint Research Centre study on digital literacy which noted that parents' attitudes towards digital technologies shape their children's attitudes (European Commission, 2018). It urged schools to 'enhance children's digital and media literacy as early as possible'. A vital component of digital and media literacy is critical thinking, which in creating 'an active filter through which media messages can be processed' (Scull et al, 2014) shores up CYP's resilience and decision-making abilities and helps them to distinguish between healthy and unhealthy relationships. Critical thinking is one of the most effective ways to counter the messages about sex, sexuality, sexiness, body image and the objectification of women that feature in digital technologies, newspapers, magazines, advertisements, films, television programmes, music videos, video games and song lyrics.

Parents can encourage their children – who are conscious of gender roles by age two (Culhane and Bazeley, 2019: 10) – to question our culture. In this Instagram era of Photoshopping and YouTubers, 'unchecked media consumption', as the author Peggy Orenstein put it, is associated with 'greater tolerance for sexual harassment, belief in rape myths, early sexual initiation, sexual risk-taking, a great number of partners, and stereotyping of women' (Orenstein, 2020: 227).

Reinforcing safeguarding and strengthening the parent–child connection

Safeguarding goes beyond parents putting in place filters, monitors, blocks and controls on their children's technology. Parents' open communication with their children around sex and sexuality is a form of safeguarding – it reduces risks and leads to positive outcomes, explained Cardiff University lecturer Dr Clare Bennett. Her assertion that 'early parent-child sexuality communication is protective' (Bennett, 2017: 37) is corroborated by the declaration by Professor Gail Dines (Silverman, 2018) that: 'From a public-health perspective, the best protective factor for anything to do with kids is having well-educated, skilled parents.' Dines founded the organisation Culture Reframed to help parents build up their children's resilience and resistance to pornography, which it deems 'the public-health crisis of the digital age' (Culture Reframed, nd).

Safeguarding also revolves around parents talking about bodies in a natural, factual way from the start and using correct terms for body parts, which can 'promote positive body image, self-confidence and parent-child communication' (Buni, 2013). Children who use anatomically correct terminology are informed – which is a deterrent to predators – and can communicate effectively if anything adverse happens to them (Kenny and Wurtele, 2008).

Early intervention is key: if young children understand that they have a right to personal space and bodily autonomy – for instance in choosing not to hug someone or not to be tickled – they will be better able to distinguish between safe and unwanted touch, to define their own boundaries and to respect other people's limits. Body safety is the forerunner of consent. Talking to older children about consent means getting them to recognise in themselves when something feels pleasurable or does not feel right, and to articulate rather than override their instinctive feelings. Communicating consent means being assertive and showing self-respect and self-knowledge; checking in about ongoing enthusiastic consent comes down to reading, responding to and respecting another person's verbal and non-verbal cues. The topics of consent and pleasure are interrelated: someone cannot know what they do not want if they cannot acknowledge what gives them pleasure (Jewett, 2020a). Although YP say that they favour sex-positive (Pandora et al, 2017) sex education, which focuses on communication, consent and pleasure (Planned Parenthood, 2018), the new guidance for England (DfE, 2019b) does not feature the topic of pleasure.

Parents model confidence about sex and relationships topics by talking openly about them with their children, which in turn gives their children confidence. Ideally parents would discuss sex and relationships within the context of love, intimacy, pleasure and consent – and within their own moral framework. Understanding their parents' moral stance gives children a chance to define their own values and the ability to know their own mind.

Parents can also empower their children by learning from them, effectively turning the tables on who is the 'expert' by using a reverse-mentoring approach – that is, asking their children questions and listening non-judgementally, and with curiosity, to their thoughts, feelings and experiences.

What underpins parents safeguarding their children and strengthening the parent–child connection is their keeping a line of communication open between them.

Countering the impact of pornography on children and young people

More than half of British children aged 11 to 13 have seen pornography (BBFC, 2019), which for many CYP has become a default form of sex education. Whether children unintentionally come across pornography, are shown it by school friends or deliberately search for it, they are being exposed – some as young as age seven (BBFC, 2019) – to explicit and often extreme images before they are ready to process or relate to what they are seeing. Watching pornography highlights concerns for new digital natives around issues such as body image, self-esteem, confidence, positive sexual identity, unrealistic expectations about sex and bodies, objectification, self-objectification, sexual dissatisfaction, respect, pleasure and consent. Teenagers' use of pornography – 88 per cent of which is violent or degrading towards women (Bridges et al, 2010) – is associated with 'more sexual aggression in terms of perpetration and victimisation' (Peter and Valkenburg, 2016). Despite the fact that 'there is evidence of a correlation between children's regular viewing of pornography and harmful behaviours' (Women and Equalities Committee, 2016: 48), studies of the impact of pornography on CYP's attitudes and behaviour have drawn contradictory conclusions (Peter and Valkenburg, 2016).

There is a generational disconnect in terms of parents' understanding of their children's exposure to pornography, as exemplified by the BBFC finding that 75 per cent of parents assumed that their children had not accessed it while 53 per cent of their children had, and a study from New Zealand which found that 54 per cent of parents were not aware that their children had been exposed to sexually explicit content while just 19 per cent were aware and 27 per cent were not sure (Pacheco and Melhuish, 2018). Parents' main online concerns were their children 'being treated in a hurtful way', sexting and seeing sexually explicit content.

The potential for their children seeing sexual content online was also among parents' top three concerns in a UK study in which 22 per cent of parents were aware that their children had seen pornography, 39 per cent would not be comfortable discussing it and 54 per cent would broach the subject 'if they were worried their children were watching it' (Internet Matters, 2018). Some parents were not sure if they had communicated messages effectively. Two in three parents wanted sex education to include the topic of pornography and wanted schools to focus on the fact that the bodies seen in pornography are not 'normal', that interactions among performers are not 'typical' of adults and that watching pornography could impact CYP's self-esteem.

The importance of emphasising the benefits of sex education

'People say parents can provide RSE learning at home. Often, they do not,' affirmed former chief prosecutor Nazir Afzal at the 2019 SEF conference. 'Young people want to be informed; they want parents to be informed. Schools must ask allies from the community how to communicate to parents – and they must relentlessly communicate at every opportunity' (Jewett, 2020b).

September 2020 saw the long-awaited implementation in England of compulsory RSE in all secondary schools (both state funded and independent), relationships education in all primary schools and health education in primary and secondary state-funded schools (DfE, 2019b). Schools were required to fulfil parental-consultation requirements on the design and delivery of their RSE policy. Affirming the importance of parental engagement in RSE, the government acknowledged: 'Schools recognise the importance of strong, constructive and open conversation with parents in the education of their children' (DfE, 2019a: 4). It is crucial, added DfE representative Helena Wright at the 2020 SEF virtual conference, that schools 'help parents to understand how they can support what their child is learning in school with their own teaching at home' (Jewett, 2020c).

A school–home partnership around RSE furthers a whole-school approach and ideally includes transparency, such as the school informing parents about what is covered in lessons and when so that they can bring up RSE topics with their children as they would other subjects, and the school sharing resources with parents so that they can 'continue the conversations started in class at home' (DfE, 2019b).

These means of building trust with parents are increasingly important in light of a concerted backlash against RSE. Most parental objections to RSE in 2018 and 2019 related to LGBTQ+ inclusivity and content, said the DfE – objections that were made manifest by the well-publicised protests by a minority of parents, and others in their communities, outside primary schools in Birmingham and Manchester. Religious groups also targeted parents through circulating anti-RSE petitions and letter templates, and in 2020 launched a judicial review with the claim that RSE was a breach of parents' rights (Jewett, 2020c).

Previously parents had the 'right to withdraw' their children from RSE; in the new guidance children have the less forceful-sounding 'right to be excused' and those who are withdrawn can opt themselves into lessons three terms before turning 16. The downside for children who are withdrawn is that they are not able to learn alongside their peers in the classroom and can end up hearing inaccurate information in the playground. Withdrawal from RSE has, moreover, long been regarded as a risk indicator or child-protection concern, with government guidance cautioning: 'Children cannot always rely on their parents to talk to them about puberty or sex' (Department for Education and Employment, 2000: 11). Currently there is no formal way to assess or monitor whether RSE is being delivered at home.

It is therefore vital that schools highlight the benefits of RSE to encourage maximum support and minimum opt-out from parents. Parental engagement in RSE upholds children's right to reliable information and improves their learning outcomes (Reed, 2017). If the majority of parents – the 92 per cent – who want schools to teach RSE (Sex Education Forum, 2019) spoke out and acknowledged its many benefits, it would be a vital counterpoint to the vocal minority who oppose RSE during these increasingly polarised times.

Conclusions

Sex education is a dynamic field. Altered by significant events such as the MeToo movement, by shifts in attitude and by advances in technology, it requires changing the conversation both at home and on a societal level. Meaningful ways forward for inclusive, sex-positive, rights-based comprehensive sex education involve collaboration – between school and home, with and among young people, and between parents and children.

Meanwhile children also change, their connection to their parents evolves and conversations become more complex. The parent–child connection – including open communication and the reverse-mentoring reciprocity of parents and children learning from each other – is proving to be a protective antidote to the mental health and safeguarding issues around sex and relationships topics that new digital natives face.

Parental engagement in children's sex education is a powerful way to spark critical thinking, fight gender stereotyping and sexual harassment, question culture and contribute to creating a society that is more equal, respectful and accepting of difference. Supporting parents in their journey alongside their children, Outspoken Sex Ed aims ultimately to help young people have confident, pleasurable and positive experiences around sex, relationships and expressing their emerging identity. If parents meet their children on the level of talking openly, they both stand to learn a lot about themselves and each other.

Points for reflection
- How can the benefits of parental engagement in their children's sex education best be championed?
- What frameworks for parental collaboration can schools put into place – for example boards with 50–50 parents and staff or steering groups of parents, staff and students?
- Are successive generations of parents more comfortable talking openly about sex and relationships topics and better able to help their children navigate digital challenges?

Further information
To find out more about Outspoken Sex Ed visit https://www.outspokeneducation.com/.

Note
[1] The reference to 'parents' includes carers throughout this chapter.

References
BBFC (British Board of Film Classification) (2019) 'Children see pornography as young as seven, new report finds', 26 September, Available from: https://www.bbfc.co.uk/about-us/news/children-see-pornography-as-young-as-seven-new-report-finds.

Bennett, C. (2017) 'Parental approaches to teaching children about puberty, relationships and reproduction in the Netherlands', Winston Churchill Memorial Trust, Available from: http://orca.cf.ac.uk/111067/1/Bennett%20C%20Report%202017%20Final.pdf.

Bridges, A., Wosnitzer, R., Scharrer, E., Sun, C. and Liberman, R. (2010) 'Aggression and sexual behavior in best-selling pornography videos: a content analysis update', *Violence Against Women*, doi: 10.1177/1077801210382866.

Buni, C. (2013) 'The case for teaching kids "vagina", "penis" and "vulva"', *The Atlantic*, 15 April, Available from https://www.theatlantic.com/health/archive/2013/04/the-case-for-teaching-kids-vagina-penis-and-vulva/274969/.

Culhane, L. and Bazeley, A. (2019) 'Gender stereotypes in early childhood: a literature review', Fawcett Society, Available from: https://www.fawcettsociety.org.uk/Handlers/Download.ashx?IDMF=e8096848-cbdb-4e16-8713-ee0dadb3dcc5.

Culture Reframed (nd) https://www.culturereframed.org/.

Department for Education and Employment (2000) 'Sex and relationship education guidance', Available from: https://assets.publishing.service.gov.uk/government/uploads/system/uploads/attachment_data/file/283599/sex_and_relationship_education_guidance.pdf.

DfE (Department for Education) (2019a) 'Parental engagement on relationships education', Available from: https://assets.publishing.service.gov.uk/government/uploads/system/uploads/attachment_data/file/884450/Parental_engagement_on_relationships_education.pdf.

DfE (Department for Education) (2019b) 'Relationships education, relationships and sex education (RSE) and health education', Available from: https://assets.publishing.service.gov.uk/government/uploads/system/uploads/attachment_data/file/908013/Relationships_Education__Relationships_and_Sex_Education__RSE__and_Health_Education.pdf.

Emmerson, L. (2018) 'Not a single issue', Sex Education Forum, [blog] 1 June, Available from: https://www.sexeducationforum.org.uk/news/blog/not-single-issue.

European Commission (2018) 'Boosting children's digital literacy – an urgent task for schools', 11 July, Available from: https://ec.europa.eu/jrc/en/news/boosting-children-s-digital-literacy-urgent-task-schools.

Guardian (2017) 'Child-on-child sexual assaults soar, police figures reveal', 9 October, Press Association, Available from: https://www.theguardian.com/society/2017/oct/09/child-on-child-sexual-assaults-soar-police-figures-reveal.

Internet Matters (2018) 'We need to talk about pornography: children, parents and age verification', Available from: https://www.internetmatters.org/wp-content/uploads/2019/06/WeNeedToTalkAboutPornography-LowRes.pdf, London: Internet Matters.

Internet Watch Foundation (2020) 'The dark side of the selfie: IWF partners with the Marie Collins Foundation in new campaign to call on young men to report self-generated sexual images of under 18s', 15 January, Available from: https://www.iwf.org.uk/news/dark-side-of-selfie-iwf-partners-marie-collins-foundation-new-campaign-to-call-on-young-men-to.

Jewett, L. (2020a) 'Conversing with kids about consent', *Outspoken Education*, [blog] 3 March, Available from: https://www.outspokeneducation.com/post/conversing-with-kids-about-consent.

Jewett, L. (2020b) 'RSE, health education and parental consultation', *Headteacher Update*, 9 January, Available from: https://www.headteacher-update.com/best-practice-article/rse-health-education-and-parental-consultation/222762/.

Jewett, L. (2020c) 'RSE and parental consultation: getting it right', *SecEd*, Available from: https://www.sec-ed.co.uk/best-practice/rse-and-parental-consultation-getting-it-right-relationships-health-sex-education-curriculum-pshe.

Katz, A. and El Asam, A. (2020) 'In their own words: the digital lives of schoolchildren, 14 October, Available from: https://www.internetmatters.org/wp-content/uploads/2020/10/Internet-Matters-CyberSurvey19-Digital-Life-Web.pdf.

Kenny, M.C. and Wurtele, S.K. (2008) 'Toward prevention of childhood sexual abuse: preschoolers' knowledge of genital body parts', in M.S. Plakhotnik and S.M. Nielsen (eds) *Proceedings of the Seventh Annual College of Education Research Conference: Urban and International Education Section*, Miami: Florida International University, pp 74–9.

Livingstone, S., Davidson, J. and Bryce, J. (2017) 'Children's online activities, risks and safety – a literature review by the UKCCIS evidence group', October, Available from: https://assets.publishing.service.gov.uk/government/uploads/system/uploads/attachment_data/file/759005/Literature_Review_Final_October_2017.pdf.

Madigan, S., Ly, A., Rash, C., Van Ouytsel, J. and Temple, J.R. (2018) 'Prevalence of multiple forms of sexting behavior among youth', *JAMA Pediatrics*, 172(4): 327–35.

Manning, S. (2020) 'Here's what you said about your kids' sex questions...', Outspoken Education, [blog] 22 April, Available from: https://www.outspokeneducation.com/post/here-s-what-you-said-about-your-kids-sex-questions.

National Education Union and UK Feminista (2017) *'It's Just Everywhere': A Study on Sexism in Schools – And How We Tackle It*, UK: National Education Union and UK Feminista.

NCB (National Children's Bureau) (2011) 'Parents and SRE: a sex education forum evidence briefing', Sex Education Forum, Available from: https://www.sexeducationforum.org.uk/sites/default/files/field/attachment/SRE%20and%20parents%20-%20evidence%20-%202011.pdf.

NCB (National Children's Bureau) (2019) 'Young People's RSE Poll 2019', Sex Education Forum, Available from: https://www.sexeducationforum.org.uk/sites/default/files/field/attachment/Young%20people%27s%20RSE%20poll%202019%20-%20SEF.pdf.

Orenstein, P. (2020) *Boys & Sex*, London: Profile Books.

Outspoken Sex Ed (nd) https://www.outspokeneducation.com.

Pacheco, E. and Melhuish, N. (2018) 'Children's exposure to sexually explicit content: parents' awareness, attitudes and actions, Available from: https://www.netsafe.org.nz/wp-content/uploads/2018/12/Parents-and-Pornography-2018_10Dec2018.pdf.

Pandora, P., Denford, S., Shucksmith, J., Tanton, C., Johnson, A., Owen, J., Hutten, R., Mohan, L., Bonell, C., Abraham C. and Campbell, R. (2017) 'What is best practice in sex and relationship education? A synthesis of evidence, including stakeholders' views', *BMJ Open*, 7(5), Available from: https://bmjopen.bmj.com/content/7/5/e014791.

Parkinson, H.J. (2015) 'Parents – talk to your kids about mental health. Even if it's awkward', *Guardian*, 1 December, Available from: https://www.theguardian.com/commentisfree/2015/dec/01/parents-mental-health-children-depression.

Peter, J. and Valkenburg, P. (2016) 'Adolescents and pornography: a review of 20 years of research', *The Journal of Sex Research*, 53: 509–31, doi:10.1080/00224499.2016.1143441.

Planned Parenthood (2018) 'That 8-letter word: including pleasure in sex education', 2 July, Available from: https://www.plannedparenthood.org/planned-parenthood-st-louis-region-southwest-missouri/blog/that-8-letter-word-including-pleasure-in-sex-education.

PSHE Association (2018) 'PSHE Association response to call for evidence on RSE and PSHE', Available from: https://www.pshe-association.org.uk/system/files/PSHE%20Association%20call%20for%20evidence%20response_0.pdf.

Reed, Y. (2017) '"What's out there for parents, putting us in a better position?" Parental needs for engagement in children's relationships and sex education', Dissertation for MA in International Child Studies, King's College London, Available from https://docs.wixstatic.com/ugd/dfbec9_1d7216e469bf4beebc58844dfc93c7a7.pdf.

Robinson, K.H., Smith, E. and Davies, C. (2017) 'Responsibilities, tensions and ways forward: parents' perspectives on children's sexuality education', *Sex Education*, Vol 17, 333–47, doi:10.1080/14681811.2017.1301904?src=recsys.

Rough, B.J. (2018) *Beyond Birds & Bees*, New York: Seal Press.

School-Home Support (2015) 'Parental engagement – a training toolkit full of useful resources for supporting parents with complex needs', Available from: https://www.schoolhomesupport.org.uk/wp-content/uploads/2015/11/SHS-Parental-engagement-toolkit.pdf.

Scull, T.M., Malik, C.V. and Kupersmidt, J.B. (2014) 'A media literacy education approach to teaching adolescents comprehensive sexual health education', *Journal of Media Literature Education*, 6(1): 1–14.

Sex Education Forum (2019) 'Relationships and sex education: briefing for parliamentarians', 25 February, Available from: https://www.sexeducationforum.org.uk/sites/default/files/field/attachment/Briefing%20on%20RSE%20for%20Parliamentarians%20-%2025%20Feb%202019%20debate.pdf.

Silverman, R. (2018) 'How to talk to kids about porn with Gail Dines', [blog] 18 June, Available from: https://drrobynsilverman.com/how-to-talk-to-kids-about-porn-with-gail-dines/.

UNESCO (2018a) 'International technical guidance on sexuality education: an evidence-informed approach', Available from: https://unesdoc.unesco.org/ark:/48223/pf0000260770.

UNESCO (2018b) 'Why comprehensive sexuality education is important', 15 February, Available from: https://en.unesco.org/news/why-comprehensive-sexuality-education-important.

Williams, S. (2020) '"Anyone popular at school has muscles": the rise of the ripped teen', *Guardian*, 9 May, Available from: https://www.theguardian.com/lifeandstyle/2020/may/09/anyone-popular-at-school-has-muscles-the-rise-of-the-ripped-teen.

Women and Equalities Committee (2016) 'Sexual harassment and sexual violence in school', House of Commons, 7 September, Available from: https://publications.parliament.uk/pa/cm201617/cmselect/cmwomeq/91/91.pdf.

YoungMinds (2017) 'Children's mental health: 10 priorities for the government', Available from: https://youngminds.org.uk/media/1746/childrens-mental-health-ten-priorities-for-the-government.pdf.

8

The Lift Off programme by Red Balloon: online learning and wellbeing support for children who self-exclude from school

Michelle Jayman and Jenny Lewis

Red Balloon Learner Centres and online programmes such as Lift Off are dedicated to supporting vulnerable children who become long-term absent from school because of bullying or other trauma, assisting their recovery and bridging their return to mainstream education or other progression pathway. Providing children with educational, wellbeing and social re-engagement programmes as an alternative to school, the charity Red Balloon offers academic lessons, counselling services, therapeutic activities and a supportive community.

Self-exclusion from school and mental wellbeing

The number of pupils in England excluded from both primary and secondary schools has significantly increased since 2010 (Marmot et al, 2020).[1] Permanent exclusions reached their highest point in nearly a decade, with just under 8,000 pupils being expelled in the academic year 2017–18. This equates to around 42 children (aged 5 to 15) per day (Partridge et al, 2020). These grim figures deservedly attract much attention and make headline news; however, less interest is given to the unknown yet significant number of children who self-exclude from mainstream education. There are multiple, often complex, reasons why children 'refuse' to attend school. According to Thambirajah et al (2008: 33): 'School refusal occurs when stress exceeds support, when risks are greater than resilience and when "pull" factors that promote school non-attendance overcome the "push" factors that encourage attendance.' Research suggests that children self-exclude due to mental health difficulties or after experiencing trauma, and there is a strong link between bullying and absenteeism (Brown et al, 2011). According to Carrie Herbert, founder and chief executive of Red Balloon, these children are liable to fall below the radar and become lost to society (*Guardian*, 2010). Moreover, despite a lack of reliable data, there are estimated to be between 6,000 and 10,000 pupils self-excluding from mainstream school at any one time.

A body of evidence shows the profound short- and long-term impact that bullying has on children: it can lead to emotional distress, low self-esteem, anxiety, self-harm and suicide (National Academies of Sciences, Engineering and Medicine, 2016). In the UK, the *Annual Bullying Survey* has been conducted since 2013 by anti-bullying charity Ditch the Label in partnership with secondary schools and colleges. Survey findings in 2019, from a sample of 2,347 respondents, revealed that one in five students had experienced some form of bullying in the previous 12 months, with 69 per cent of victims agreeing that this had negatively impacted on their mental health. 'Verbal bullying' was identified as the most common (30 per cent of victims had experienced this 'sometimes'; 8 per cent 'often') with 'physical assault' and 'cyberbullying' showing the same pattern of incidence, with young people experiencing it either 'sometimes' (8 per cent) or 'often' (2 per cent) (Ditch the Label, 2019). The survey also found that 24 per cent of respondents had 'anticipatory anxiety' and were fearful about being abused online in the future.

New digital natives (NDNs) have access to an ever-expanding array of social networks and online spaces where cyberbullying can take place – spaces which schools and parents/carers find extremely difficult to monitor. The digital landscape has fundamentally changed the way young people now experience bullying (Law et al, 2012). The ability to exist anonymously online and the potential to inflict almost constant abuse makes cyberbullying – which takes place in chat rooms and through instant messaging, social media and other spaces NDNs inhabit – functionally different from traditional bullying. Greater access to electronic devices and less online supervision have contributed to a rise in digital forms of bullying among adolescents, while evidence suggests that cyberbullying provides a channel for further victimisation of those already experiencing traditional types of bullying (Waasdorp and Bradshaw, 2015). While both cyberbullying and traditional bullying appear to cause psychological distress independently, the effects may be greatest on individuals who experience both (Waasdorp and Bradshaw, 2015).

For some children, the trauma of being bullied is so severe that they self-exclude from mainstream school or are withdrawn by their parents/carers due to physical safety and mental wellbeing concerns (Centre for Social Justice, 2016). Absenteeism can exacerbate the damage already inflicted by bullying, reducing children's sense of belonging to the school community and their engagement with peers. This can induce feelings of social isolation and alienation, leading to emotional and behavioural difficulties (Carroll, 2013). A systematic review by Epstein et al (2020) found that school absenteeism was associated with both self-harm and suicidal ideation in young people. Worryingly, children who are at home during the school day are more likely to be online for longer periods of time and therefore more at risk from cyberbullying (Royal College of Psychiatrists, 2020).

Learning and achieving: academic challenges and alternative education provision

Persistent school absence can result in significant barriers to learning, and a decline in achievement is associated with any degree of absence; as Hancock et al (2013) observed, *every* day counts. Children can quickly fall behind in acquiring key skills and reaching attainment goals, while at secondary school level there is higher risk of school dropout (Allensworth and Easton, 2005). It can be difficult for pupils who have experienced bullying to return to their existing schools, therefore they have diminished opportunities to develop academically. Figures show that bullied children achieve substantially lower key stage 4 results (at age 16) than non-bullied children (Green et al, 2010). Lack of confidence is also associated with falling behind academically, and this can combine and cluster with other factors which further affect children's mental wellbeing (Mentally Healthy Schools, nd). While prevention strategies that enable pupils to remain in school are always preferable to remedial action, children who are not attending school, for whatever reason, need an immediate and effective support system. Graham et al (2019) insist that no pupil excluded from school, either at the school's request or self-imposed, should be given up on; every child has the right to high-quality educational provision that meets their need for a 'good' education.

Local authorities have a legal duty to arrange education (at school or otherwise) for those children of compulsory school age who are not receiving suitable education for any period. For bullied children who self-exclude, this duty can be met through pupil referral units (PRUs). However, the majority of PRUs are highly unsuitable environments for bullied children, as they are often populated by children removed from mainstream education because they are perpetrators of bullying (Centre for Social Justice, 2016). According to the House of Commons Education Committee (2018: 3) non-mainstream provision is often seen as 'a forgotten part of the education system, side-lined and stigmatised as somewhere only the very worst behaved pupils go'. However, there needs to be greater awareness that good-quality alternative provision can be transformational for pupils when mainstream school is either inappropriate or unacceptable; providers of this type of schooling should be seen as integral to the education system (Centre for Social Justice, 2018). Specialist education caters for children who self-exclude from their existing school, and Red Balloon is an example of the type of quality provision desperately needed.

Red Balloon: specialist alternative education

Since Red Balloon was founded in 1996, approximately 300 children and young people have attended one of its four

Learner Centres in England. At least 90 per cent of children who participate in the Red Balloon recovery programme for six weeks or more return to mainstream education or enrol on an apprenticeship scheme. Students vary in age, background, ability and interests, but most are aged between 14 and 15. A common characteristic is that they had stopped going to mainstream school because they felt scared, believed that they would be targeted and humiliated or were fearful that they would be assaulted. In many cases pupils have been out of school for weeks or months and, for some, years. In line with research on absenteeism cited earlier (Epstein et al, 2020), over 50 per cent of the students at Red Balloon centres have either seriously thought about or attempted suicide.

Red Balloon offers students a personalised, holistic recovery programme which comprises academic learning, personal development and wellbeing support. The intention is to create a learning experience that is relevant and fun, challenging but not pressured, in an environment where everyone is treated with unconditional positive regard and respect. Programmes can be accessed through one of the Learner Centres or via Red Balloon of the Air (RBAir), an online distance-learning option in which the student and teacher are physically separated. Although the roots of distance learning stretch back to the 1800s,[2] its rapid expansion began in the late 1990s with the exponential growth and advancement of digital technology. Teaching and learning are facilitated through a combination of technologies such as email, audio, video, digital screens and the internet (Roffe, 2004). 'The primary objective of distance education is to create educational opportunities for the under-represented and for those without access to a traditional educational institution' (Jonasson, 2001, cited in Kentnor, 2015: 23). RBAir satisfies this definition with the tailored service it offers; its provision has been adapted and its primary engagement is online. The intention is to benefit a wider reach of children and effectively meet their learning needs, encompassing both academic progress and socio-emotional development.

The Red Balloon approach: theoretical underpinnings and Mantle of the Expert (MoE)

The ethos of Red Balloon is rooted in education that places student voice at the centre of all learning, recognising the pluralism in children's perspectives and the need to both *hear* and *attend to* their views. This approach encourages students to direct and develop bespoke learning pathways supported by teaching staff. There is a strong focus on students' mental wellbeing alongside academic learning, underpinned by the belief that the two are closely interwoven. This premise is supported by a body of literature (for example Gutman and Vorhaus, 2012). Of central importance is for all students to feel that they belong to the Red Balloon community, having shared the negative experience of being disconnected from mainstream school and their peer group. Feeling connected is considered particularly important for adolescents, who increasingly look to peers and adults outside their family for support (Cowie and Oztug, 2008). Red Balloon nurtures connectedness by providing a safe environment, offering opportunities for meaningful input and creative engagement and matching activities with students' interests – factors conducive to fostering a sense of belonging (Whitlock, 2006).

Individual agency is at the heart of the Red Balloon philosophy and is embedded in Mantle of the Expert (MoE), a pedagogy that uses drama and enquiry to create imaginary contexts for learning. MoE was originally developed in the 1970s and 80s by Dorothy Heathcote, a staunch advocate of creative, child-centred teaching methods (Heathcote and Bolton, 1995). In relation to fostering individual agency, Covey (1989) described 'circles of concern' (the multiple factors in life which affect us – for example for a child this includes family, friends and school) and 'circles of influence' (factors over which we have control). Tim Taylor, author of *A Beginner's Guide to Mantle of the Expert* (2016), argues that everyone has limits to their circle of influence. However, whether this causes stress depends on the amount of agency people have; less agency means more stress and more agency means less (Taylor, 2017). In the 'real-world', hierarchical power structures mean that pupils in mainstream school have very small circles of influence. This is particularly poignant for bullied children. While there is little scope for children to increase their circle of influence in real life, 'it is productive to introduce imaginary worlds into the equation. In imaginary worlds children can take on the roles of people with far more influence' (Taylor, 2017).

Children who self-exclude from school often lose confidence communicating with peers and adults, and many arrive at Red Balloon quiet and withdrawn, believing that their views and opinions are worthless. Applying a MoE pedagogy encourages children to experiment and experience what it is like to have power and be in a position of authority as the ones making decisions and taking on responsibility. This approach draws on students' underlying strengths: children work collaboratively *with* adults, not for them, and on tasks that have meaning and purpose in the present. Real-life situations can be explored and discussed from inside a 'safe space' created by the fictional setting. This gives students the chance to look at the kinds of challenges they meet in their own lives without having to discuss them directly. A body of research describes the therapeutic benefits of drama-based activities. For example, Miller (2011) identified how storytelling can be used to construct situations and explore the various ways the narrative could end. In this way, the child has a position of leadership concerning the characters, the situation and the resolution, allowing the child to work through their own experiences. Co-constructed learning and student voice are at the heart of the MoE approach, in which dialogue is carefully created to bring out children's strengths, building up self-esteem, improving communication skills and making students feel respected and valued.

Face-to-face MoE sessions have been successfully delivered in Red Balloon learning centres since they were set up. However, the challenge arose to transfer the principles of MoE into a programme that worked online – and, crucially, provided comparable, good-quality support that was deemed acceptable and beneficial to a generation of NDN learners. The RBAir trial programme, Lift Off, took place in autumn 2018 and is presented in the next section.

Red Balloon of the Air (RBAir): a Lift Off programme case study

The Lift Off programme comprises core online provision with some bespoke aspects of face-to-face support. What is offered in each component depends on what individual students feel comfortable with and the stage they have reached in their educational journey. RBAir can accommodate students from anywhere in the country who can access the portal from home. Each learning 'pod' accommodates up to 30 students at a time, and groups of around four or five work together as a smaller unit. Digital learning resources include instant messaging using type and voice chat (and video where appropriate), Voice over Internet Protocol (VoIP), avatars navigating a virtual world, collaborative documents (for example Google Docs and Google Slides on a shared drive) and a 3D building environment. Face-to-face elements may involve home visits from a mentor, meeting another student with a mentor or a small group local outing such as a museum visit.

Delivering Red Balloon sessions online raised some initial concerns among staff: these included practical issues – for example managing timetables with rolling admissions – and issues related to student engagement and motivation, for example encouraging regular remote attendance and students' active participation in online lessons. While there are some problems common to both face-to-face and online teaching and learning, difficulties can be exacerbated in a virtual classroom when, for example, students remain silent for prolonged periods and no visual cues are available. Red Balloon staff were keen to avoid new students experiencing stressful encounters in the virtual learning environment in which lack of confidence and low self-esteem make it difficult for students to engage in the first place. Nonetheless, staff had conviction in the appeal of the programme which not only gave learners agency over their own academic curriculum and personal development, but offered a digital context that would open up a whole new realm of creativity and discovery through MoE. Staff hopes that students would be willing to engage in the Red Balloon online learning experience were realised, as one of the programme's projects described in the next section serves to illustrate.

The Lift Off programme: MoE and the virtual castle project

The Castle was a virtual project led by two experienced Red Balloon staff members in which five students participated. A fictional medieval castle (inspired by Harlech Castle in Wales) was chosen as the scenario for the students to explore and develop using a narrative co-created with their teachers. The project was delivered on a limited budget and was relatively 'low tech' in terms of presentation. The storyline – based on an earl's family who lived in the castle in 1350 – was written and designed using PowerPoint presentations alongside teachers' ideas for curriculum tasks and links to other learning resources. PowerPoint was chosen as the presentation platform because students were familiar with it, and it was cost free and compatible with the type of voice chat software that Red Balloon was already using. The story unfolded using carefully tailored text and images in order to be accessible to students with a range of interests and abilities.

The main focus of the story was the falling fortunes of the resident earl of the castle, his relationship with the king and the proposed arranged marriage of the earl's daughter to a young nobleman. The teachers and students were to explore the environment in the guise of a traveller on an important mission. This background provided an appealing narrative that has modern parallels (for example arranged marriage, gender roles, power relations and more) and facilitated a rich assortment of cross-curricular learning opportunities. The characters were created to ensure a spread of non-stereotypical strong roles across the sexes. Students were given a great deal of freedom to explore the narrative and investigate the context. For example, they could add to the material elements (fixtures, fittings and resources), invent new stories from the castle's mythical past or study the real history of castles. Each student was given a detailed physical plan of the castle which enabled them to track the movements of the characters. Based on this prototype, a virtual world castle was digitally created for students to explore independently and carry out curriculum-linked quests. A physical resource box was sent to each student containing various items, for example a sealed letter, a quill pen and bottles for mixing potions. A combination of real and virtual teaching resources served to feed students' curiosity, drawing them into the learning environment, where they connected with fellow distance learners journeying 'remotely' through the castle, thus fostering cohesiveness and a sense of belonging to the online community.

Preliminary feedback from key stakeholders

Preliminary feedback gathered by Red Balloon from students participating in the Castle project suggested that the programme was well received and effective for supporting academic learning and socio-emotional development. Moreover, a virtual platform was deemed to be a desirable format for delivery. These positive findings were echoed by both parents/carers and the staff delivering the sessions. This data collected from key stakeholders with respect to their perceptions and experience of the virtual castle project were integrated and organised under four main themes: translating to digital delivery, empowering independent learners, building confidence and developing social skills and making connections.

Theme 1: translating to digital delivery

Students embraced the digital interface, a familiar environment for them to connect with, and the technical aspects of delivery went smoothly (for example students readily communicated with staff and each other using a range of electronic methods and were proficient users of the software). The creation of a forum for learning which combined digital and physical learning resources was unanimously popular:

- 'I liked the format of the lessons … The story is a really nice way to introduce someone to the online school.'
- 'The story has been really fun … The pouring and making of the herbal remedies was also a blast (though they were a little stinky!)'

- 'I love the quill! I also like how everyone is so nice here, and not stressy and shouty like in my other schools.'

Staff were impressed by the scope students had to develop ideas and complete learning tasks that the online programme allowed:

> 'We are very happy with the near-limitless potential of Google Slides and our imaginations!'

> 'We have also had a tour of the Virtual World castle this week – it is truly stunning.'

Benefits for students were quickly observed and by the end of the third week (halfway through the programme) teachers reported that: '[students] continue to challenge themselves and to be engaged and interested, and we are seeing steps forward in their confidence in their learning!'

Digital and hands-on learning tasks were effectively integrated to achieve learning goals:

> 'Student A made a herbal remedy this week for a nervous headache for one of the characters in the story and recorded a time-lapse video of herself doing so.'

> 'Student C got involved with preparations for the King's feast in the story by completing tasks on medieval make-up and fashion including an outfit that she would have liked to have worn to a feast.'

Parents/carers' comments indicated that online sessions had helped to re-engage their children with learning and encourage them back into a study routine: 'She enjoys her sessions and has really taken to you [staff]. She hasn't been in school for so long and this is really helping to give her focus and purpose in her day.'

Theme 2: empowering independent learners

Student accounts showed that the young people had taken responsibility for their own learning and were proactive and self-motivated completing activities. This suggests that a MoE pedagogy implemented through an online delivery method was effective in facilitating learners' progress: 'I enjoyed using my imagination with the story line … expressing my creativity through thinking about what the character is going to act, look, be like (I drew how my character would look in my spare time).'

Staff reports provided further evidence of students' self-motivated, independent learning:

- 'This week she has started to keep her own 'to-do lists' for [her] work. She needs very little input from me … while at the same time she enjoys and will initiate a discussion.'
- 'Student B has been writing a scene with a theme of arranged marriage … She dramatised and recorded it herself, working out how to use Audacity [software] pretty much on her own, and recording herself playing the guitar to add some incidental music.'
- 'Student C continues to create skilful, imaginative pieces of writing … She has also enjoyed using her painting skills to create a stop-motion joust! She is very self-motivated and will often continue working on a project in her own time.'

Parents/carers felt that personalised learning programmes allowed the needs of individual children to be accommodated, encouraging independence and leading to successful outcomes: 'She can work [independently] without me sat there now'; 'With lessons and mentor visits and also her counsellor online, Student H's needs are well met'; 'We are all enjoying seeing the real H emerging again.'

Theme 3: Building confidence

Alongside learners exhibiting increased levels of academic engagement throughout the duration of the programme, there were also objective and subjective reports of students' increased confidence in their abilities. Confidence is associated with self-efficacy, broadly recognised as a key determinant of adolescent wellbeing (Caprara et al, 2006). According to staff:

- 'Student D has become confident enough this week, during the Mantle of the Expert sessions, to offer answers to more open-ended questions, poking her intellectual toe into the realm of speculation and possibilities, rather than staying solely within the certainties which are her comfort zone.'
- 'Student C, who last week did some writing for the first time in a long time, was much more confident expressing her thoughts in writing this week.'
- '[I'm] very proud of their ability to know exactly what they're doing and get on with things!'
- 'She was very pleased with her stop-motion joust, saying that she doesn't usually like to show her creative side and is proud that she's done so.'

Students' personal reflections aligned with teacher observations: 'I was very shy and scared to start, and I was worrying quite a lot. Then when I did it, I felt really proud of myself'; 'It was really enjoyable and made me not feel like the most stupid in the group anymore!' Parents/carers agreed: 'My daughter visibly relaxed over the lessons from being weepy, nervous and unconfident to laughing, singing and giving more and more.'

Theme 4: Developing social skills and making connections

Additional components associated with positive wellbeing were elicited from stakeholder accounts of learners' experiences. Emergent factors included improved social skills (Sapra, 2019) and a sense of belonging/connectedness to the group (Goodenow, 1993). One student revealed: 'I have finally found a school that I fit in.'

Parents/carers welcomed the opportunities that their children had for making social connections and interacting with peers that the programme facilitated: 'She has been positive since the beginning. It's great that she is getting to interact with other pupils too.'

Staff also reported socio-emotional gains for learners and concluded that even initially reluctant students had made improvements in this domain:

> Student D has also been learning (through the story) about small talk and skills such as how to politely leave a conversation!
>
> This week we had a session with students talking in a group chat, working on the same slides, sharing work with one another ... I was especially thrilled that Student D, who has previously been very against the idea of groups because 'I don't want to talk to anyone', joined in. At first, she said she'd just say 'hi' but was soon chatting away! My 'heart-warming highlight' was the spontaneous reassurance she gave to another student.

Conclusions and wider implications of the work

Red Balloon provides alternative education to vulnerable children who self-exclude from school, and its Lift Off programme demonstrated that high-quality provision can be successfully delivered online. RBAir augments existing face-to-face provision by extending the reach of support services and catering to the unique needs of individual children, including those who might only re-engage with learning through an online facility. A MoE pedagogy, used in Red Balloon learning centres as well as in mainstream schools in the United Kingdom and internationally, can be applied to a distance-learning model. The fundamental principles of agency, creativity and child-directed learning which underpin MoE were effectively embedded within a digital learning context. Growing up with technology, students were accustomed to operating in the digital domain and this offered a comfortable and familiar space to re-engage them with learning. The online environment opened up myriad opportunities for students to exercise agency, direct their learning according to their interests and preferences and exploit their creativity and imagination. Several instances of this were demonstrated in the stakeholder feedback.

Beyond this virtual project case study there is a body of evidence to show the impact of MoE on students of all abilities and ages, from very young children to adults (Red Balloon Learner Centres, nd). The scope is boundless, as the contexts can take place during any time period (eg neolithic, 1700s, present day, in the future) and in any place (eg underwater, outer space, in another country). Students are able to try out a vast range of roles and occupations, for example archeologists, writers, television producers, private investigators, space explorers and animal carers, to name a few. In mainstream schools, MoE has been shown to effectively engage students who find conventional learning difficult or have problems coping with the demands of the curriculum. As this chapter has described, RBAir online programmes have successfully utilised a MoE pedagogy to reconnect school self-excluders with learning, crucially helping them make new connections with peers and form important social bonds. By making these connections to a social unit, children develop key skills that are transferable to other settings (Bernat and Resnick, 2009). With respect to RBAir, this experience could help facilitate students' return to mainstream education.

Research highlights the importance of concerted efforts to prevent all forms of bullying as a means of reducing school refusal (Havik et al, 2015). Nevertheless, self-excluders are a category of school non-attenders who remain largely invisible (Thambirajah et al, 2008). These students commonly lack swift access to the support they need, and high-quality alternative education provision is not always available locally (Centre for Social Justice, 2018). RBAir online programmes present one solution to this dilemma – and plans exist to extend this pioneering work and increase capacity to help these vulnerable children, who are not in the headlines or counted in official statistics but who are nonetheless desperately in need of both learning and wellbeing support.

Points for reflection

- How can student voice be effectively engaged to help design and develop future RBAir programmes (and other organisations' programmes) to best meet the needs and preferences of a generation of new digital native learners?
- What role can parents/carers play in supporting their children and ensuring a joined-up approach to alternative education?
- What can be done to help prevent children from self-excluding in the first place, and if they do, to make sure they receive swift, appropriate and acceptable alternative provision?

Further information

To find out more about Red Balloon learning centres and RBAir visit: https://www.redballoonlearner.org.

To find out more about the Mantle of the Expert education approach visit: https://www.mantleoftheexpert.com.

Notes

[1] A fixed-period exclusion is when a child is temporarily removed from school; permanent exclusion means that a child is expelled from school and no longer allowed to attend.

[2] The earliest known reference to 'correspondence' education (via the postal service) was in the US in 1728 (see Kentnor, 2015).

References

Allensworth, E. and Easton, J.Q. (2005) *The On-Track Indicator as a Predictor of High School Graduation*, Chicago: UChicago Consortium on School Research.

Bernat, D.H. and Resnick, M.D. (2009) 'Connectedness in the lives of adolescents', in R.J. DiClemente, J.S. Santelli and R.A. Crosby (eds) *Adolescent Health: Understanding and Preventing Risk Behaviors*, San Francisco, CA: Jossey-Bass, pp 375–89.

Brown, V., Clery, E. and Ferguson C. (2011) 'Estimating the prevalence of young people absent from school due to bullying', *National Centre of Social Research*, 1: 1–61.

Caprara, G.V., Steca, P., Gerbino, M., Paciello, M. and Vecchio, G.M. (2006) 'Looking for adolescents' well-being: self-efficacy beliefs as determinants of positive thinking and happiness', *Epidemiology & Psychiatric Sciences*, 15: 30–43.

Carroll, H. (2013) 'The social, emotional and behavioural difficulties of primary school children with poor attendance records', *Educational Studies*, 39(2): 223–34.

Centre for Social Justice (2016) *Bullying and Self-Exclusion: Who Cares?*, Roundtable report, London: Centre for Social Justice.

Centre for Social Justice (2018) *Providing the Alternative: How to Transform School Exclusion and the Support that Exists Beyond*, London: Centre for Social Justice.

Covey, S. (1989) *The Seven Habits of Highly Effective People*, New York: Free Press.

Cowie, H. and Oztug, O. (2008) 'Pupils' perceptions of safety at school: pastoral care in education', *An International Journal of Personal, Social and Emotional Development*, 26(2): 59–67.

Ditch the Label (2019) *Annual Bullying Survey*, UK: Ditch the Label.

Epstein, S., Roberts, E., Sedgwick, R., Polling, C., Finning, K., Ford, T., Dutta, R. and Downs, J. (2020) 'School absenteeism as a risk factor for self-harm and suicidal ideation in children and adolescents: a systematic review and meta-analysis', *European Child & Adolescent Psychiatry*, Sep 29(9): 1175–94.

Goodenow, C. (1993) 'The psychological sense of school membership among adolescents: scale development and educational correlates', *Psychology in the Schools*, 30: 79–90.

Graham, B., White, C., Edwards, A., Potter, S. and Street, C. (2019) *School Exclusion: A Literature Review on the Continued Disproportionate Exclusion of Certain Children*, London: Department for Education.

Green, R., Collingwood, A. and Ross, A. (2010) *Characteristics of Bullying Victims in Schools*, London: Department for Education.

Guardian (2010) 'Self-exclusion of bullied children', [online], Available from https://www.theguardian.com/society/2010/aug/20/self-exclusion-bullied-children.

Gutman, L.M. and Vorhaus, J. (2012) *The Impact of Pupil Behaviour and Wellbeing on Educational Outcomes*, London: Institute of Education, University of London.

Hancock, K.J., Shepherd, C.C.J., Lawrence, D. and Zubrick, S.R. (2013) *Student Attendance and Educational Outcomes: Every Day Counts*, Canberra: Australian Government Department of Education.

Havik, T., Bru, E. and Ertesvåg, S.K. (2015) 'School factors associated with school refusal- and truancy-related reasons for school non-attendance', *Social Psychology Education*, 18: 221–40.

Heathcote, D. and Bolton, G. (1995) *Drama for Learning: Dorothy Heathcote's Mantle of the Expert Approach to Education*, Portsmouth: Heinemann.

House of Commons Education Committee (2018) *Forgotten Children: Alternative Provision and the Scandal of Ever Increasing Exclusions*, London: House of Commons.

Kentnor, H. (2015) 'Curriculum and teaching dialogue', *Digital Commons @ DU* [online], 17, (1 & 2), Available from: https://digitalcommons.du.edu/law_facpub/24/.

Law, D.M., Shapka, J.D., Hymel, S., Olson, B.F. and Waterhouse, T. (2012) 'The changing face of bullying: an empirical comparison between traditional and internet bullying and victimization', *Computers in Human Behavior*, 28(1): 226–32.

Marmot, M., Allen, J., Boyce, T., Goldblatt, P. and Morrison, J. (2020) *Health Equity in England: The Marmot Review 10 Years On*, London: Institute of Health Equity.

Mentally Healthy Schools (nd) 'Absenteeism', *MHS*, Available from: https://www.mentallyhealthyschools.org.uk/risks-and-protective-factors/school-based-risk-factors/absenteeism/.

Miller, E. (2011) 'Notes on "Using storytelling for Therapy"', *World Story Telling Institute*, Available from: http://www.storytellinginstitute.org/72.html.

National Academies of Sciences, Engineering and Medicine (2016) *Preventing Bullying Through Science, Policy, and Practice*, Washington, DC: The National Academies Press.

Partridge, L., Landreth Strong, F., Lobley, E. and Mason, D. (2020) *Pinball Kids: Preventing School Exclusions*, London: RSA.

Red Balloon Learner Centres (nd) 'Red Balloon – does it work and is it worth it?', Available from: https://www.redballoonlearner.org/wp-content/uploads/2020/06/Red-Balloon-Does-It-Work-and-Is-It-Worth-It-5efa0b4c8a300.pdf.

Roffe, I. (2004) *Innovation and E-Learning: E-Business for an Educational Enterprise*, Cardiff, UK: University of Wales Press.

Royal College of Psychiatrists (2020) 'Technology use and the mental health of children and young people', Available from: https://www.rcpsych.ac.uk/docs/default-source/improving-care/better-mh-policy/college-reports/college-report-cr225.pdf.

Sapra, R. (2019) 'Social and emotional skills as scaffold for mental well-being of children and adolescents: a construct', *Indian Journal of Health and Wellbeing*, 10(10–12): 334–6.

Taylor, T. (2016) *A Beginner's Guide to Mantle of the Expert: A Transformative Approach to Education*, San Diego, CA: Singular Publishing.

Taylor, T. (2017) 'Creating a learning environment to reduce stress for students', Proceedings from BERA Social Emotional Well-Being and Mental Health of School-Aged Children, Oxford, 28 April [PowerPoint presentation at conference].

Thambirajah, M.S., Granduson, K.J. and De-Hayes, L. (2008) *Understanding School Refusal. A Handbook for Professionals in Education, Health and Social Care*, London and Philadelphia: Jessica Kingsley.

Waasdorp, T.E. and Bradshaw, C.P. (2015) 'The overlap between cyberbullying and traditional bullying', *Journal of Adolescent Health*, 56: 483e488.

Whitlock, J.L. (2006) 'Youth perceptions of life at school: contextual correlates of school connectedness in adolescence', *Applied Developmental Science*, 10(1): 13–29.

9

The LifeMosaic project: supporting wellbeing and empowering pupils through design, development and research

Michelle Jayman and Kyrill Potapov

Technology and children's agency in a digital age

The nature of childhood and adolescence is characteristically social, complex and in constant flux. This is further intensified for new digital natives (NDNs) by the ubiquity of digital technologies which shape their unique, rapidly changing experiences. While there are myriad possibilities for digital technologies to be utilised in supporting the mental and physical wellbeing of children, it would be over-simplistic to consider such technologies in an exclusively instrumental light. Harnessing these opportunities requires some understanding of how digital technologies work and the ways in which children perceive and use them. Sakr (2020) adopts the term 'affordances' to describe the physical properties and social associations of any tool children use to learn and play, digital or otherwise.[1] In this sense, affordances refer not only to an object's physical potential but also to the social and cultural messages which define appropriate forms of engagement. As Sakr (2020) and others (for example Ruckenstein, 2013) suggest, a socio-cultural perspective can help our understanding of how digital activities are mediated by social, cultural and material contexts.

Human agency involves volition and intentionally making things happen by one's actions – for Bandura (2001) this involves evaluating socio-cultural opportunities and constraints and regulating behaviour accordingly. Human agency inevitably influences the interface between digital technologies and learning outcomes; however, within formal education settings, structures and rules dictate what adults and children can actually do. Hierarchical teacher–pupil power relations still commonly prevail in classrooms in the United Kingdom, and varying constraints exist in terms of how digital technologies are taken up within local educational contexts. Structure and agency are thus intricately entwined. Agency is a central component of the constructivist theories that position learners as active and productive agents (Kucirkova, 2019). Children's agency becomes manifest through resources, such as digital technologies, and activities, such as design and research, which support children's own choices, motivations and independence (Vygotsky, 1997). This chapter considers how a collaborative partnership between pupils and their teacher harnessed technology to support children's wellbeing through an innovative digital design project which placed children's agency at its core.[2] LifeMosaic is a personal informatics (PI) wellbeing app designed, developed and evaluated by members of the youth population it aims to support.[3] The LifeMosaic project aligns with theoretical perspectives that are rooted in positive psychology (Seligman, 2002) and advocate a strengths-based approach to wellbeing with a focus on building socio-emotional competencies.

Mental wellbeing: concepts, components and competencies

Self-determination is broadly defined as our personal motivation in the choices we make (Deci and Ryan, 2012). Both self-determination and human agency have been associated with concepts of wellbeing which extend beyond hedonic notions of happiness, such as experiencing pleasure and enjoyment and incorporate eudaimonic aspects (Ryan and Deci, 2000). These refer to the pursuit of psychological growth and development, and to the ultimate condition of human flourishing. Specific supports and nutriments from one's social environment facilitate this process – for instance, autonomous rather than controlled behaviour is associated with positive mental wellbeing. Specific socio-emotional competencies linked to both hedonic and eudaimonic wellbeing are identified as particularly pertinent to an early-adolescent population – a positive sense of self, self-control, decision-making and prosocial connectedness (Guerra and Bradshaw, 2008). A body of research (for example Hui and Tsang, 2012) suggests that programmes and initiatives, like LifeMosaic, which nurture youth autonomy and self-determination have a positive impact on wellbeing and motivation.

Harnessing digital technologies to support wellbeing in schools

A tide of digital technologies has swept through both formal and informal learning environments, and while a significant minority is not adept in using them, the majority of children are highly proficient and thus fully equipped, in a practical sense, to function well in a hi-tech society. In their personal lives, NDNs often exercise considerable agency over the technologies they use, and the online world epitomises their natural learning environment (Dingli and Seychell, 2015). Social media technologies increasingly enable young people (YP) to create content and share experiences which are meaningful to them. This can have a positive impact on their mental wellbeing and sense of belonging, making them feel part of a community (Davis, 2012). Pupils in the LifeMosaic team reported how they had learned about mental wellbeing through digital platforms such as Instagram and Reddit and described how online spaces provided a haven in which to connect with peers and engage with issues they often felt restricted talking about in school. On the flip side, they also felt that some sites presented false or unsupportive information, potentially exacerbating existing issues that YP were experiencing. Evidence from the literature (eg Shakya and Christakis, 2017) reflects these concerns. Nonetheless, according to Calvo and Peters (2014: 2), multi-disciplinary efforts to support wellbeing and optimise human flourishing have spurred concerted thinking around the role of technology. These authors describe 'positive computing' as 'the design and development of technology to support wellbeing and human potential'. Technology is undeniably connected to the sense of agency and self-determination that children experience, and the ways in which technologies are designed and implemented can either facilitate or restrict such experiences.

Schools have a pivotal role in supporting the mental wellbeing of pupils as well as staff (Department of Health and Department for Education, 2017). However, within formal learning spaces, structural, cultural and technological challenges exist which can hinder the selection and implementation of effective strategies to support children's wellbeing in ways that are meaningful to them. Pupils in England have traditionally learned about wellbeing through personal, social, health and economic education (PSHE). Research suggests that PSHE has been poorly regarded in many schools and therefore not prioritised, with some lessons delivered by teachers who did not feel comfortable or competent to do so (Evans and Evans, 2007; Formby and Wolstenholme, 2012). With the Department of Education's (DfE) introduction of a new relationships and sex education (RSE) and health education curriculum in England from September 2020 (DfE, 2019: 31), new statutory responsibilities were placed on schools to provide an 'integrated, whole-school approach to the teaching and promotion of health and wellbeing'. This presented a timely opportunity for schools to shift to a more student-centric approach to wellbeing education (Emmerson, 2020). To build a whole-school, mentally healthy culture requires actively including *all* stakeholders. In line with this approach, pupils should be seen as more than passive recipients of services; instead they should be considered valued co-researchers and contributors to the process of developing appropriate strategies. With this in mind, the LifeMosaic project, which was intended to help augment existing mental wellbeing resources in school, is presented as a case study of good practice.

Introducing the LifeMosaic project

The LifeMosaic PI app was the outcome of a project, Design for Wellbeing, involving four pupils aged 14 to 16 (one girl;

three boys) in partnership with their teacher. Often in youth product design, YP are recruited at the end of the cycle for review purposes, but rarely are they invited to contribute to the creative process. Conversely, with LifeMosaic, the youth design team were able to pursue their own ideas and motives, establishing co-ownership and fostering meaningful collaboration from the outset. The project began as a team entry to a national competition focused on youth-led innovations to address real-world problems. Team members comprised pupils at a secondary school in West London who had voluntarily attended a weekly lunchtime club facilitated by a teacher to generate ideas. Pupil-led discussions on topics affecting YP's daily lives resulted in the proposal to design a PI app to support wellbeing. Several pupils reported first-hand experience of helping friends with emotional difficulties, and some were familiar with existing online wellbeing apps. A number of these are commercially available to children across different age groups from four years to adolescent. Content typically comprises activities to induce calm and relaxation or to manage feelings (for example breathing exercises and visualisations) and can be centred around a theme that is perceived to be popular for that age group (for example *Sesame Street* for four- to seven-year-olds, *Harry Potter* for 7- to 11-year-olds and zombies for children aged 12 and above). Other available options are children's versions of apps originally designed for adult users. At the cusp of the new millennium, Druin (1999) insisted that developers needed to ensure that their technologies supported children in ways that made sense to them as learners and avid technology users. However, as Kucirkova (2019) pointed out, app design and personalised algorithms can be based on adult assumptions about the intended user which may simply not apply to children. To address this serious oversight, children should be included as legitimate stakeholders in the design, development and evaluation of any new technologies aimed at them. This was a key tenet underpinning the LifeMosaic project, and in line with this ethos, the voices of the youth design team and the pupils who participated in the pilot research have been privileged throughout the following account of the LifeMosaic story so far.

The LifeMosaic app: personal informatics to support youth wellbeing

Most PI tools designed by adults for a youth market have tended to be prescriptive and focus on instigating specific behaviour change – for example encouraging exercise to maintain a healthy weight (Jensen et al, 2016). However, there is huge potential for PI tools to support children's learning, including socio-emotional development, and for informing and fostering tailored wellbeing practices. Involving YP in the design process generates ideas that adult developers would not necessarily predict and can therefore embrace technology in authentic ways to support youth users (Calvo and Peters, 2014). The next section will illustrate this process by describing the organic development of LifeMosaic, a non-prescriptive app which allows YP to track what is important to them and the multiple factors that can affect their mental wellbeing.

LifeMosaic users select one aspect, or more, of their life which they wish to focus on and monitor routinely 'as part of a tentative and ongoing process of self-understanding ... [for young people] to learn about their own wellbeing' (Potapov and Marshall, 2020: 8). Criteria such as diet, health and mood are default suggestions, but individual preferences can be incorporated (see Figure 9.1). Enabling customisation was a major design consideration for the team. Adults can erroneously assume that children's voice is homogenous; however, participants were sensitive to the disparate values, identities and constructions of meaning held within their peer group. 'LifeMosaic aims to put the user in control ... expressing themselves in a way that's more meaningful to them' (Xian, age 16). For example, in contrast to typical PI apps, which assume that a higher step count is of value to everyone, LifeMosaic enables the user to set their own evaluation criteria: 'For some people doing an hour's exercise might be ridiculous ... you can say you've done 10 minutes and still be proud of yourself' (Geordie, age 16).

Personal data is recorded by simply logging the number of times an activity or experience occurs, allowing the user to record significant aspects of their day. For example, the user chooses a wellbeing focus (such as sleep or mood) and then rates their day along a scale by pressing combinations of two buttons which correspond to positive and negative poles of the scale ('I slept well'/'I slept badly' or 'I managed my anxiety'/'I didn't manage my anxiety'). The two buttons are assigned a colour and the combination of button presses is represented as a blend of colours which creates a daily 'tile' or visual diary of YP's lives (see Figure 9.2). Data can be collated to generate a monthly overview – a life mosaic – for the user to reflect on how their month is going, notice patterns and set personal goals. Each unique mosaic generates 'a ticket for meaningful discourse' (Potapov and Marshall, 2020: 7). These individual data visualisations can be shared and used as a starting point for conversations with friends or a mentor, either in a designated online forum or a physical classroom setting: 'We just aim to facilitate people connecting with other people about who they are' (Xian). Using the LifeMosaic app was compared with the young designers' own experiences with popular youth platforms:

Figure 9.1: Users select a default or bespoke tracking focus

Figure 9.2: The daily tile is a visual diary

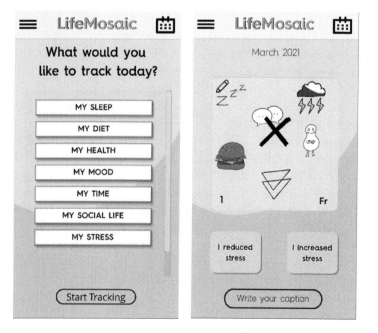

'Instagram believes that social desirability and having many friends is the most valuable thing and they use a "likes" system to represent that ... [whereas] LifeMosaic is purely ... opening discussions' (Xian). Young people were critical of the token economies of 'likes', which they felt got in the way of genuine and meaningful connections. They also acknowledged the fear of being judged or bullied on social media and the value of being supported by peers, which an app like LifeMosaic can help facilitate: '[LifeMosaic] would help you understand it's not just happening to you' (Esme, age 14).

Developing adult–pupil partnerships with participatory action research

There is consensus among critics (for example Koch and Kralik, 2006; McNiff and Whitehead, 2006) that the main purpose of action research is to impart social change through a specific action or actions. For Attwood (1997), participatory action research acknowledges the importance of involving the local community to participate *meaningfully*. The 'problem' originates within the community and is defined, analysed and solved by the community (Selenger, 1997). The impetus for LifeMosaic was to create a digital technology that would make YP's lives better. Although initially several problem areas were discussed, the pupils unanimously chose to focus on youth mental wellbeing. The project evolved through the process of collaborative meaning-making, in which design and implementation choices are steered by young people's own experiences to reflect their personal values and ideas, acknowledging them as experts in their own lives. Consistent with participatory action research methodology (Koshy, 2009), pupils were engaged in all aspects of the project. As key stakeholders and beneficiaries, the youth team were vital contributors to the change process. The LifeMosaic project was envisioned as effecting real change, with the potential to support personally relevant classroom learning around the new RSE and health education curriculum (DfE, 2019); this type of approach sits firmly within a social justice framework (Schubotz, 2020).

The youth designers concurred that: 'Most [young people] think you have to have a very serious [mental health] problem before you get [help] counselling' and referred to the 'embarrassment of talking about your problems' (Geordie). After some discussion, the team decided to create a tech-based solution that could raise awareness and help tackle stigma around these issues. They agreed that a smartphone app would be 'discreet' (as most YP have a personal mobile), readily available and easy to use. The ways in which NDNs think about technology and exploit its application is naturally inspired by their use of devices in their daily lives (OECD, 2019), and a smartphone app emerged as the likeliest solution: 'Most of your life and the things causing you to feel some way is probably on your phone or computer' (Seth, age 16).

In discussions about the design of the app, YP were keen not to medicalise the concept of wellbeing or impose language with clinical connotations. This aligns with research conducted by The Children's Society (2019: 1) which found that YP aged 11 to 21 preferred to be asked about their 'feelings and behaviour' rather than questions specifically on 'mental health'. A central concern for the LifeMosaic team was enabling users of the app to feel in control. They agreed that users should be able to choose any aspect of their life to track and to decide how this focus was articulated: 'Rather than saying "This is how you should change" or even "This is bad" or "This is good", the most important thing was how can you understand for yourself and just learn more about yourself every day' (Seth). Enabling users to monitor and express aspects of their lives which they personally value increases the effectiveness of this type of digital resource, as well as YP's willingness to discuss their experiences (Hong et al, 2018). LifeMosaic is essentially a 'meaning-making' tool that helps users make sense of everyday experiences and affords them personal agency in presenting their stories. The team's desire to facilitate high levels of agency was a fundamental design principle. This was both implicit in their design choices (for example embedding bespoke features) and explicit in the group's pledge at the start of the project: 'We want to empower young people to deal with challenges of every shape and size' (LifeMosaic designers).

For participation to be meaningful to YP and effective in influencing change, it must be embedded in relationships and ways of working, thus creating a culture of participation (Kirby et al, 2003). Moreover, the project team, or community of enquiry, requires all members to be sensitive and responsive to the different forms of leadership required at various times in the project (Gillis and Jackson, 2002). Here, the YP directed the design process and design choices were based on the lived experiences of team members. This reflected findings from the wider literature which supports children's desires to be active agents in decisions about interventions and services that target them:

> We're the experts; start listening to us ... Don't do this as a tokenistic gesture ... Listen to us because we are the ones who really know what it's like. Make sure we are at the heart of planning, commissioning, and evaluating. (Services et al, 2010, cited in Children's Commissioner, 2017: 12)

The teacher's role in the project team was to 'seek clarification or prompt ideas already in the youth discourse' (Potapov and Marshall, 2020: 5). This illustrates how the 'professionals' can scaffold work while the key knowledge initiative rests with the YP (Groundwater-Smith and Mockler, 2016). In this way, experiences were co-constructed throughout the process. Likewise, when other adult collaborators were invited in at different stages – for example parent volunteers provided workshops on fundraising and branding – ownership of the project was retained by the YP.

Participatory action research offers a radical alternative to knowledge development (Wakeford and Sanchez Rodriquez, 2018) and acknowledges children as competent agents who are participants in, and producers of, social and cultural change rather than passive recipients. Children's authentic contribution involves analysis, interpretation and the co-construction of knowledge (Waller and Bitou, 2011). With respect to the LifeMosaic project, this was facilitated through the design, development and evaluation of the PI wellbeing app. For the pilot research, presented in the next section, children's words were privileged in the analysis, and youth researchers helped develop themes to meaningfully express the findings. Space was created for genuine dialogue to take place, to clarify the meaning of the findings and to allow any differences of opinion to be voiced and agreement to be reached.

Pilot evaluation study

Following a successful crowdfunding campaign, the LifeMosaic design team secured the services of a freelance developer and the first iteration of the app was produced. A small pilot study was conducted involving a convenience sample of seven year 8 pupils aged 12 to 13 years (four girls; three boys) who were invited to trial the app for one week, using it to track their sleep patterns (none had prior knowledge of LifeMosaic). A focus group method was selected as it offers a less intimidating and more supportive research encounter than personal interviews, especially for children (Kamberelis and Dimitriadis, 2013). As part of the co-construction process (Tay-Lim and Lim, 2013), the teacher was nominated to facilitate the session and the youth team members contributed to the analysis and interpretation of the findings. This level of participation was congruent with the choices of the young people and deemed both appropriate and desirable, underlining how meaningful participation is a process and not simply an isolated activity or event (Kirby et al, 2003).

A 30-minute session took place on school premises following the trial. The aim was to capture pupils' experiences of using the app and to explore its potential as an effective resource to support existing school mental wellbeing strategies. Discussion was guided by the facilitator, but participants directed the flow and interaction of the discourse. Member checking was regularly employed to ensure that the data remained true to the children's views. An audio recording of the session was transcribed and a thematic analysis of the data was conducted (Braun and Clarke, 2013). All team members were consulted, and the emergent themes were agreed: functionality, behaviour change, and technology and wellbeing.

Functionality

Participants reported varying levels of engagement with the app, from everyday use as a detailed sleep diary to more sporadic practice. This highlights an inherent limitation with all PI apps – they require sufficient commitment to regular use to fulfil their potential. Nonetheless, data that had been recorded enabled respondents to reflect on their sleep behaviours and demonstrated how LifeMosaic operated as a functional tool, enabling users to observe, reflect on and develop greater self-awareness about aspects of their life. Data showed a common pattern among participants – that of using technologies at night, which interrupts a healthy sleep routine. Several children reported staying awake watching video websites on school nights. Others reported staying up late chatting with friends, playing online games or using social media. The negative impact on sleep habits was acknowledged alongside the resignation that: 'You get sucked in' (participant 3).

Poor quality sleep was recognised as contributing to having a 'bad day' (participant 2) or generally affecting pupils' mood, which in turn impacted on social interactions (participants 5 and 6). Connections were made between stress, poor sleep and unhealthy eating habits: 'Just because you're stressed so you want to buy yourself some [fast food] chicken' (participant 3); 'Let's say you don't sleep. Then your brain isn't focusing properly, and you can't be bothered to get healthy food' (participant 5). These exchanges, prompted by sharing PI data in a safe space, demonstrated how LifeMosaic can be effectively employed as a 'ticket to talk'.

Behaviour change

Specific behaviour change, prompted by greater awareness of personal sleep hygiene, was not widely demonstrated. Only one pupil admitted to actively doing something to improve their sleep quality: using a blue light filter on their phone to reduce the impact of screen light on their level of alertness. Although not linking it to specific positive action, another participant reported how they felt simply using LifeMosaic: 'Helped my sleep a bit because I knew I was tracking it' (participant 5).

Technology and wellbeing

Participants' reflections on their sleep mosaics exposed how different the relationships with technology were between young people and older generations (for example parents/carers and educators). One participant described how their parents had encouraged them to charge their phone during the night to avoid the temptation of late-night usage. Fellow participants reacted vehemently to the suggestion of being separated from their phone overnight despite the apparent logic and positive intention of this measure enabling better quality sleep. Knock-on effects of poor sleep in relation to wellbeing emerged. One participant described feeling more 'vexed' about sitting an exam after suffering from poor sleep.

Overall, findings highlighted the centrality of technologies in children's lives and their potential to impact both positively and negatively on wellbeing.

Conclusions from the LifeMosaic project and implications of the research

The world of rapidly changing technologies is familiar territory for NDNs. However, they rarely get to participate in designing, developing and evaluating the latest products and resources aimed at them. As they are key stakeholders and the beneficiaries of technologies within a youth market, this is a serious oversight. The LifeMosaic app was developed through participatory action research, which is deemed to be based on democratic, equitable, liberating and life-enhancing principles (Koch and Kralik, 2006). In this regard, the LifeMosaic project has shown how a pupil–teacher partnership led to the creation of a PI app that empowers children through technology and positions them as independent agents of action.

Utilising personal informatics via a smartphone app to support children's wellbeing is an emerging field with huge potential to benefit large numbers of users. Children have a different technological habitus to older generations: the ways in which children engage with digital technologies have been framed by their exposure to them during their formative years. As the experts in their own lives, children are best placed to consider the most effective solutions to the issues which affect them and, moreover, how to harness digital technologies to their benefit. Adult assumptions about what is meaningful or important for children often falsely subsume children into one homogenous group (Murray, 2019). Conversely, the LifeMosaic youth designers were insistent that their wellbeing resource should be sensitive to users' individual as well as collective selves.

It is clear that wellbeing is an important issue for young people who want to be active in supporting their own mentally healthy lives. Technology, for NDNs, is a natural tool for achieving this end. Nonetheless, having access to a digital app such as LifeMosaic is not enough in itself to accelerate progress. Socio-cultural messages are inextricably bound to different technologies and inevitably influence users' digital activity. Human agency was at the heart of the design process and users are encouraged to self-reflect on aspects of their lives which are uniquely important and meaningful to them, practise self-care and seek support on their own terms. The LifeMosaic app is not envisaged as a panacea to solve socio-emotional difficulties, but it does enable users to engage first-hand with their own wellbeing and can help create a wider school culture which values and destigmatises mental health. Furthermore, a body of research (for example Eisenstein et al, 2019) supports the effectiveness of peer-to-peer initiatives to convey public health messages.

Understandably, pupils can be sceptical about participatory and consultative practices, especially if nothing changes or improves as a result. Initiatives for change in schools have typically reflected top-down approaches, with government administrators and school leaders deciding which practices to introduce, staff being tasked with implementing them and pupils being expected to accept and follow them. Contrasting with this tradition, the LifeMosaic case study suggests that a true commitment to working in partnership with pupils can disrupt hierarchies of power and significantly increase the likelihood of achieving positive, meaningful change. The LifeMosaic project helped inform the school's wellbeing strategies and the app has been adopted in pastoral practice to complement an existing 'buddy system'. This involves a year 12 student meeting with a younger pupil on a weekly basis to check in on how they are doing and to support them in achieving personal goals. Some of the year 12 mentors and mentees have chosen to integrate the LifeMosaic app into their sessions. Research on the benefits of this use of the tool is ongoing. In addition, the youth team have disseminated information about LifeMosaic to other schools, and several institutions have expressed an interest in implementing it locally. Good practice initiatives are sorely needed in schools (Brown, 2018) and LifeMosaic is at the vanguard of innovative wellbeing strategies to support today's new digital natives.

Points for reflection
- How can self-tracking technologies (such as PI apps) be enhanced to encourage YP to reflect on and articulate their experiences to support their own wellbeing?
- What further opportunities are there for digital technologies such as LifeMosaic to be integrated into existing practices and augment whole-school strategies for socio-emotional learning in accordance with the RSE and health education curriculum?
- What practical steps can schools take to promote and support pupils to be participatory agents and engage authentically in the change process?

Further information
To find out more about LifeMosaic visit lifemosaicapp.me. This site provides updates on new iterations of the app.

Notes
[1] The concept of affordances was introduced by Gibson (1961, cited in Sakr, 2020) to describe how humans perceive objects in terms of their use and best function.
[2] We gratefully acknowledge the youth team which led the project for their central contribution to this chapter: Esme O'Brien Thomas, Xian Stewart, Geordie Shepley and Seth Ashby Hawkins.
[3] Personal informatics refers to technology and practices that 'help people collect personally relevant information for the purpose of self-reflection and gaining self-knowledge' (Li et al, 2010: 557).

References

Attwood, H. (1997) 'An overview of issues around the use of participatory approaches by post-graduate students', *Participatory Research, IDS PRA Topic Pack*, Brighton, UK: IDS, University of Sussex.

Bandura, A. (2001) 'Social Cognitive Theory: an agentic perspective', *Annual Review of Psychology*, 52: 1–26.

Braun, V. and Clarke, V. (2013) *Successful Qualitative Research: A Practical Guide for Beginners*, London: SAGE.

Brown, R. (2018) *Mental Health and Wellbeing Provision in Schools*, London: Department for Education.

Calvo, R.A. and Peters, D. (2014) *Positive Computing: Technology for Wellbeing and Human Potential*, Cambridge, MA: MIT Press.

Children's Commissioner (2017) 'Children's voices: the wellbeing of children with mental health needs in England', [report] Available from: https://www.childrenscommissioner.gov.uk/wp-content/uploads/2017/10/Voices-Mental-health-needs-1_0.pdf.

Davis, K. (2012) 'Friendship 2.0: Adolescents' experiences of belonging and self-disclosure online', *Journal of Adolescence*, 35(6): 1527–36.

Deci, E.L. and Ryan, R.M. (2012) 'Self-determination theory', in P.A.M. van Lange, A.W. Kruglanski and E.T. Higgins (eds) *Handbook of Theories of Social Psychology*, Thousand Oaks, CA: SAGE, pp 416–36.

Department of Health and Department for Education (2017) *Transforming Children and Young People's Mental Health Provision: A Green Paper*, London: Crown.

DfE (Department for Education) (2019) *Relationships Education, Relationships and Sex Education (RSE) and Health Education*, London: Crown.

Dingli, A. and Seychell, D. (2015) 'Who are the digital natives?' in *The New Digital Natives*, Berlin: Springer, pp 9–22.

Druin, A. (1999) *The Design of Children's Technology*, Burlington, MA: Morgan Kaufmann Publisher.

Eisenstein, C., Zamperoni, V., Humphrey, N., Deighton, J., Wolpert, M., Rosan, C., Bohan, H., Kousoulis, A.A., Promberger, M. and Edbrooke-Childs, J. (2019) 'Evaluating the peer education project in secondary schools', *Journal of Public Mental Health*, 18(1): 58–65.

Emmerson, L. (2020) 'RSE: What do young people want and need?', *SecEd*, 2020(1): 40.

Evans, C. and Evans, B. (2007) 'More than just worksheets? A study of the confidence of newly qualified teachers of English in teaching personal, social and health education in secondary schools', *Pastoral Care in Education*, 25(4): 42–50.

Formby, E. and Wolstenholme, C. (2012) 'If there's going to be a subject that you don't have to do… Findings from a mapping study of PSHE education in English secondary schools', *Pastoral Care in Education*, 30(1): 5–18.

Gillis, A. and Jackson, W. (2002) *Research for Nurses: Methods and Interpretation*, Philadelphia, PA: F.A. Davis Company.

Groundwater-Smith, S. and Mockler, N. (2016) 'From data source to co-researchers? Tracing the shift from "student voice" to student–teacher partnerships in educational action research', *Educational Action Research*, 24(2): 159–76.

Guerra, N.G. and Bradshaw, C.P. (eds) (2008) 'Linking the prevention of problem behaviors and positive youth development: core competencies for positive youth development and risk prevention', *New Directions for Child and Adolescent Development*, 122: 1–17.

Hong, M.K., Lakshmi, U., Olson, T.A. and Wilcox, L. (2018) 'Visual ODLs: co-designing patient-generated observations of daily living to support data-driven conversations in pediatric care', Proceedings of the 2018 CHI Conference on Human Factors in Computing Systems, New York [paper], 21–26 April, doi:10.1145/3173574.3174050.

Hui, E.K. and Tsang, S.K. (2012) 'Self-determination as a psychological and positive youth development construct', *The Scientific World Journal*, 2012:759358, doi:10.1100/2012/759358.

Jensen, C.D., Duncombe, K.M., Lott, M.A., Hunsaker, S.L., Duraccio, K.M. and Woolford, S.J. (2016) 'An evaluation of a smartphone-assisted behavioral weight control intervention for adolescents: pilot study', *JMIR Mhealth Uhealth*, 4(3): e102.

Kamberelis, G. and Dimitriadis, G. (2013) *Focus Groups: From Structured Interviews to Collective Conversations*, London: Routledge.

Kirby, P., Lanyon, C., Cronin, K. and Sinclair, R. (2003) *Building a Culture of Participation: Involving Children and Young people in Policy, Service Planning, Delivery and Evaluation*, London: Department for Education and Skills.

Koch, T. and Kralik, D. (2006) *Participatory Action Research in Health Care*, Malden, MA: Blackwell Publishing.

Koshy, V. (2009) *Action Research for Improving Educational Practice: A Step-by-Step Guide*, London: SAGE.

Kucirkova, N. (2019) 'Children's agency by design: design parameters for personalization in story-making apps', *International Journal of Child-Computer Interaction*, 21: 112–20.

Li, I., Dey, A.K. and Forlizzi, J. (2010) 'A stage-based model of personal informatics systems', Proceedings of the SIGCHI Conference on Human Factors in Computing Systems (CHI '10), Atlanta [paper] 10–15 April, doi:10.1145/1753326.1753409.

Murray, J. (2019) 'Hearing young children's voices', *International Journal of Early Years Education*, 27(1): 1–5.

McNiff, J. and Whitehead, J. (2006) *All You Need to Know About Action Research*, Thousand Oaks, CA: SAGE.

OECD (2019) 'What do we know about children and technology?', [report] Available from: https://www.oecd.org/education/ceri/Booklet-21st-century-children.pdf.

Potapov, K. and Marshall, M. (2020) 'LifeMosaic: co-design of a personal informatics tool for youth', 21–24 June, London: Proceedings of the Interaction Design and Children's Conference.

Ruckenstein, M. (2013) 'Spatial extensions of childhood: from toy worlds to online communities', *Children's Geographies*, 11(4): 476–89.

Ryan, R.M. and Deci, E.L. (2000) 'Self-determination theory and the facilitation of intrinsic motivation, social development, and well-being', *American Psychologist*, 55(1): 68.

Sakr, M. (2020) *Digital Play in Early Childhood: What's the Problem?*, London: SAGE.

Selenger, D. (1997) *Participatory Action Research and Social Change*, New York: Cornell University.

Seligman, M.E.P. (2002) 'Positive psychology, positive prevention, and positive therapy', in C.R. Snyder and S.J. Lopez (eds) *Handbook of Positive Psychology*, Oxford, UK: Oxford University Press, pp 3–9.

Shakya, H.B. and Christakis, N.A. (2017) 'Association of Facebook use with compromised well-being: a longitudinal study', *American Journal of Epidemiology*, 185(3): 203–11.

Schubotz, D. (2020) 'Participatory Action Research', in P. Atkinson, S. Delamont, A. Cernat, J.W. Sakshaug and R.A. Williams (eds) *SAGE Research Methods Foundations*, [online] Available from: https://pure.qub.ac.uk/en/publications/participatory-action-research-3.

Tay-Lim, J. and Lim, S. (2013) 'Privileging younger children's voices in research: use of drawings and a co-construction process', *International Journal of Qualitative Methods*, 12(1): 65–83.

The Children's Society (2019) 'Reaching out: children and young people's views of mental health support, [report] Available from: https://www.childrenssociety.org.uk/information/professionals/resources/reaching-out.

Vygotsky, L.S. (1997) *The Collected Works of LS Vygotsky: The History of the Development of Higher Mental Functions*, Berlin: Springer Science and Business Media.

Wakeford, T. and Sanchez Rodriquez, J. (2018) 'Participatory action research: towards a more fruitful knowledge', in K. Facer and K. Dunleavy (eds) *Connected Communities Foundation Series*, Bristol, UK: University of Bristol/AHRC Connected Communities Programme.

Waller, T. and Bitou, A. (2011) 'Research with children: three challenges for participatory research in early childhood', *European Early Childhood Education Research Journal*, 19(1): 5–20, doi:10.1080/1350293X.2011.548964.

10

Building better mental wellbeing for children: rebel thinking and innovative practice

Michelle Jayman

'The health and wellbeing of today's children depend on us having the courage and imagination to rise to the challenge of doing things differently' (Marmot, 2010, p 29)

Children and young people's mental wellbeing is one of the most critical health issues the world is facing today. Enjoying a mentally healthy life is inextricably linked to the environment in which we grow and develop. In the early decades of the 21st century, digital technologies are often tightly interwoven into everyday life from infancy, spawning a unique generation of new digital natives (NDNs). The digital realm is vastly networked and many children are exposed to a world far beyond their immediate family, school and friendship groups.[1] The ubiquity of digital technologies and their mediating role across crucial aspects of children's lives has generated keen interest in the implications for their mental and physical wellbeing. Studies which suggest a raft of nefarious effects on children's wellbeing have been criticised for methodological flaws (Orben and Przybylski, 2019), yet such research has influenced key policy decisions including restrictive measures which attempt to limit children's access to technologies. Nonetheless, powerful evidence, including research by Twenge et al (2019) linking mood disorders and suicide-related outcomes among younger generations with digital technology use, supports adopting a cautionary approach. Certainly, research in this area is still emerging and the relative benefits vis-à-vis the potential risks and harm to children continue to be fiercely debated.

In 2020, a deadly virus arrived in the midst of our everyday lives, spreading indiscriminately across the globe. The impact of COVID-19 on the subject matter of this book has been profound: the pandemic has adversely affected children's mental wellbeing while simultaneously triggering their greater reliance on, and immersion in, the digital realm. Technology has been children's gateway to learning, living and staying connected with the world. The original intention of this book was to consider children's mental wellbeing in the context of growing up in a highly digitalised world. In the wake of a 21st-century pandemic, this principal focus has assumed an even greater resonance. The urgent need for effective, meaningful interventions to support and protect a generation of children is more pressing now than ever.

A snapshot of children's mental wellbeing: pre-existing and emerging concerns

The magnitude of mental health issues affecting children worldwide was evident prior to the pandemic, with figures for those experiencing difficulties estimated at 10–20 per cent (WHO, 2020a). Other evidence (Inchley et al, 2020) showed that children's mental wellbeing dipped between 2014 and 2018 in many countries. However, there was substantial variation, highlighting the influence of different cultural, policy and economic factors. In England, 11.2 per cent of 5- to 15-year-olds were identified with a clinically diagnosable mental health disorder in 2017; roughly one in nine children, with emotional difficulties in particular increasingly common (Sadler et al, 2018). The Children's Society (2020) reported that 15-year-olds in the United Kingdom were less happy and satisfied with life than their counterparts in 21 other European nations. Data used in the report were largely collected before the pandemic; undoubtedly, disruptions to education and forced periods of lockdown and isolation in the wake of COVID-19 have further diminished children's subjective wellbeing. A survey by the Prince's Trust (2020) revealed that 43 per cent of over 1,000 respondents had experienced elevated anxiety levels since the outbreak of the pandemic. This mirrors findings from an international study (Save the Children, 2020) comprising almost 6,000 children and parents/carers from the US, Europe and Asia. Children reported feeling anxious, confused and unhappy and those with pre-existing difficulties were more likely to be affected. Their situation was worsened by reconfigured services and limited or no access to their usual support systems: 'My mental health has deteriorated so much that I'm often not able to do my now online therapy session and I haven't had contact with my psychiatrist since lockdown began' (YoungMinds, 2020: 5).

Universal disruption to lives but disparate experiences and outcomes

It appears that some children experienced general anxiety and low mood for the first time in their lives due to the 2020 pandemic. While there are collective stressors, children's experiences can vary greatly depending on their social and economic circumstances. Most educational institutions around the world were forced to replace face-to-face lessons with remote teaching and learning. This disruption to education was unprecedented and students were, on average, forecast a subsequent learning deficit (Di Pietro et al, 2020). Nonetheless, the switch to online learning had greater repercussions for children from disadvantaged backgrounds, who were already more at risk of falling behind. School-related stresses included children's access to digital and other resources (such as a laptop/computer and broadband internet connection and a quiet personal space to study from home), as well as available support from parents/carers or other family members. At the start of UK school closures, approximately 10 per cent of pupils did not have access to either a digital device or the internet (Teacher Tapp, 2020). Emerging evidence suggests that children's disparate engagement with the curriculum will have variable consequences on both their academic progress and mental wellbeing in the short and longer term (Lucas et al, 2020).

Social isolation and loneliness

A systematic review (Loades et al, 2020) examining the impact of social isolation and loneliness on previously healthy children identified increased risk of depression and anxiety. While the study also concluded that children's shared experience of containment could help mitigate any negative effects, other evidence found that heightened feelings of loneliness and isolation were common as opportunities for informal support from friends or trusted adults, including teachers, were compromised (Office for National Statistics, 2020). Children reported missing face-to-face contact with significant people in their lives: 'Last week I saw my group of friends, we went on a cycle and it made me feel a lot happier as although we have been facetiming at home before, it was nice to have conversations and catch up and laugh in real life' (YoungMinds, 2020: 5).

Friends were reported as providing the most support for children during the first wave of lockdown in the UK (YoungMinds, 2020). Healthy relationships with friends and peers are crucial for socio-emotional development, and evidence suggests that children are more vulnerable than adults when routines and social rhythms are interrupted (Dyregrov et al, 2018). Moreover, regular, positive interactions with teachers and peers are associated with children's higher self-esteem and self-confidence (Orth et al, 2012). The collapse of typical formal and informal structures that education and after-school activities provide removed many children's normal sense of stability and security, replacing it with disruption and uncertainty.

Conversely, a significant minority of adolescents reported improved wellbeing, which related to having unanticipated extra time for hobbies and to connect online (Prince's Trust, 2020). Others with pre-existing difficulties associated better wellbeing with freedom from school, where they had felt under pressure from academic stress, bullying or other factors (YoungMinds, 2020). Nonetheless, a body of evidence (eg Huebner and

Figure 10.1: 'I miss my friends' (Lily, age 8)

Arya, 2020) shows that in the wake of the pandemic substantial numbers of youth were experiencing fresh anxieties and growing concerns about their own mental wellbeing:

> And I feel like this pandemic, as we are all aware, is exacerbating existing inequalities, and existing forms of oppression. And I feel like, I can probably understand why young people feel anxious, when it feels like their whole, like, their whole generation is being wasted. (Mental Health Foundation, 2020: 8)

Supporting mental wellbeing during a pandemic: the rise of technologies

In the UK, Child and Adolescent Mental Health Services (CAMHS), counsellors in schools and others responsible for mental wellbeing support were struggling to meet demand prior to the COVID-19 crisis. The onset of the pandemic witnessed a dramatic shift to online provision in a bid to continue vital services. First-hand accounts from children suggested that their experiences were mixed. For some, accessing support on the phone or via video calls, online forums and apps was welcomed: 'I have downloaded a mood tracker app, which provides insights and online help' (YoungMinds, 2020). Others had poor experiences, finding remote services either inferior and/or difficult to access: 'Unfortunately there is no way for me to do my therapy online as there is no place in my home I can talk about my problems without people hearing. This has meant I've had to go without therapy' (YoungMinds, 2020). Undoubtedly, the limitations and challenges associated with digital and virtual service delivery are critical considerations in providing effective and appropriate mental wellbeing support beyond the 2020 pandemic.

Building back better: social models and holistic approaches

A life-course approach to mental wellbeing has an emphasis on prevention and holistic support. According to the WHO (2013), responsibility for promoting mental wellbeing and preventing problems arising extends across every sector of society and all sovereign government departments. Beyond this, the responsibility lies at the heart of all our institutions, our communities and our families.

Nonetheless, the biomedical model of mental health remains dominant in Western societies, driving service provision and research agendas. The underpinning premise is that individuals need 'treatment' for an illness. Yet the WHO (2018) states: 'Health is a state of complete physical, mental and social wellbeing and not merely the absence of disease or infirmity.' Social models recognise mental health as encompassing this state of positive wellbeing and thus, alongside restorative treatments, the promotion and protection of mentally healthy lives are imperative. The contexts within which people live must be examined, and social models are grounded in the belief that both prevention and recovery are best implemented in a holistic way by working with individuals and communities.

Listening to the voices of those who use mental health services and those experiencing difficulties is an essential component underpinning social models of health which are couched within a rights-based agenda. This contrasts sharply with perceptions of the traditional biomedical model which has been described by adult service users as stripping them of control, and as being stigmatising and unhelpful (Beresford et al, 2009, 2016). Furthermore, service users felt that negative perceptions had distorted public understanding of mental health and engendered a culture of 'labelling'. A report by the Children's Commissioner (2017) showed that negative impressions were even harboured among primary school children who revealed highly stereotyped notions of mental ill health which they associated with bizarre and unpredictable behaviour that was frightening, aggressive and violent: 'Mentally ill for me is like ... that gives me a picture of someone who's really screwy in the head' (Plaistow et al, 2014, cited in Children's Commissioner, 2017: 8). These findings suggest that fear and stigma are ingrained at an early age. Furthermore, The Children's Society (2019) highlighted youth concerns regarding accessible and acceptable language for talking about mental wellbeing issues.

Adult service users saw education as key to changing negative attitudes (Beresford et al, 2016: 23), underlining the pivotal role of schools for introducing the topic of mental health early on: 'just so you know that having mental distress is part of normal life. That we all get mentally distressed when certain circumstances are too much for us, and it's getting that message across in schools'. As we saw in Chapter 3, Book of Beasties aims to encourage primary school children to talk about their emotions and regulate behaviour through a play-based programme. Utilising staff to deliver mental wellbeing initiatives helps to cascade good practice across the broader curriculum and foster a school-wide culture of promotion, prevention and support. In a similar vein, in Chapter 7 on Outspoken Sex Ed, we saw how imperative communication and open dialogue at home between children and their parents/carers is in negating misperceptions and the creation of harmful stereotypes.

Voice gives agency and social media platforms allow those with personal experience to share their narratives, helping tackle discrimination and stigma (Beresford et al, 2016). Collaboration in research is also an important channel, giving service users a chance to shape and improve provision. Such 'democratising' of the research agenda is underpinned by the belief that individuals should have more control over their own wellbeing, should be listened to and should be able to make informed choices, and this includes children. Involving the beneficiaries of any intervention in its design and development facilitates more meaningful and effective provision, which we saw in Chapter 9 with the secondary school pupils who were at the core of the LifeMosaic project.

The Children's Commissioner (2019) has called for renewed investment in early-intervention services after years of austerity, and for more attention to be given to the type of 'low-level' support that community initiatives and school-based programmes comprise. The contributors to this book passionately support this plea for urgent action and agree that efforts should be directed towards the ways in which society can be enabling for children, supporting their wellbeing and allowing them to flourish. To that end, the collection of interventions and initiatives in this book was brought together.

Towards effective mental wellbeing strategies

The 2020 pandemic exacerbated the demand for mental wellbeing services from a system that was already struggling to cope. However, it is increasingly recognised that a multi-disciplinary and multi-sectoral response is required, one that can offer a range of support to suit the differing needs of children. The interventions and initiatives presented in this book are just a snapshot; nonetheless, regardless of the nature of provision, it is imperative that the views of children are sought and used to inform commissioning decisions and modes of delivery. A future vision of mental wellbeing support should be tailored to the needs of children from diverse backgrounds and delivered across school, community and domestic settings. The key factors which are crucial to this progressive future provision, and which our case studies highlight, are now briefly considered.

Embedding a whole-school culture

School can be a haven for children and an ideal setting for mental wellbeing support. In England, the Department for

Education (DfE) guidance for schools recommends a graduated response to meeting children's needs, ranging from universal approaches in the classroom to targeted interventions for pupils with more complex needs (DfE, 2018). Yet, as many educators have insisted, there is huge disparity among schools in terms of ability and resources to provide such support. The new mandatory relationships and sex education (RSE) and health education curriculum (DfE, 2019) aligns with a 'whole-school approach' and incorporates lessons on emotional literacy and mental wellbeing for both primary and secondary school pupils.

By the end of primary education children should know 'how to recognise and talk about their emotions [and] ... how to judge whether what they are feeling and how they are behaving is appropriate and proportionate' (DfE, 2019: 31). To help fulfil their statutory requirements, school leaders are advised to commission work and build relationships with external providers: 'Working with external organisations can enhance delivery ... bringing in specialist knowledge and different ways of engaging' (DfE, 2019: 18). According to Cooper (2011), schools are often overwhelmed by the range of mental wellbeing programmes available and implementation decision making is not always based on the strength of the evidence. Greater responsibility on schools has demanded more scrutiny of specific interventions and prompted government calls for models of good practice to share (Brown, 2018). Pyramid Club (Chapter 2) and Book of Beasties (Chapter 3) are programmes designed to suit the varying needs, capacities and resources of individual schools and to operate within existing frameworks of wellbeing support. Both programmes can be delivered by school staff or paraprofessionals and are relatively low cost and easy to implement compared with interventions which require specialist staff and often have excessively long waiting times.

Recognising children as 'experts' in their own lives

Fattore et al (2019) insist that for children's mental wellbeing to be fully understood, children themselves must be authentically acknowledged as active beings both in everyday life and within research. However, significant challenges remain for integrating children's perspectives and ensuring that they are legitimately involved in measuring, understanding and monitoring wellbeing (Huynh and Stewart-Tufescu, 2019). Traditionally, children were regarded as inherently poor informants and the views of adults who cared for, educated or worked with them were sought in order to understand their lives (Johnson, 2004). More recently, the repositioning of childhood within a rights-based, social justice framework has seen a notable shift, with efforts to engage children of all ages (Huynh and Stewart-Tufescu, 2019). Johnson, nonetheless, warned that researchers' assumptions imposed on children's actions or words produce poor evidence, and if used to inform policy can lead to inadequate services and not what children want or need. Therefore only research genuinely undertaken *with* children or *by* children can generate evidence for policy-making based on children's authentic views. This means creating effective partnerships with children to both develop and evaluate mental wellbeing interventions.

For Groundwater-Smith and Mockler (2015: 162), 'Authentic student voice work involves the building of generative relationships and the just engagement of adults and young people in the research enterprise.' However, strategies for co-construction require critical reflection on processes and protocols, otherwise children can become disempowered and their contribution tokenistic (Johnson, 2004). Nonetheless, genuine collaborations have the reformatory power for pupil voice to be championed through pupil-led action research, as the LifeMosaic case study (Chapter 9) has demonstrated. This project encapsulates the transformative potential of children's voice through the design, development and evaluation of an innovative mental wellbeing initiative. Schools can be an ideal site for social change (Brydon-Miller and Maguire, 2009) but this requires a shift in culture from one based on hierarchy and power to one which upholds the tenets of participation, collaboration and equal relationships. While all stakeholders bring their knowledge and experience to the venture, the mantle of 'expert' must ultimately belong to the children.

Of course the responsibility for children's mental wellbeing stretches beyond the school gates – and community initiatives, which we turn to next, can provide different types of support including those involving more physical activities which have become increasingly restricted during school hours.

Facilitating opportunities for outdoor and community activities

There is a strong link between mental and physical wellbeing, and meta-analyses have shown that physical activity can prevent or reduce anxiety and depression (Larun et al, 2006; Bell et al, 2019) and increase levels of self-esteem in children (Ahn and Fedewa, 2011). Survey findings revealed that over a quarter of parents/carers believed that lack of accessible outdoor play facilities contributed to their child experiencing poor mental wellbeing (Association of Play Industries, 2020). The frequently occupied online realm is associated with greater sedentary behaviour among NDNs, while heightened parental concerns regarding outdoor play (largely attributed to fear of traffic accidents and 'stranger danger') have helped to reinforce this undesirable trend.

Opportunities for children to enjoy physical play, team sports and outdoor space were vastly reduced during the 2020 pandemic, and tragically any associated benefits for mental wellbeing were lost. In the United States, the Center for Disease Control and Prevention (CDC) recommended caution and that parents/carers should avoid setting up playdates to maintain social distancing (CDCP, 2020); however, the American Academy of Pediatrics (AAP) recognised a different concern and urged parents to allow children to play outside so they did not miss out on physical activity and the chance to explore and experience nature (Glassy and Tandon, 2020).

Natural outdoor environments are good for physical and mental wellbeing, and Chapter 5 (Forest School) and Chapter 6 (Girlguiding) have contributed to a wealth of evidence demonstrating myriad positive effects. Simply experiencing nature is uniquely de-stressing and children can enjoy a rich variety of activities that are not reliant on digital technologies. Moreover, physical exercise has been shown to help improve sleep patterns in children (Dolezal et al, 2017), another contributory factor to positive wellbeing.

The multiple advantages of being outdoors and exposed to nature were appreciated by parents/carers, educators and children themselves in our case studies. Offline life operates at a slower pace, allowing 'time out', and some children found this a welcome relief from the intensity of their constantly connected digital lives. Arguably, it is not the digital world itself that is the biggest threat to children's wellbeing, but the huge opportunity costs – the increasing dominance of screen-mediated activities suggests that NDNs are growing up ever more removed from nature and outdoor adventures. Nonetheless, as discussed in Chapter 1, technology providers have begun to offer 'blended' experiences whereby digital game apps incorporate tasks to complete in the physical world, for example discovering local streams and rivers or searching for bugs and wildlife. Children themselves are applying technologies in creative, exploratory ways; this was illustrated by the young people at Forest School who used their digital skills to embrace novel experiences in the woodland environment. In a similar vein, digital apps have become part of the Girlguiding experience, supporting traditional activities like stargazing. Furthermore, in the wake of the COVID-19 pandemic a number of Girlguiding units turned to virtual meetings to stay 'connected' and continue traditional activities such as building dens and setting up a tent, albeit in the home or garden. While it seems that digital technologies can augment some outdoor activities and were able to offer a degree of continuity during lockdown, children's first-hand experience of nature and outdoor play cannot be paralleled, and nor can the associated benefits for their mental wellbeing.

Harnessing digital technologies to promote and support mental wellbeing

The 2020 pandemic saw an explosion in digital activity across all sectors of society and with it a growing reliance on technological solutions to learn, live and stay connected. This exposed a world where technologies were a necessity, not a commodity. Prior to the COVID-19 context, many interventions for children offered some, or all, of their content remotely. A rapid review of the literature on virtual and digital delivery programmes for children in the UK (EIF (Early Intervention Foundation), 2020) identified 116 in total. The majority (58 per cent) were education focused; five offered mental wellbeing support, although only two of these were found to be evidence based (ie demonstrably effective) according to the EIF's own criteria.[2]

A review of 50 studies from nine countries (James, 2020) discovered several benefits associated with remote mental wellbeing support for children. These included increased flexibility, lack of waiting time and not having to rely on parents/carers for transportation to services. Also, disadvantaged and traditionally repressed groups (such as the LGBTQ+ community) and those living in remote locations found digital services easier to access. Perceptions of increased confidentiality and anonymity were identified; children reported feeling 'safer' and less at risk of stigma and judgement and this was highly valued. Nonetheless, the review authors concluded that many children simply do not 'suit' remote provision and therefore face-to-face services could never be completely replaced.

A report commissioned by the Children and Young People's Mental Health Coalition (CYPMHC) (Abdinasir and Glick, 2020) described mixed responses to the digital migration of counselling, therapy and treatment services in the wake of the pandemic. While some children preferred online help, others struggled to engage, finding it more difficult to 'open up' when conversations were not held in person. Building a trusted relationship – a therapeutic alliance – between practitioner and client is crucial and deemed increasingly so the more adverse the individual's circumstances (Moore, 2017). Evidence suggests that the quality of this relationship is more strongly linked to positive wellbeing outcomes than specific therapy components (Lambert and Barley, 2001), while clients who feel listened to and treated with respect are more likely to attend and complete intervention programmes (Lindsay et al, 2014). Chapter 4 (the School Counselling Partnership) highlighted the importance of building trusting relationships, not just with individuals but with staff and the whole school community, in fostering an inclusive culture of self-care and mental wellbeing support for all.

Certainly the transition from face-to-face to remote provision was not a uniform experience for children. Although relatively smooth for some, for others increased traffic to websites and helplines meant longer waiting times than before the pandemic (YoungMinds, 2020). Some children expressed their anxiety and wanted the option of face-to-face support: 'I got a lot of support from a few teachers at my school and trusted them with what I was telling them. Now I can no longer speak to them and have been isolating myself from speaking to anyone else' (YoungMinds, 2020: 9). The British Association of Counselling and Psychotherapy (2020) highlighted the need for specific training for therapists delivering online treatment as different skills are required and new protocols must be established. There is a gap in the literature on the impact of remote mental wellbeing support, and long-term studies are urgently required. Nonetheless, it remains the case that a significant minority of children lack access to the appropriate resources, including technology, to receive support from these services in the first place.

The burden of digital poverty: debunking the digital native myth

Children living in poverty are already significantly disadvantaged compared with their wealthier peers and the gap is widening, with the 'digital divide' now more apparent than ever (Guernsey et al, 2020). It is true that continuous and quality access to technology is not the reality for many marginalised children and their families, with some households having to share digital devices and others without any at all. An estimated 9 per cent (almost one in ten) families in the UK do not have a laptop, desktop or tablet (Children's Commissioner, 2020). Many others are living with restricted or no internet access. In disadvantaged households, parents sometimes lack basic digital skills, and this deficit can be passed on because children miss out on regular exposure to technologies in the home (Umar and Jalil, 2012). At the height of lockdown restrictions, the sudden and overwhelming reliance on home education left hundreds of thousands of school-aged children in a learning wilderness. Reports from head teachers suggested that very few disadvantaged pupils had engaged with online learning: 'As a Mum said, it was pay the wi-fi or feed the children this month' (University of Cambridge, nd). Heads also reflected on some parents' inability to help their children use the most appropriate learning platforms due to their own digital skills deficit.

Crucially, digital exclusion linked to poverty not only leaves a significant minority of children behind with their learning but also denies them access to both formal and informal channels of vital wellbeing support. In the absence of regular and reliable online connections, vulnerable and marginalised children do not experience the sense of belonging generated from staying in touch with their friends, teachers and the wider school community. The WHO (2020b) declared poverty the single largest determinant of health for both adults and children. Living in poverty increases the likelihood of vulnerabilities and adverse childhood events that are themselves known risk factors for poor mental wellbeing. Digital exclusion highlights the profound social and economic inequalities that currently exist in our society – a reality which puts children at risk of multiple poor outcomes.

In the same way that Prensky's (2001) original notion of the digital native could not encompass all young people of that era, today's 'new digital native' does not define a homogenous generation of children. There are myriad differences in how and why children engage with digital technologies, as discussed in Chapter 1, and as we have seen in this chapter, the degree of children's exposure to and experience with digital technologies is a crucial factor that determines NDN credentials. Nonetheless, the 2020 pandemic vastly accelerated the extent to which societies worldwide are embracing technologies, and policy makers, educators and parents/carers must take into account the increasingly important mediating role played by digital technologies for children's play, education, social relationships and mental wellbeing.

Future focus: holistic, preventative care with children at the heart of provision

The full impact of COVID-19 on the mental wellbeing of children worldwide is still unfolding; forecasts indicate that it is likely to be profound (O'Shea, 2020). However, a mental wellbeing crisis preceded this tumultuous event and the urgent need for action, although magnified, has not recently surfaced. Traditional biomedical approaches to mental health in the UK have been characterised by crisis response and late intervention, and policy and research in this area have been predominantly reactive. Social models of mental wellbeing are grounded in the belief that with the right help and support those experiencing mental difficulties can flourish in society and, moreover, primary focus is given to building individual strengths and implementing effective preventative strategies. It is now widely accepted that children's mental wellbeing can be affected by multiple social and environmental factors, and promoting protective factors and mitigating risk factors should be acknowledged as a global priority. Child-centred, preventative approaches must be given the high status they deserve, and the case studies presented in this book champion this plea for action.

The diversity of initiatives and interventions discussed in earlier chapters underline the importance of looking holistically at supporting children's mental wellbeing – in schools, in the community, at home and in other spaces that children occupy, including the digital realm. In popular discourse, digital technologies have given rise to neuromyths and are often made a scapegoat for children's deteriorating wellbeing. A more nuanced view celebrates the benefits and unique affordances of digital technologies which, for example, offer a platform for online communities to give support and connectivity and can be a lifeline for children who are isolated. Moreover, as we saw in Chapter 8 (Red Balloon), providing a digital space can help re-engage vulnerable children with learning who would otherwise be excluded from education. A balanced approach, while embracing the positives, recognises the negative aspects that are specific to the digital realm and seeks ways to address them, for example by tapping into children's digital expertise, drawing upon NDNs' experiences and insight to develop literacies and strategies which children can then apply online. A digital wellbeing focus involves educating children about digital health as part of the broader mental wellbeing curriculum, and should sit alongside RSE and health education in all schools.

Nonetheless, strategies to support children's mental wellbeing, whether in schools, community settings or in the home, will only be effective if educators, practitioners and parents/carers have the skills and confidence to enact them and are given the training, resources and ongoing support they need.

Looking to the future, authentic collaborations among children, education and health professionals, community workers, researchers and parents/carers are needed to ensure that mental wellbeing initiatives and interventions are relevant, meaningful and effective. 'Rebel thinking' involves genuinely listening to children and building back better mental wellbeing support by creating a system that offers varied and tailored provision to suit the unique needs of every child. More than this, any recovery plan must be multifaceted and address not just service provision but also the social determinants of wellbeing. Reducing socio-economic inequalities should be a universal priority. Perhaps then, in the aftermath of the 2020 pandemic, the new decade will be marked as the time when mental wellbeing care for children and young people was truly and meaningfully transformed.

Notes

1   The term 'children' used throughout this chapter includes young people.
2   The programme has evidence from at least two rigorously conducted evaluations (Randomised Control Trial/Quasi-Experimental Design).

References

Abdinasir, K. and Glick, O. (2020) *CYPMHC Annual Report 2020*, London: CYPMHC.

Ahn, S. and Fedewa, A.L. (2011) 'A meta-analysis of the relationship between children's physical activity and mental health', *Journal of Pediatric Psychology*, 36(4): 385–97.

Association of Play Industries (API) (2020) 'Children are indoors too much and need more playgrounds, say parents', API [online] 4 August, Available from https://www.api-play.org/posts/children-are-indoors-too-much-and-need-more-playgrounds-say-parents/.

Bell, S.L., Audrey, S., Gunnell, D., Cooper, A. and Campbell, R. (2019) 'The relationship between physical activity, mental wellbeing and symptoms of mental health disorder in adolescents: a cohort study', *International Journal of Behavioral Nutrition and Physical Activity*, 16: 138.

Beresford, P., Nettle, M. and Perring, R. (2009) *Towards a Social Model of Madness and Distress?: Exploring what Service Users Say*, York, UK: Joseph Rowntree Foundation.

Beresford, P., Perring, R., Nettle, M. and Wallcraft, J. (2016) *From Mental Illness to a Social Model of Madness and Distress*, London: Shaping Our Lives.

British Association of Counselling and Psychotherapy (2020) 'Coronavirus (COVID-19): Guidance and resources for members', BACP [online] 27 November, Available from: https://www.bacp.co.uk/news/news-from-bacp/coronavirus/.

Brown, R. (2018) *Mental Health and Wellbeing Provision in Schools*, London: Department for Education.

Brydon-Miller, M. and Maguire, P. (2009) 'Participatory action research: contributions to the development of practitioner inquiry in education', *Educational Action Research*, 17(1): 79–93. doi:10.1080/09650790802667469.

CDCP (Center for Disease Control and Prevention) (2020) 'Caring for children: tips to keep children healthy while school's out', CDCP [online] 17 September, Available from: https://www.cdc.gov/coronavirus/2019-ncov/daily-life-coping/children/protect-children.html.

Children's Commissioner (2017) *Children's Voices: A Review of Evidence on the Subjective Wellbeing of Children with Mental Health Needs in England*, London: Children's Commissioner.

Children's Commissioner (2019) *Early Access to Mental Health Support*, London: Children's Commissioner, Available from: https://www.childrenscommissioner.gov.uk/wp-content/uploads/2019/04/Early-access-to-mental-health-support-April-2019.pdf.

Children's Commissioner (2020) 'Children without internet access during lockdown', *Children's Commissioner*, [online] 18 August, Available from: https://www.childrenscommissioner.gov.uk/2020/08/18/children-without-internet-access-during-lockdown/.

Cooper, P. (2011) 'Educational and psychological interventions for promoting social-emotional competence in school students', in R.H. Shute, P.T. Slee, R. Murray-Harvey and K.L. Dix (eds) *Mental Health and Wellbeing: Educational Perspectives*, Adelaide, AU: Shannon Research Press, pp 29–40.

DfE (Department for Education) (2018) *Mental Health and Behaviour in Schools*, London: Crown.

DfE (Department for Education) (2019) *Relationships Education, Relationships and Sex Education (RSE) and Health Education*, London: Crown.

Di Pietro, G., Biagi, F., Costa P., Karpiński Z. and Mazza, J. (2020) *The Likely Impact of COVID-19 on Education: Reflections Based on the Existing Literature and Recent International Datasets*, Belgium: Publications Office of the European Commission.

Dolezal, B.A., Neufeld, E.V., Boland, D.M., Martin, J.L. and Cooper, C.B. (2017) 'Interrelationship between sleep and exercise: a Systematic Review', *Advances in Preventive Medicine*, 2017:1364387, doi:10.1155/2017/1364387.

Dyregrov, A., Yule, W. and Olff, M. (2018) 'Children and natural disasters', *European Journal of Psychotraumatology*, 2018;9(Suppl 2): 1500823.

EIF (Early Intervention Foundation) (2020) *Covid-19 and Early Intervention: Evidence, Challenges and Risks Relating to Virtual and Digital Delivery*, London: EIF.

Fattore, T., Fegter, S. and Hunner-Kreisel, C. (2019) 'Children's understandings of well-being in global and local contexts: theoretical and methodological considerations for a multinational qualitative study', *Child Indicators Research*, 12: 385–407.

Glassy, D. and Tandon, P. (2020) 'Information for caregivers: getting children outside while social distancing for COVID-19', *American Academy of Pediatrics* [online] 17 September, Available from: https://www.healthychildren.org/English/health-issues/conditions/chest-lungs/Pages/Getting-Children-Outside.aspx.

Groundwater-Smith, S. and Mockler, N. (2015) 'From data source to co-researchers? Tracing the shift from "student voice" to student–teacher partnerships in educational action research', *Educational Action Research*, 24(2): 159–76.

Guernsey, L., Ishmael, K. and Prescott, S. (2020) 'Online learning in the wake of COVID-19 tips and resources for PreK-12 with equity in mind', New America [online] 16 March, Available from: https://www.newamerica.org/education-policy/edcentral/online-learning-wake-covid-19/.

Huebner, C. and Arya, D. (2020) 'The new pessimism: how COVID-19 has made young people lose faith in their own agency', LSE [online] 11 September, Available from: https://blogs.lse.ac.uk/covid19/2020/09/11/the-new-pessimism-how-covid-19-has-made-young-people-lose-faith-in-their-own-agency/.

Huynh, E. and Stewart-Tufescu, A. (2019) '"I get to learn more stuff": children's understanding of wellbeing at school in Winnipeg, Manitoba, Canada', *International Journal of Emotional Education*, 11(1): 84–96.

Inchley, J., Currie, D., Budisavljevic, S., Torsheim, T., Jåstad, A., Cosma, A., Kelley, C., Már Arnarsson, A., Barnekow, V. and Weber, M.M. (eds) (2020) *Spotlight on Adolescent Health and Well-Being. Findings from the 2017/2018 Health Behaviour in School-aged Children (HBSC) Survey in Europe and Canada. International Report. Volume 1. Key Findings*, Copenhagen: WHO Regional Office for Europe.

James, K. (2020) *Remote Mental Health Interventions for Young People: A Rapid Review of the Evidence*, London: Youth Access.

Johnson, K. (2004) *Children's Voices: Pupil Leadership in Primary Schools*, Australia: National College for School Leadership.

Lambert, M.J. and Barley, D.E. (2001) 'Research summary on the therapeutic relationship and psychotherapy outcome', *Psychotherapy*, 38: 357–61.

Larun, L., Nordheim, L.V., Ekeland, E., Hagen, K.B. and Heian, F. (2006) 'Exercise in prevention and treatment of anxiety and depression among children and young people', *Cochrane Database of Systematic Reviews*, 3(3): CD004691.

Lindsay, G., Cullen, M.A., Cullen, S., Totsika, V., Bakopoulou, I., Goodlad, S., Brind, R., Pickering, E., Bryson, C., Purdon, S., Conlon, G. and Mantovani, I. (2014) *CANparent Trial Evaluation: Final Report*, London: Department for Education.

Loades, M.E., Chatburn, E., Higson-Sweeney, N., Reynolds, S., Shafran, R., Brigden, A., Linney, C., McManus, M.N., Borwick, C. and Crawley, E. (2020) 'Rapid systematic review: the impact of social isolation and loneliness on the mental health of children and adolescents in the context of COVID-19', *Journal of the American Academy of Child and Adolescent Psychiatry*, 59(11): 1218–39.e3.

Lucas, M., Nelson, J. and Sims, D. (2020) 'Schools' responses to COVID-19: pupil engagement in remote learning', NFER [online] 16 June, Available from: https://www.nfer.ac.uk/schools-responses-to-covid-19-pupil-engagement-in-remote-learning/.

Marmot, M. (2010) *Fair Society, Healthy Lives: The Marmot Review Executive Summary*, London: The Marmot Review.

Mental Health Foundation (2020) *Coronavirus: The Divergence of Mental Health Experiences During the Pandemic*, Scotland: Mental Health Foundation.

Moore, T.G. (2017) *Authentic Engagement: The Nature and Role of the Relationship at the Heart of Effective Practice. Keynote Address at ARACY Parent Engagement Conference – Maximising Every Child's Potential*, Melbourne, AU: Centre for Community Child Health.

Office for National Statistics (2020) 'Coronavirus and loneliness, Great Britain: 3 April–3 May 2020', ONS [online] nd, Available from: https://www.ons.gov.uk/peoplepopulationand community/wellbeing/.

Orben, A. and Przybylski, A.K. (2019) 'The association between adolescent well-being and digital technology use', *Nature Human Behaviour*, 3: 173–82.

Orth, U., Robins, R.W. and Widaman, K.F. (2012) 'Life-span development of self-esteem and its effects on important life outcomes', *Journal of Personality and Social Psychology*, 102(6): 1271.

O'Shea, N. (2020) *Covid-19 and the Nation's Mental Health: Forecasting Needs and Risks in the UK: October 2020*, London: Centre for Mental Health.

Prensky, M. (2001) 'Digital natives, digital immigrants', *On the Horizon*, 9(5): 1–6.

Prince's Trust (2020) *Young People in Lockdown: A Report by the Prince's Trust and YouGov*, London: Prince's Trust.

Sadler, K., Vizard, T., Ford., T., Marcheselli, F., Pearce, N., Mandalia, D., Davis, J., Brodie, E., Forbes, N., Goodman, A., Goodman, R., McManus, S. and Collinson, D. (2018) *Mental Health of Children and Young People in England, 2017*, London: NHS Digital.

Save the Children (2020) 'Children at risk of lasting psychological distress from coronavirus lockdown', Save the Children [online] 8 May, Available from: https://www.savethechildren.net/news/%E2%80%98children-risk-lasting-psychological-distress-coronavirus-lockdown%E2%80%99-save-children.

Teacher Tapp (2020) 'Learning (or not) from afar: the first week of school closures', Teacher Tapp [online] nd, Available from: https://teachertapp.co.uk/learning-or-not-from-afar-the-first-week-of-school-closures/.

The Children's Society (2019) *Reaching Out: Children and Young People's Views of Mental Health Support*, London: The Children's Society.

The Children's Society (2020) *The Good Childhood Report 2020*, London: The Children's Society.

Twenge, J.M., Cooper, A.B., Joiner, T.E., Duffy, M.E. and Binau, S.G. (2019) 'Age, period, and cohort trends in mood disorder indicators and suicide-related outcomes in a nationally representative dataset, 2005–2017', *Journal of Abnormal Psychology*, 128(3): 185–99.

Umar, I.N. and Jalil, N.A. (2012) 'ICT skills, practices and barriers of its use among secondary school students', *Procedia – Social and Behavioral Sciences*, 46: 5672–6.

University of Cambridge (nd) '"Pay the wi-fi or feed the children": coronavirus has intensified the UK's digital divide', University of Cambridge [online] nd, Available from: https://www.cam.ac.uk/stories/digitaldivide.

WHO (World Health Organization) (2013) 'Mental health action plan 2013–2020', WHO [online] 6 January, Available from: https://www.who.int/publications/i/item/9789241506021.

WHO (World Health Organization) (2018) 'Mental health: strengthening our response', WHO [online] 30 March, Available from: https://www.who.int/news-room/fact-sheets/detail/mental-health-strengthening-our-response.

WHO (World Health Organization) (2020a) 'Adolescent mental health', WHO [online] 28 September, Available from: https://www.who.int/news-room/fact-sheets/detail/adolescent-mental-health.

WHO (World Health Organization) (2020b) 'Poverty and social determinants', WHO [online] nd, Available from: https://www.euro.who.int/en/health-topics/environment-and-health/urban-health/activities/poverty-and-social-determinants.

YoungMinds (2020) *Coronavirus: Impact on Young People with Mental Health Needs*, London: YoungMinds.

Index

Note: References to figures appear in *italic* type; those in **bold** type refer to tables.

Index